DISCARD

Bilingual Children

Are you raising your child bilingually, or planning to do so in the future, but are unsure how to proceed? Using a question-and-answer format, this practical and reassuring guide will enable you to make informed decisions about how to raise your child with two or more languages. To grow up bilingually is a necessity or an opportunity for more children today than ever before. However, parents are frequently uncertain about what to do, or even fear that they may be putting their child's development at risk. Disentangling fact from myth, it shows that a child can acquire more than one 'first' language simultaneously and that one language need not have negative effects on the other. Each chapter is devoted to a question typically asked by parents in counselling sessions, followed by a concise answer, summaries of the evidence and practical tips.

Jürgen M. Meisel is Professor Emeritus and former Chair of the Research Center on Bilingualism at the University of Hamburg, as well as Adjunct Professor and Distinguished Fellow, Faculty of Arts, University of Calgary. He has been engaged in parent counselling for more than 35 years. He is a founding editor of the journal *Bilingualism: Language and Cognition* (Cambridge) and author of seven books and numerous articles.

DISCARD

Bilingual Children

A Guide for Parents

JÜRGEN M. MEISEL
University of Hamburg and University of Calgary

CAMBRIDGE
UNIVERSITY PRESS

CAMBRIDGE
UNIVERSITY PRESS

University Printing House, Cambridge CB2 8BS, United Kingdom

One Liberty Plaza, 20th Floor, New York, NY 10006, USA

477 Williamstown Road, Port Melbourne, VIC 3207, Australia

314–321, 3rd Floor, Plot 3, Splendor Forum, Jasola District Centre, New Delhi – 110025, India

79 Anson Road, #06-04/06, Singapore 079906

Cambridge University Press is part of the University of Cambridge.

It furthers the University's mission by disseminating knowledge in the pursuit of education, learning, and research at the highest international levels of excellence.

www.cambridge.org
Information on this title: www.cambridge.org/9781107181366
DOI: 10.1017/9781316850329

© Jürgen M. Meisel 2019

This publication is in copyright. Subject to statutory exception and to the provisions of relevant collective licensing agreements, no reproduction of any part may take place without the written permission of Cambridge University Press.

First published 2019

Printed in the United Kingdom by TJ International Ltd, Padstow Cornwall

A catalogue record for this publication is available from the British Library.

ISBN 978-1-107-18136-6 Hardback
ISBN 978-1-316-63261-1 Paperback

Cambridge University Press has no responsibility for the persistence or accuracy of URLs for external or third-party internet websites referred to in this publication and does not guarantee that any content on such websites is, or will remain, accurate or appropriate.

For Susanne, of course.

Contents

Preface

Raising children bilingually still leads to controversial and emotionally loaded debates, among parents, other family members, or educators who care for children growing up with two or more languages. Remarkably enough, it also arouses the interest of many not directly concerned, and all those expressing their opinions on this issue tend to be strongly committed to their respective points of view. This is perhaps not all that surprising, after all, because it is an issue that concerns the well-being of young children. Since the viewpoints expressed in family conversations, in the popular media and even in research reports defend diverging, and sometimes mutually exclusive, views on bilingualism in early childhood, there is obviously a need for information and clarification. My goal is to respond to this need, offering information that can resolve controversies and inform parents about the possibilities and limits of child bilingualism.

A rapidly increasing number of parents raise their children bilingually or trilingually, either because they view multilingualism as an advantage for children or because they find themselves in a situation where exposure to more than one language is inevitable. To the extent that they have a choice in this matter, they need to know whether exposing young children to two or more languages simultaneously entails risks for children's linguistic or cognitive development. Once they have decided in favour of bilingualism, the challenge is to create an environment that is most beneficial for bilingual development. In this situation, one can turn to friends for advice or search the internet for relevant information. In fact, I know from many years of counselling that parents are usually well informed about the pros and cons of child bilingualism. The reason why they seek counselling is that they are not 100 per cent sure. Doubts remain about the trustworthiness of their sources of information, especially if these do not agree on what they advise. Some parents fear that warnings against possible risks for children's linguistic and cognitive development might not be unfounded after all, if simultaneous exposure to two languages happens in early childhood. More frequently, however, requests for counselling ask for information about how to support children's bilingualism, or they ask whether the current settings in the family and in the wider social context are indeed favourable for their children's bilingual development. I have learned this in the course of my counselling activities. Interacting with parents and educators, I have gained a better idea of which concerns are most relevant for them, and I hope to have succeeded in addressing them all in this book.

In fact, most of the questions concerning alleged risks or benefits of child bilingualism can be answered today with much confidence, based on results of research by linguists and psychologists. Systematic studies began almost exactly 100 years ago, and research activities increased dramatically as of the 1980s. I believe that parents and other caregivers should be informed about the many findings obtained by this research, and this is what I am trying to achieve with this book.

The choice of topics addressed here and the thematic focus on language development during the first five to six years is largely determined by the questions raised in face-to-face counselling sessions, in emails addressed to the counselling service I have offered for 35 years, or in private conversations. However, it is also influenced by research findings. Sometimes, research studies address issues and obtain results that are relevant for those looking after children growing up bilingually, even if parents have not asked about them. In other words, in some cases I offer answers to questions you did not know you wanted to ask.

The kind of questions to which you, the readers, want to find answers will depend on, among other things, the type of linguistic knowledge and skills you would like your children to attain. Should they become native speakers in more than one language or merely develop basic communicative skills in one of the languages, or do you want your children to reach an intermediate proficiency level? The kind of support children need depends crucially on how one answers these questions. Yet although I have tried to indicate alternative solutions that exist in different settings, it is unfortunately not always possible to deal with them in much detail. I have therefore opted for an approach that starts from the assumption that children exposed to two or more languages from birth are expected to acquire competences equivalent to those of monolingual native speakers of these languages. This does not mean that I am propagating linguistic perfectionism. Rather, it is an attempt to determine what can be achieved in principle and to ask subsequently what other alternatives exist if this goal is either not attainable or not the one set by parents.

To be quite explicit: my intention is not to coax parents into raising children bilingually but to help them make informed decisions when setting goals for their linguistic education. If they do want to raise them bilingually, I offer advice on how to reach this goal, focusing on the linguistic development during preschool years.

Ideally, the information on child bilingualism presented in this book should be sufficiently detailed to allow readers to find answers to questions arising in the specific settings of their families. They obviously do not want to be bored by expositions containing only well-known information. On the other hand, they probably do not want to become immersed in details of linguistic or psycholinguistic research. Still, one can ask if some such details would be of interest after all, if they can be argued to shed light on the questions to which readers want to find answers. I may be wrong, but based on my counselling experience, I am convinced that the readers of this book expect to be offered more detailed information and less superficial treatments of the issues at stake than what they can find searching the internet, in blogs or on Wikipedia. Quite obviously, I am merely guessing what the main interests of the readership may be. But although you, the readers, do not constitute a homogenous group with respect to your interests and needs, there is one thing you do have in common: you read books. And you are willing to expose yourself to a book-length discussion of child bilingualism.

Nevertheless, in an attempt to accommodate different needs and allow for flexibility when reading the book, the chapters are all organized in an identical fashion. The first section presents the problems to be dealt with in the chapter and, whenever possible, questions are answered in this section in a concise fashion. The second section then summarizes some research results on which these answers are based. These research reports are presented in an as non-technical fashion as possible. Accordingly, readers who are primarily looking for practical guidelines can skip the second section of every chapter. The third section formulates guidelines that follow from the recommendations given in the first section. Although no additional reading is required in order to be able to follow the discussion presented in the book, section 4 offers reading suggestions for those who want to get some first-hand experience with the research on which the recommendations are based. Moreover, Chapters 3 to 8 need not be read in this order; rather, each of these chapters can be read independently. Note that Chapter 1, section 1.3 contains some more remarks on how to use the book.

In case you are wondering what qualifies me to write a guide for parents of children growing up bilingually, I have to admit that I myself did not grow up bilingually, at least not in the common sense of the term. I grew up in Germany as a dialect speaker, and I learned Standard German later in school. At the age of 10, I started learning my first 'real' second language, and a few others, later on. As a linguist studying Romance languages, I have been working on language acquisition since 1973. Over the years, I directed a number of research projects investigating various acquisition types, first adult and child second language acquisition by immigrant workers, and as of 1980 the simultaneous acquisition of languages by children exposed to two languages from birth, French – German, Spanish – Basque, and Portuguese – German. This is why examples from these languages are cited throughout the book; they are taken from the data collected by these research projects.

I have been engaged in various counselling activities since 1982, initially answering letters by concerned parents of bilingual children, addressed to the editors of the German magazine *Eltern* ('Parents'). Later on, I gave numerous talks addressing non-academic audiences in Germany, France, Spain, Canada, the US, and Brazil. In the late 1980s, I set up a counselling service at the University of Hamburg, initially as a telephone hotline and as of 1999 on the university website. A similar service continues to be offered at the University of Calgary and can be found at the following address: http://arts.ucalgary.ca/pcs. These exchanges with parents are the main motivation for this book.

This brings me to the last point of this preface. I cannot end it without mentioning at least some of the people who encouraged and supported me when writing this book. First of all, the friends and colleagues who discussed with me the issues dealt with here and who advised me on how to present them, having read parts of the text or the entire manuscript, most importantly Susanne E. Carroll (University of Calgary) and Regina Mahlmann (University of Hamburg). I also want to thank Andrew Winnard (Cambridge University Press) who encouraged me in my plan to write a guide for parents raising children bilingually. Finally, I am grateful to both the past and the current director of the Language Research Centre (LRC, University of Calgary) for allowing me to use the logo from the LRC's Parent Counselling Service, 'Sometimes, two is better than one'.

Abbreviations

*	Signals that a construction is not grammatical
2L1	Bilingual first language (acquisition)
2P2L	Both parents speak both languages
AOA	Age of onset of acquisition
cL2	Child second language (acquisition)
CP(H)	Critical period (hypothesis)
CV	Consonant–vowel
fem	Feminine
fMRI	Functional magnetic resonance imaging
L1	Monolingual first language (acquisition)
L2	Second language (acquisition)
LAD	Language Acquisition Device
LMC	Language Making Capacity
masc	Masculine
ML	Majority language
mL	Minority language
mL@H	Minority language at home
ML/2L	Majority language spoken by one parent, two languages by the other one
mL/2L	Minority language spoken by one parent, two languages by the other one
MLU	Mean length of utterances
OPOL	One person, one language
OV	Object–verb
PLD	Primary linguistic data
SLI	Specific Language Impairment
SOV, SVO	Subject–object–verb, subject–verb–object
SV	Subject–verb
UG	Universal grammar
V2	Verb-second order

*V3	Ungrammatical verb-third order
VO, VOS	Verb–object, verb–object–subject
VS	Verb–subject
XSV	Variable element–subject–verb
WL	Weak(er) language

1 Bilingualism in Early Childhood

Disentangling Myths and Facts

1.1 Myths or Facts?

Monolingualism is curable – El monolingüismo es una enfermedad curable – Le monolinguisme, ça se guérit – Monolinguismus ist heilbar! A provocative and defiant statement, sprayed as graffiti on walls or flaunted on T-shirts, primarily in parts of the world where languages are spoken that are not recognized as official languages or are not languages of instruction in the educational systems of their speakers' countries. The claim is not only that learning more than one language is possible and indeed recommendable. It rather suggests that failing to do so results, due to one's own fault, in an impoverished state of one's mental capacities, because we all have the ability to become bilinguals.

But is this assumption correct? Is it a fact or a myth? The fact is that, worldwide, monolingualism is indeed not the norm, if defined in terms of number of speakers. There exist some 200 states (193 member states of the United Nations, and SWIFT, the Society for Worldwide Interbank Financial Telecommunication, connects 214 states and territories), but more than 7000 languages are spoken in the world, more precisely 7099, according to Ethnologue (2017), the reference work that catalogues all known living languages. Consequently, many states must be multilingual, even if there are only some 20 with more than one official language – India alone has 19 official languages and South Africa 11. Admittedly, the fact that two or more languages are spoken in a country does not necessarily mean that a large part of its population is bilingual. Rather, speakers of a minority language normally also speak the majority language and are thus bilingual or multilingual whereas speakers of majority languages are frequently

1

monolinguals. Still, these facts suggest that bilingualism is more common than monolingualism.

The answer to the question of how widespread bilingualism is depends, in part at least, on who counts as a bilingual. UNESCO, for example, defines bi- and multilingualism as the use of more than one language in daily life. In other words, for someone to be considered to be bilingual does not necessarily require that this person have an equally good command of two languages. This definition reflects the linguistic reality of many bilingual societies, and it takes into account the fact that bilingualism is no longer confined to multiethnic societies. Rather, because of political and economic changes, bilingual societies have emerged in many other parts of the world, including countries that had previously been linguistically and ethnically homogeneous. Labour migration and movements of political refugees played an important role in this process, but this does not mean that these changes affect only economically disadvantaged groups. Rather, local mobility within and across national borders is currently a requirement at many workplaces, especially for highly qualified people. Although the social, economic and even political status of these temporary labour migrants differs substantially from that of migrant workers in Europe during the second half of the twentieth century, they face similar linguistic challenges. So-called guest workers were expected to stay for a limited time in the host countries, and for many of them this was initially their own expectation, too. They eventually became bilinguals, using two languages in daily life, but because of the uncertainty about their duration of stay, they did not necessarily attribute a high priority to the task of acquiring the language of the host country, at least not from early on. Those sent to a foreign country by their employers today find themselves in a rather similar situation: they live in bilingual settings, but only temporarily. Some experience this as an excessive demand; others see it as a welcome opportunity to acquire another language. At any rate, local mobility in modern societies, no matter what its causes are – politics, economy, even tourism or student exchanges – generates new types of potentially bilingual settings. These are not only situations of social but also of family bilingualism where a language is spoken in the family that is not the one of a mostly monolingual ambient society. Either all family members speak this language, as in the case of immigrants, or one of them speaks a different language, as is the case in binational marriages.

To return to the question of what is myth and what is fact in claiming that everyone can or rather should become bilingual, it is not only a fact that many countries in the world are multilingual but indeed also a fact that the majority of the world's population is bilingual. Moreover, bilingualism is an issue for all social classes, albeit in different fashions, depending not merely on social and economic status but also on attitudes towards bilingualism that vary considerably from country to country and across social groups within countries.

This means that becoming bilingual is not always an inevitable necessity. Particularly in cases of potential family bilingualism, there are choices to be made. However, well-founded

Monolingualism is curable

choices require adequate information about the advantages and risks possibly entailed by each option. Being told that monolingualism is curable can hardly count as such. For adults who are already native speakers of at least one language and who consider learning another one, obtaining information about the benefits or possible problems related to bilingualism is perhaps not a crucial issue. However, the decision on whether to raise children bilingually, either simultaneously from birth or successively during their first years of life, is clearly a very different matter that does raise concerns among parents and other caregivers. Rumour has it that acquiring more than one language during early childhood might contain risks for the children's linguistic, cognitive or social development or that early bilinguals might get confused and will not be able to function in each of their languages in the same way as monolinguals. Quite obviously, such concerns need to be taken seriously. Are they, too, facts or merely myths emanating from prejudices or misconceptions? Knowing that the majority of the world's population is bilingual does not really help in this case because we do not know how proficient these bilinguals are in each of their languages. This will not do for parents who decide to raise their children bilingually and who want to be sure that these children will become fully competent speakers of at least one and preferably both languages.

Unless they know with reasonable certainty that this goal can be achieved, parents are likely to decide against a bilingual education for their children, even if they have a favourable attitude towards bilingualism and do not reject the other language. A well-known example is the adoption of Proposition 227 (English Language in Public Schools Statute) in California in 1998 that effectively eliminated bilingual classes in most cases. Parents from linguistic minorities supported this proposition because they wanted to make sure that their children develop a knowledge of English that allows them to participate fully in all domains of the larger community. Proposition 227 was largely reversed by Proposition 58 (November 2016), but it is by no means a unique case of minority parents following this kind of reasoning and deciding against bilingualism. In fact, such concerns are known to have contributed in significant ways to the decline of regional languages that had served for centuries as the dominant or even only language of their communities.

Occitan, spoken in the southern half of what is today France, is one example at hand. It was the first literary language in Modern Europe, with a writing system developed in the tenth century and an internationally read literature, especially the poetry of the troubadours of the twelfth and thirteenth century. It was also the first and preferred language of King Richard I of England (the Lionheart). When the County of Toulouse was incorporated into the French kingdom (1271), Occitan became one of the languages of France, and with the incorporation of other Occitan-speaking regions, e.g. the previously English territory in the fifteenth century and the Provence, annexed in 1547, it was the one with the largest number of speakers.

For a long time, being part of France did not change significantly the linguistic situation of its speakers, not even when French became the only official language of the country (1539). In their daily interactions, they continued to use Occitan, which was also the first language of most of the bilinguals among them. Although French was now the largely dominant means of national interaction, in court dealings and other public functions, not many people could actively use that language. In fact, even at around 1800, less than one out of five citizens of France were able to speak and understand French. This only began to change in the nineteenth century with the introduction of compulsory military service, exposing large parts of the male population to various French dialects, other regional languages, and the national language. Finally, with the introduction of compulsory school attendance (1881), all children were exposed to French. Until the 1940s, most of them learned it as a second language at primary school.

In 1930, there were still 14 million speakers of Occitan. Yet at the beginning of the twenty-first century, UNESCO lists it as a seriously endangered language. It is estimated that it is currently used in everyday life by one or two million people, and that approximately 100,000 persons are native speakers, mostly bilinguals who acquired it simultaneously with French. Sociolinguistic studies suggest that a major reason for this dramatic decline is that parents were concerned that bilingualism might be a risk for their children's achievements in school. Note that minority languages were long banned from the public school system in France. Only as of 1951 could they be offered as an optional subject, yet not as a medium of instruction. Bilingual Occitan-French classes in a small number of public schools in southern France are an achievement of the twenty-first century – and they are still a matter of considerable political controversy. It is easy to see why parents worry that raising children bilingually might lead to problems when they enter an educational system where only French matters.

The decline of Occitan in France is just one blatant example of how concerns that bilingualism might cause problems for children affect social bilingualism. Although lack of support by the educational system played a major role in this case, this does not explain why parents, especially those who themselves speak another language in addition to the official one, should come to believe that it could be disadvantageous for children to know another language, in addition to the one taught and used in school. The main reason for such concerns and for why parents decide against a bilingual education for their children seems to be that they have doubts over whether it is possible to develop competences in two or more languages in early childhood, equivalent to those of monolinguals. This is clearly a concern that needs to be taken seriously. If it proved to be well founded, it would indeed be a reason to be reluctant to opt for a bilingual education of young children. But is this really the case? Is it difficult or even impossible for young children growing up with two or more languages to acquire in each of them the kind of linguistic knowledge and the linguistic skills that characterize monolinguals? Or worse, do they run the risk of not developing a native competence in any of their languages?

The question of how children exposed to more than one language from early on can become native speakers of these languages is one of the main topics of this book. It is an issue that, understandably, triggers highly emotional debates because what is at stake is children's linguistic development or perhaps even their well-being more generally. As a result, one finds strongly opposing views, among parents and caregivers as well as in newspaper articles and other media contributions dealing with child bilingualism. Whereas some voices warn against early bilingualism, pointing to possible risks, others see no limits to children's linguistic capacities and find only benefits in childhood multilingualism. Quite obviously, these views cannot both be correct because they make a number of contradictory claims or interpret the observations on which they agree differently. However, this does not necessarily mean that one view is entirely right and the other one completely wrong. Rather, it is precisely in this controversy that we face the challenge of disentangling myths and prejudices about child bilingualism from facts. In order to be able to do so, one needs to examine in some detail the alleged risks and benefits, and this is what I will do in the following chapters.

Let us nevertheless have a brief look right away at some of the issues to be discussed. In the two boxes below, I have summarized several of the more fundamental issues, beginning with possible problems and risks, followed by benefits attributed to a bilingual upbringing. The claims listed here are concerns expressed by parents, caregivers in daycare and preschool facilities, speech therapists and paediatricians, and in questions addressed to counselling services.

Possible Risks of Early Child Bilingualism

- Children exposed to more than one language at an early age cannot keep them apart. They fuse – temporarily or permanently – the two linguistic systems into a single one.
- Even if they do succeed in developing separate linguistic systems for their languages, they will confound them

when using them in everyday communication, speaking a macaronic language mix.

• Rather than becoming bilinguals, they end up as semilinguals in two languages, with incomplete competences in each of them.

• The competence attainable in the weaker language resembles that of foreign language learners; it is incomplete in comparison to monolingual native speakers.

• The rate of linguistic development in bilinguals is considerably slower than in monolinguals. This delay can have negative effects on children's success in preschool and in school.

• Balanced bilingualism is not possible – one language will always be stronger than the other one.

• If parents or caregivers communicate regularly in a foreign language with children, the children will not be able to become native speakers of that language.

• The task of acquiring two languages simultaneously puts excessive strain on the mental capacities of young children.

• Fusion of linguistic systems can cause problems, affecting children's cognitive development in general.

• Confusion about languages negatively affects children's psychological development. Individuals torn between languages and cultures experience difficulties in developing their personal identities.

These critical remarks on child bilingualism paint an extremely negative picture. If only half of them could be shown to be based on facts, one would indeed have to warn against a bilingual upbringing of children. Yet this is not the case. In fact, some of these comments reflect ideologically motivated biases and prejudices rather than problems documented in the course of bilingual development. There exists no evidence, for example, that exposure to two languages confuses children and causes cognitive or psychological disorders. The ideological nature of such claims becomes evident when they serve as arguments against risks of an undefined nature in only some contexts but not in others. A clear example of this kind of biased view is that of a French politician who warned against negative consequences of bilingualism in France but who supported, only a few days later, French-English bilingualism in Québec. A similar case is when scholars argue that bilingualism is an unrealistic goal for most children but recommend it for the happy few, i.e. those growing up in economically and educationally privileged families.

To the extent that rejections of this kind are at all based on facts, they rely on studies carried out during the second third of the twentieth century that reported on cases of lack of success in school by children from economically disadvantaged immigrant families. They confound effects of socioeconomic factors with those attributable to bilingualism. Nevertheless, this does not mean that all objections raised by critics of child bilingualism can safely be ignored. Rather, they must be examined carefully in the light of research findings provided by studies of child bilingualism over the last years, and this is what I will do, beginning in Chapter 3. Quite obviously, this critical examination must also be extended to the alleged benefits of bilingualism, some of which are listed in the following box. Only the ones supported by empirical research qualify as possible arguments in favour of a bilingual education of very young children.

Alleged Benefits of Early Child Bilingualism

- Children exposed to more than one language from birth become native speakers of all their languages.
- Even if onset of acquisition happens later in childhood, children can attain a perfect knowledge of this language.
- Bilinguals are more successful than monolinguals in learning further languages at a later age.

- Bilinguals outperform monolinguals in their reading and mathematical abilities.
- Bilinguals achieve higher scores in intelligence tests.
- Bilinguals tend to make better financial decisions than monolinguals.
- Bilingualism helps to delay neurological disorders like Alzheimer's disease and other types of dementia.

These by no means exhaustive lists of claims – some outright contradictory – concerning risks and benefits of child bilingualism illustrate the dire need for clarification. Parents and caregivers must be able to find out which of the alleged risks are real and whether they can be avoided. Moreover, they need to know what to do and what not to do in order to support the linguistic development of the children in their care. The question thus is whether we know enough about bilingualism and how it is acquired in early childhood to be able to disentangle facts from myths and offer the required guidance to parents and other caregivers. The answer is decidedly an affirmative one: it is indeed possible to give reliable answers to most of the questions underlying the lists of risks and benefits. Linguists, psychologists and other scholars have studied childhood bilingualism for more than one hundred years. Over the past 30 years, this research has increased dramatically, accumulating a huge amount of facts and providing many new insights. This is not to say that all problems are solved. Rather, as is typically the case in scientific research, for some of them there is a broad consensus among researchers concerning their explanation; for others, plausible solutions have been proposed, but further investigations are needed, and still others are topics of considerable controversy.

A guide for parents that bases its recommendations on insights gained by scientific research will necessarily reflect this state-of-the-art. In other words, some of the questions underlying the concerns and expectations of parents and educators can be answered with great certainty; for others, the answers rely on solid research results, but some aspects still need to be confirmed, and in some cases, only tentative answers can be offered. However, most of the problems invoked by the list of possible risks belong to the first group of well-studied issues for which satisfactory or even conclusive explanations can be given, because many investigations carried out during the last 20 years of the twentieth century focused precisely on these potentially problematic aspects of child bilingualism.

1.2 Searching for Facts in Research on Child Bilingualism

Recent research results will thus serve as the basis of the explanations and recommendations that I will propose in the following chapters. The focus lies on the *development* of bilingualism because most of the above-mentioned concerns relate to various aspects of language acquisition. I will therefore report on relevant research findings and summarize the results of some studies that succeeded in establishing facts in domains where previously prevailing uncertainties had caused concerns among parents and educators. These summaries are intended for the benefit of readers who want to find out to what degree and in what way research results actually support particular claims or recommendations. It should therefore be useful to offer some information about goals pursued and methods employed in studies of language acquisition. In fact, some basic information on which aspects of child bilingualism are investigated may also be of interest for readers primarily looking for a hands-on approach to child bilingualism and practical guidance, and who are less concerned with the research results underlying such recommendations.

The problem is that language is a complex and heterogeneous phenomenon – so much so that the term *language* is not particularly useful as a characterization of an object of scientific activities. Just as stating that biology investigates 'life' does not reveal much about this science, asserting that the language sciences study 'language' does not inform you about their research interests, even if the assertion is trivially true. In fact, one can approach this topic in many different ways, varying according to the perspective one adopts, and none of these approaches can be argued to be the correct or most appropriate one. They can focus on structural properties, social functions, communicative efficiency, and so forth, depending on one's interests. Importantly, these interests necessarily shape the questions that one can ask about the object of study, and the answers that one may expect to receive depend, in turn, on the kind of questions asked. For the present purpose of collecting information about child bilingualism, it is indispensable to understand what characterizes a native speaker of a language and to find out whether the same characteristics can be detected in bilinguals and, if this is the case, how they are acquired.

Keeping this in mind, a possible question to start out with is to ask: What does it mean to say that someone speaks language X? What kind of knowledge or skills are we ascribing to this individual? Quite obviously, such a person is able to communicate with others who know that language. However, this observation does not answer the question. It extends the ascribed capacity to other individuals, referring indirectly to a speech community whose members are able to interact successfully among each other, precisely because they share similar kinds of knowledge and are proficient in that language. The latter distinction is indeed particularly important for the description of the linguistic capacity of a person. Quite obviously, speakers of a language must have a good knowledge of its properties, but they must also be able to put this knowledge to use. This may appear self-evident, but the gap between knowing and doing can be considerable. Linguists refer to this observation by distinguishing between *competence* and *performance*, terms that will recur frequently in the following chapters.

The most crucial components of speakers' linguistic *knowledge* are the *lexicon* and the *grammar*. These are technical terms whose meanings can differ significantly from equivalent expressions in everyday language. Speaking of linguistic knowledge, for example, does not imply that a person is aware of the content of a body of knowledge or that one can access it via introspection. Native speakers of English 'know', for example, that a word with the initial consonant cluster *pt–* cannot be part of the lexical repertoire of their language, although it can be a loan from another language, e.g. 'Ptolemaic'. Yet, except for linguists, few of them are aware of this fact or can explain why this is so. We are thus dealing with *implicit* rather than explicit *knowledge*.

As for the term 'mental *lexicon*', it indeed refers to the lexical stock of a language, but it contains more information than the alphabetically ordered dictionaries with which we are familiar, and it is organized differently. Similarly, a mental *grammar* resembles only remotely grammar books. It is conceived as a *system* of rules or principles specifying the formal properties that shape a language. It is a system in that its parts are interdependent – if one element changes, significant parts of the system function differently. Just think of board games: if you remove a castle from a chessboard, the result is not merely an empty space but a substantially different strategic situation in the game.

Moreover, grammars are not monolithic systems; they rather comprise subsystems specifying sound (*phonology*), word (*morphology*) and sentence (*syntax*) structures of languages. Together, these constitute the grammatical competence of a speaker. Note that 'speaker' is a convenient shorthand expression that refers not only to oral language but to other modes as well, e.g. signing or reading. Importantly, it refers to both speech production and comprehension, as is suggested by the more explicit but somewhat clumsy term *speaker-listener*. Finally, lexical or grammatical *competence* refers to the knowledge of a speaker as well as to the description of this knowledge by linguists. We hope, of course, that the latter renders adequately the crucial properties of the former, but since we do not have direct access to competences, linguists' grammars can only be approximate accounts of the mental representations of the linguistic competences of speakers.

As may have become apparent from these last remarks, the goal of linguistic research is not merely to document linguistic behaviour. Rather, it aims at revealing the knowledge and the skills on which speakers rely when using their languages. However, since we do not have direct access to underlying principles and mechanisms, an important first step is to describe and analyse actual speech events. In other words, linguists write grammars whose rules should capture the implicit knowledge of speakers as it manifests itself in their speech. Importantly, this is a *descriptive*, not a prescriptive, procedure. Put differently, the goal is not to impose norms of what might be considered good or correct language. Grammars are not normative systems – they explain what speakers do, not what they are supposed to do. Only errors are filtered out. Identifying such errors is not always as easy as it may seem at first sight, but this issue need not concern us here. However, another one, linguistic variation, must be mentioned briefly, because it bears directly on attempts to compare the linguistic proficiency of various types of learners.

Languages like English, Spanish or German are not homogeneous objects. Not only are different varieties spoken in different countries, they also exhibit variation within national boundaries. *Dialects*, regional varieties of languages, can differ quite significantly from each other and from the national standard, not merely in pronunciation or lexical repertoires, but in all aspects of grammar. In some languages, like Italian or German, such dialectal differences can even lead to mutual incomprehensibility. Moreover, variation also occurs across social groups (*sociolects*) and within individuals who adopt their language use to specific situations (*registers*), e.g. depending on whether one interacts with one's boss, a child or a pet, in court or in a bar.

What this means is that we all, monolinguals as well as bilinguals, are *multilectal* because we speak several varieties of our native languages: various sociolects and registers, and perhaps even more than one dialect. At least the latter case is comparable to bilingualism, as dialects differ in their underlying grammars; bidialectal speakers thus possess more than one grammar. These may share a considerable number of rules, more than grammars of unrelated languages like Spanish and Basque, but not necessarily more than grammars of related ones like Dutch and German or Spanish and Portuguese. Irrespective of whether one wants to compare multilectal to multilingual speakers, the fact is that all of them, even monolinguals, can switch between different varieties of their languages. This must be taken into account when one analyses speech behaviour with the goal of formulating hypotheses about properties of mental grammars. The point is that a specific type of observed language use cannot simply be taken as evidence of a property of the grammar of language X. Rather, one must determine which variety of language X it belongs to, and apparent inconsistencies in language use may actually reflect a switch of varieties.

This multilectal perspective on language undoubtedly complicates matters, but problems do not disappear if we ignore them. In fact, linguistic variation and multilectal competences are highly relevant issues for our present purpose, because the discussions and recommendations in this book are based largely on studies contrasting different types of speakers: children, adults, monolinguals, bilinguals, first or second language learners, and so forth. It is therefore crucial to determine whether differences observed in the speech of different speakers actually indicate distinct types of grammatical knowledge or a switch between varieties. In fact, such differences need not reflect different grammatical properties at all – they may very well be an indication of how speakers put their knowledge to use, in which case they would have to be interpreted as performance phenomena.

Remember that competent speakers possess not only lexical and grammatical knowledge of their languages, they are also able to activate this competence when using the language in communicative interaction. This is by no means a trivial statement. What is self-evident is that performance presupposes that there is something to be performed, in our case linguistic knowledge. Yet although this is a necessary condition, it is not a sufficient one for performance to be possible. The well-known tip-of-the-tongue phenomenon can serve as an illustration of this claim. Speakers experiencing it are momentarily not able to retrieve a word that they have used many times before and that they can use in spontaneous speech shortly afterwards. Thus, they obviously do know it. In fact, when offered a list of words, they reject the wrong ones. Even more interestingly, they may be able to identify certain properties of the word, like its initial sound, its number of syllables, or its meaning; or they can cite words that are similar in sound or meaning. This shows that the irretrievable element is not missing; yet it is only partially, not fully, accessible. It furthermore suggests that items in mental lexica can be retrieved in a number of different ways, not merely by their initial sounds.

What matters in the present context is that the principles and rules that structure our lexical and grammatical knowledge do not suffice when it comes to activating this knowledge in comprehension and production. Rather, the skills that make proficient use possible require additional mechanisms. In order to convey a thought or communicative intention, an array of appropriate lexical items must be organized according to the grammar of the language and then be uttered – in oral speech – as a sequence of sounds. Conversely, comprehending an utterance requires attributing to a sequence of sounds a sentence structure that can be assigned meaning. The crucial point is that online processing of utterances cannot proceed step-by-step through the rules of grammar. Rather, for the sake of speed of processing, procedures are used that are possibly less exhaustive but more efficient in generating sentence structures. Importantly, comprehension is not production in reverse. Consequently, we must think of the processor as comprising a *parser* as well as a *formulator*, and the mechanisms of these components are not the same. As should be apparent by now, performance mechanisms are not merely collections of ad hoc strategies for language use; they rather constitute systems comprising subsystems, similar to mental grammars. Language learners must therefore develop both a grammatical competence and the proficiency to put it to use in a wide array of communicative contexts.

> **To Sum Up: Competence and Performance of Native Speakers of a Language**
>
> - The focus of our discussions lies on the development of the implicit grammatical and lexical knowledge of one or more languages.
> - (Mental) grammars comprise subsystems specifying sound (*phonology*), word (*morphology*) and sentence (*syntax*) structures.
> - Languages are not homogeneous objects. They consist of various sociolects, registers and dialects that differ in their grammatical properties.
> - Therefore, even monolinguals must acquire more than one grammar and more than one lexicon.
> - They are multilectal: they know and are able to understand and produce more than one variety of their language.

Let me briefly summarize some points that are most pertinent for the presentation of research findings in the following chapters of this book. We want to know what it means for a child to become and to be bilingual, what is unique to bilinguals, what they share with monolinguals, and which of these properties are possibly reasons for concerns or rather represent benefits, as compared to monolinguals. The search for answers to these and related questions requires comparing various types of speakers: child and adult monolinguals, simultaneous and successive bilinguals, and so forth. These comparisons cannot refer to norms established for standard languages but need to relate to the linguistic knowledge and proficiency of speakers of the languages in question. Distinguishing between competence and performance is crucial in order to determine whether differences between bilinguals and monolinguals, as observed in their speech, reflect differences in their mental lexica or grammars, or whether they differ in how they use this knowledge.

As will become apparent in later chapters, most of the issues discussed there concern the acquisition of linguistic competences, overwhelmingly, in fact, of grammatical knowledge. Nevertheless, the development of performance systems of native speakers of a language also plays an important role, and the psycholinguistic skills involved in language processing are of particular relevance. I should add that habituation of mechanisms and routines is a decisive factor in language processing. When the frequency with which they are activated decreases significantly, activating them again later requires more effort, they tend to operate at a slower rate and are prone to more variability in successful performance. Interestingly, the grammatical knowledge on which processing mechanisms draw are not subject to such frequency effects – they remain unchanged even if they are not activated for an extended time.

To avoid misunderstandings, I should add that although the focus of the discussions in this book will be on linguistic knowledge, speakers must obviously be able to access other types of knowledge as well, in order to be able to interact adequately and successfully with other members of their speech community. In part, this knowledge is specific to particular social or linguistic groups, and it is acquired in the course of socialization. Other aspects are universal and thus invariant across linguistic or social groups. If, for example, someone asks 'Do you know where the Eiffel Tower is?', answering 'In Paris.' is perfectly legitimate – unless this exchange happens in the streets of Paris. Both utterances are grammatically correct, but if uttered in Paris, the answer violates what linguists call *pragmatic* principles. In the present example they account for the fact that this question is not a general request for information but a request for street directions. It is a somewhat peculiar case because its interpretation depends on the location where the exchange takes place. Nevertheless, it is not a language-specific or culture-specific problem. Assuming that two interlocutors know where they are, the addressee of the question is able to deduce that this location is not the requested information.

As for cases where social norms determine the use of linguistic expressions, just think of languages that mark linguistically various degrees of formality or politeness. Japanese is a well-known example of a language with a large array of honorific suffixes, expressions that are attached to proper nouns. However, even in languages that only offer two options, formal and non-formal address, the choice of the adequate verb form depends on an intricate network of social criteria, including social status, seniority, age, sex, etc. In fact, the degree of formality depends furthermore on whether one combines the formal/informal verb form with the first or the last name of the addressee. Not surprisingly, second language learners may encounter difficulties trying to discover the underlying sociolinguistic regularities. Such was the case when a native speaker of English ordered the dog off the sofa, shouting 'Descendez!' – to the amusement of native French bystanders who would never use the polite form with their pet. On the other hand, English speakers may be irritated to find that German speakers use the non-formal verb form when addressing God. The sociolinguistic knowledge on which native speakers rely in these and similar situations is acquired in childhood. In this process, they draw on their linguistic competence and on their familiarity with the social and cultural values of the speech community into which they have been socialized. Quite obviously, bilinguals face these tasks in both their languages. If successful, they are therefore bicultural as well as bilingual.

In sum, adequate and successful verbal communication presupposes that speakers are able to access multiple types of knowledge, in addition to their linguistic competence: pragmatic, sociolinguistic, and so forth. As mentioned above, I will primarily report on studies that investigate the development of the linguistic competence of bilingual children, because the overwhelming majority of the questions on possible risks and benefits of bilingualism refer to these issues. This is also the reason why Chapter 2 is dedicated entirely to an outline of processes of grammatical development, thus providing a background against which bilingual acquisition can be evaluated. Nevertheless, sociolinguistic topics and issues relating more generally to biculturalism will also be addressed, if only briefly.

At this point, I would like to clarify a terminological choice. For the sake of simplicity, I use the term *bilingual* also for those who speak more than two languages. Consequently, I only use the term *multilingual* when referring specifically to the acquisition or use of three languages or more. In instances where the exact number of languages spoken by an individual is a pertinent issue, I use the terms *trilingual* or *quatrolingual*. Let me add that the term *bilingualism* is also neutral with respect to the type of bilingualism: family bilingualism in predominantly monolingual environments, social bilingualism in multiethnic countries, bilingualism resulting from labour migration, simultaneous and successive bilingualism, whether onset of acquisition happens at an early or at a later age, and so forth. I will return to these different types in the following section and then repeatedly in later chapters of this book. At any rate, I introduce explicit terminological distinctions only when these become relevant at a given point of our discussion. When dealing with the role of age of onset of acquisition, for example, see Chapter 7, it is necessary to distinguish between those acquiring two languages from birth and those first exposed to a second language either in childhood or as adults.

Before concluding this section, I should add a note on research methodology. As will become obvious in the following chapters, a large number of studies on early childhood bilingualism consist of investigations of a small group of children, sometimes even of a single child. One may wonder whether findings by such *case studies* are at all reliable and whether they can be generalized to bilingual children in general. The answer is that they are indeed of particular interest because they allow us to look at minute details of the acquisition process, as if under a microscope. Moreover, these are typically *longitudinal* studies, i.e. they follow the development of small groups of children over an extended period, thus providing us with insights into the actual progress of developmental processes. It would simply not be feasible to carry out such detailed research over months or years with a large number of individuals. Nevertheless, claims and hypotheses based on longitudinal case studies can be tested in *cross-sectional* studies that examine the linguistic capacities of larger groups of subjects at a given point of time. In other words, these two types of studies serve as controls for one another. In fact, the various case studies serve a similar function for each other.

A tentative and almost certainly non-exhaustive count of research papers and books published over the course of more than 30 years since 1985 reveals that more than 70 different children acquiring two or more languages simultaneously have been investigated in case studies. Most of these cover periods of several years. Altogether, they deal with a large number of languages and language pairs. Although the majority of the languages studied belong to the Indo-European family, non-Indo-European languages are also well represented, e.g. Basque, Cantonese, Hebrew, Inuktitut, Korean, Mandarin and Quechua.

Methodologically, these studies take different approaches in yet another respect: whereas all longitudinal and many cross-sectional studies collect *spontaneous* speech samples, a large and rapidly increasing number of experimental studies apply *controlled* data collection procedures that enable them to test narrowly defined hypotheses and to gain insights about constructions rarely used in spontaneous speech.

In sum, we can draw on a large body of research that investigated acquisition processes by early bilinguals as well as the knowledge and skills that they attained. These studies followed different theoretical approaches and applied a variety of research methods, analysing genetically and typologically distinct languages, looking at different types of bilingual settings. As for case studies, the ones published to date already report on a considerable number of individuals, and the number of such studies is rapidly increasing. It is therefore safe to say that the currently available research results provide a solid basis on which claims about the risks and benefits of childhood bilingualism can be assessed. Not surprisingly, though, some issues remain controversial whereas there exists a broad consensus on others. It goes without saying that the recommendations made in this book must reflect this situation. At any rate, statements asserting that 'research has proven such and such' should always be taken with a grain of salt. Insights gained by scientific research represents at best the current state of knowledge; in other words, it is subject to further scrutiny – and this is obviously true for the language sciences, as well.

1.3   Goals of This Book – and How to Use it

The goal of this book is to help parents and other caregivers to achieve their goals for their children's multilingual education, focusing on the linguistic development during preschool years. In fact, the discussion of possibilities and limits of child bilingualism is also designed to enable parents who are still hesitant as to whether they should raise their children bilingually to make informed decisions when defining the educational goals that they intend to pursue. These will obviously reflect individual aspirations as well as societal values and specific needs resulting from particular settings. Since the latter can vary considerably, parents' needs for information will vary accordingly.

Children of immigrant workers, for example, are often exposed to only one language during early years, the heritage language, especially if a sizeable number of people in the host country speaks it. This preschool monolingualism in a bilingual context is problematic on the individual as well as on the societal level if the long-term perspective of the children is to live in the country whose language they begin to learn at age 5, 6 or even later. Parents are not necessarily aware of the fact that it is possible to acquire more than one 'first' language in early childhood and that the simultaneous acquisition of another language has no negative effects on the heritage language, whereas attaining a full native competence becomes increasingly more difficult at later ages of onset of acquisition. This kind of information should be made available to parents, notwithstanding the fact that other factors, too, play a decisive role when it comes to making decisions on whether children should be raised bilingually.

A basic understanding of simultaneous and successive acquisition of bilingualism is indeed necessary for caregivers to be able to make responsible decisions on children's linguistic education, in every imaginable multilingual context. If, for example, one parent accepts a temporary assignment to a position abroad, children are immersed or born into a bilingual context where the family language differs from that of the societal majority. Since this situation is intended to last for only a limited number of years, the need for a bilingual upbringing is perhaps less pressing. However, parents may see bilingualism as an advantage for their children and view this setting as an exceptionally good opportunity to achieve this goal.

The same observation applies to multilingual families living in predominantly or exclusively monolingual environments. Binational families are the ones who most frequently ask for advice from counselling services. A rapidly increasing number of these inquiries come from families living in a third country, referring thus to trilingual settings. In fact, cases where a fourth language is present are also not rare, either because parents do not speak each other's language and resort to one which is not the community language (e.g. Greek mother, Russian father, living in France, communicating in English) or because other family members speak a different language. In these situations, the desire to stay connected with the heritage languages and cultures and to enable children to communicate with their grandparents represent strong motivations for a multilingual upbringing of children. The particular challenge for these types of family bilingualism is to provide the quantitatively and qualitatively adequate input necessary for the development of multiple first languages. A similar issue arises when linguistically homogeneous families in a monolingual environment want to expose their children to a language of which the parents themselves are not native speakers.

Parents and other caregivers of children in situations like the ones mentioned here are the primary addressees of this book. It should also be useful for families living in bilingual societies like the Basque Country, Belgium or Québec, even if they can rely on a number of local sources of information and on communal support and are less likely to look at books for guidance.

In fact, the willingness to opt for bilingualism and the need for guidance depend not only on the accessibility of support outside the family, most importantly bilingual daycare facilities and schools, but also on attitudes towards multilingualism and multiculturalism prevalent in the social environment. In Australia and Canada, for example, these ideas are widely supported, though not generally accepted, whereas in the United States 'English only' attitudes are widespread. Therefore, heritage languages are more endangered in the US, being at risk to be attrited in the second generation and lost in the third generation. Similar differences exist in other parts of the world as well. We have already seen an example in section 1.1 where I mentioned the decline of Occitan in France. Further support for this claim comes from the fact that Basque or Catalan bilingualism fares considerably better in Spain than in France. The need for guidance, as expressed in requests for counselling by parents and caregivers raising children bilingually, varies accordingly.

In the recommendations suggested in the following chapters, I try to take this into account. I distinguish between various kinds of bilingual settings, e.g. family or social bilingualism, simultaneous or successive language acquisition, different ages at the onset of acquisition, trilingualism. I also consider differences between educational goals, most importantly with respect to the linguistic knowledge and skills that the children are expected to attain. Should they become native speakers in more than one language or merely develop basic communicative skills in one of the languages, or aim at a level in between these options? The kind of support needed in order for bilingual education to succeed depends crucially on how one answers these questions.

In this book, I make suggestions on how to proceed in order to enhance children's linguistic development in two or more languages. In doing so, I adopt a perspective that is clearly favourable towards bilingualism, but the purpose of this guide is not to impose this view on its readers or to talk people into raising children bilingually. Whether they want to opt for a bilingual education is, of course, solely the parents' decision. I do believe, however, that it is possible to demonstrate that this is a feasible option and that early bilingualism can indeed be advantageous for children. As argued in the first section of this chapter, it is certainly possible to distinguish between myths and facts in most cases concerning alleged risks or benefits of early child bilingualism. Nevertheless, not all problem areas are equally well researched, and this state-of-the-art will be reflected by the recommendations given in the following chapters and in the discussion of the issues addressed there. I will state explicitly which suggestions or pieces of advice are backed by broadly accepted research results and which ones still require further investigations. However, all the recommendations in this book are founded on reliable research findings, and I refrain from giving advice in cases where I am not convinced by the conclusions that have been drawn from the available findings.

The organization of this book and of its individual chapters takes these considerations into account. As mentioned earlier, Chapter 2 is dedicated to a description of some crucial aspects of acquisition processes, focusing on grammatical development. This should help to determine in what way bilingual acquisition differs from other acquisition types – if at all.

The following chapters all start with a first section in which problems are outlined that are addressed in questions raised by parents in requests for counselling. Whenever possible, tentative answers to these questions are given in this same section. It thus offers answers to questions that parents ask, and, in some cases, answers to questions that should be asked. Section 2 then offers summaries of research results on which these answers are based – for those readers who want to know more about the studies enabling us to give these answers. I have made great efforts to present these research reports in plain language and in a non-technical fashion. Admittedly, certain arguments cannot be reproduced without mentioning some details of the linguistic analyses. Note, however, that the purpose of these more detailed discussions is to justify and explain claims and recommendations in sections 1 and 3. Yet the latter are perfectly intelligible without this information. Section 3 then focuses on more practical aspects and suggests guidelines in accordance with the recommendations given in the first section. Section 4, finally, offers reading suggestions for those who want to get some first-hand experience with the research on which the answers and recommendations are based. Let me emphasize, however, that no additional reading of research papers is required in order to be able to follow the discussion in this book.

In sum, readers can focus on the parts of a chapter that are most relevant to them, depending on their specific needs and interests. Those who are less interested in the research underlying the recommendations and who are primarily looking for practical guidance can skim or omit altogether the second section of a chapter, limiting their attention to sections 1 and 3. Moreover, Chapters 3 through 8 need not be read in the order in which they appear. In fact, each chapter can be read independently, following the interests of the readers rather than the logic intended by the author. Whenever necessary, cross-references point to the discussion of related issues in other chapters.

1.4   Reading Suggestions

The preschool years are the foundation for subsequent developments, and early bilingualism might influence later educational processes. The following paper evaluates the outcome of bilingual education for literacy, academic achievements and language levels. It concludes that 'there is no evidence for harmful effects of bilingual education and much evidence for net benefits in many domains'.

Bialystok, E. (2016). Bilingual education for young children: Review of the effects and consequences. *International Journal of Bilingual Education and Bilingualism*, 21(6), 656–79. http://dx.doi.org/10.1080/ 13670050.2016.1203859

The following article offers a summary of research on grammatical aspects of early bilingual development. Although it focuses on research activities during the period from 1995 through 2002, it is still worth reading.

De Houwer, A. (2005). Early bilingual acquisition. In J. F. Kroll & A. M. B. de Groot (Eds.), *Handbook of bilingualism*, pp. 30–48. Oxford: Oxford University Press.

2 How Infants Become Native Speakers

2.1 The Human Language Making Capacity

Children are all different – yet in some respects, they are very much the same. This is not a contradictory statement, and it is not as trivial as it may sound. Rather, it is a reminder that we need to acknowledge both the common traits that we share with others and the particular ones that distinguish us from others. It is also an incentive to search for the underlying causes that result in either commonalities or particularities. These questions are of considerable interest if we want to understand our linguistic capacities, the linguistic competence of adults as well as children's language acquisition. Parents know, of course, about differences between children, even within the same family and in spite of very similar if not identical family contexts and educational styles. One sibling may begin to walk months earlier than the other one, and one child utters their first words at a much younger age than another one. Generalizing over children is not impossible, but difficult. Even the widespread belief that early walkers are early talkers is not correct: early walkers may be late talkers, and vice versa. Moreover, they can take different routes in advancing through the language acquisition process. Some produce a continuous flow of speech sounds soon after they begin to utter their first words, although adults may find it difficult to identify words of the target language in this speech stream. Others produce few but almost perfectly pronounced words of the adult language. In spite of these and many other individual differences, these children, in fact all children, follow identical developmental paths in other respects; see section 2.2 for an explanation of what exactly this means.

It goes without saying that both similarities and differences across individual children or distinct acquisition settings can inform us about the nature of language development, and a comprehensive treatment of acquisition would have to deal with all these aspects of language acquisition. However, for our purposes, commonalties are of particular interest, especially the ones characterizing the development of children's grammatical competences. After all, the major concern motivating questions about the risks and benefits of child bilingualism is whether bilinguals are somehow special, possibly in a negative sense. This reveals that bilingualism is commonly assessed in comparison to monolingualism and that the monolingual child is the benchmark for bilingual acquisition. One might be inclined to reject this approach, pointing out that the larger part of the world's population speaks more than one language and that researchers as well as many bilinguals themselves emphasize that bilingualism must not be represented as an instance of deviance from monolingual norms. Yet this is precisely the issue that needs to be clarified, and this clarification requires careful comparisons of simultaneous and successive bilinguals with monolinguals. I will therefore adopt this contrastive perspective, asking whether these acquisition types differ and, if they do, what the differences are. I believe that this is the most fruitful approach in a guide for parents – it means that their concerns are taken seriously, not that monolingualism is considered as the gold standard of language acquisition. The purpose of this second chapter is thus to present a summary of what we know about important milestones characterizing monolingual and bilingual development.

The following outline of the course of first language acquisition is primarily concerned with the development of grammatical knowledge. I will therefore explain briefly what the relevant components of grammar are and which linguistic phenomena reveal how grammatical knowledge develops. In order to do this, I will have to introduce a few linguistic terms and explain what they mean. This is not intended as a crash course in linguistics. Rather, it should lead to a better appreciation of the achievements attained by the language-learning child. Moreover, some familiarity with this terminology should come in handy when reading the summaries of research reports in the second sections of the following chapters.

The decision to focus on the acquisition of mental grammars is motivated by several considerations. First, the grammar is the core component of linguistic competence, as explained in the previous chapter (section 1.2). Most importantly, it exhibits most of the developmental commonalities across children that we are looking for, because the course of grammatical acquisition is least dependent on factors that cause variation, such as the frequency with which a particular phenomenon occurs in the input that children receive. On the other hand, the development of some crucial parts of grammar is subject to age-dependent changes. This means that, in order to be able to acquire a native competence, children need to be exposed to the language at an early age. Quite obviously, the question of how maturation and other age-related changes affect children's capacity to acquire language is of considerable importance for those bilinguals who acquire their languages successively. I will therefore deal with this issue at some length in Chapter 7.

In this chapter, I will only refer to children who acquire languages from birth, either in monolingual (section 2.2) or in bilingual (section 2.3) settings. However, before asking how linguistic knowledge develops through the first three years of life, a few general remarks about acquisition are in order. Probably the most important observation is that first language acquisition is *always successful*. This may appear to be self-evident and hardly worth further discussion. However, if we consider for just a moment the very substantial differences that characterize not only the learning contexts but also the learners themselves, it is indeed quite remarkable that all children, leaving pathological cases aside, develop a full native competence in every language present in their environment. Just imagine the differences in what individuals bring to the task of language acquisition: some are more intelligent than others, some are more outgoing personalities than others, and so forth. Moreover, they grow up in socially and emotionally profoundly different contexts, experiencing different communicative styles, etc. Yet all they need in order to succeed in this formidable task is exposure to the target language in meaningful interactions with caregivers or peers. In other words, what matters is that the children are spoken to and have plenty of opportunities to speak, preferably in an emotionally positive and supporting environment. No teaching is required, not even corrective feedback.

To be sure, many parents try to foster children's linguistic development by correcting their grammatical errors. It seems, however, that this has little effect on acquisition processes – these children do not fare better than those whose parents do not correct them. In fact, they may not even understand the purpose of the corrections, interpreting them as contradicting the content of their utterance, as referring to *what* they said rather than to *how* they said it.

Another way in which parents hope to facilitate children's acquisition task is by using what has been called *baby talk* or *motherese*. Adults, quite generally, tend to adapt their language use to the limited linguistic abilities of children. Motherese varies according to children's age, but in all its realizations it is intended to catch the attention of the child, e.g. by talking in a higher pitched voice to infants and toddlers, to enhance interaction, e.g. frequently asking pseudo-questions like 'where is our little girl?', or to facilitate comprehension by means of hypercorrect pronunciation, choice of basic vocabulary or avoidance of complex structures. Whether this really enhances language acquisition is an open question. Some researchers believe that it accelerates the rate of acquisition, whereas others warn that structural simplification results in an impoverished linguistic environment.

I see no reason to discourage caregivers from correcting children's speech or from modifying their own speech according to what they feel is more adequate in interactions with children. But they should know that language acquisition succeeds equally well without this kind of support. After all, not all parents resort to this kind of language use, certainly not in all cultures. Thus, acquisition success does not depend on linguistic support by adults – the only necessary requirement is sufficient exposure to the target language. This is even more impressive if one considers the fact that children are able to develop grammatical competences even though the linguistic input to which they are exposed is deficient. This is to say that a certain percentage of the utterances produced by adults does not conform to the norms of the target grammar: performance errors, false starts, incomplete sentences, elliptic but colloquially acceptable constructions (*can't find it*), and so forth. Somehow, these are ignored or reinterpreted by children in the process of grammar construction. An amazing feat, indeed.

But that is not all. First language acquisition is not only successful; it happens within a relatively short period. What is to be understood by 'short period' depends essentially on how one determines the onset of acquisition. First exposure occurs already before birth since the sounds of the target languages are perceived *in utero*. The question is whether this can trigger acquisition processes. The answer is almost certainly an affirmative one, because neonates have been shown to be able to distinguish between the sounds of their ambient languages as opposed to unfamiliar ones, although they do not, of course, understand the meaning of anything that is said, as yet. Subsequently, during the first year of life, they tune in to the specific characteristics of the languages to which they are exposed and develop the ability to perceive some of their formal properties, as we will see in section 2.2.

There can be no doubt that language acquisition is well underway during the first months of the first year, although children do not utter their first words, or rather what resembles words of the adult language, until approximately age 1;0 (years; months). At around age 3;0, they have acquired a basic grammar; and by age 4;0, most of the target grammar is in place. Word learning, however, never ends in the course of a lifetime; this is why lexical acquisition is not mentioned in this context. Thus, although it is not possible to define precisely the beginning and end of acquisition, grammatical development happens largely within three or four years. Considering the magnitude and complexity of the task, it is perhaps not an exaggeration to view this as a fast acquisition rate. After all, adults who move to a place where a language other than their first one is spoken, and who have the opportunity to communicate every day in the new language, rarely acquire it at a similar rate, and certainly not as successfully.

Still, the third quality of first language (L1) acquisition that must be mentioned here, uniformity of grammatical development, is even more significant than the fast acquisition rate; it is on a par with the first one, ultimate success of all learners. Developmental uniformity means that children proceed through identical developmental phases and behave in an identical fashion in the way in which they acquire the grammars of their target languages. At this point, I will not elaborate on this topic, for section 2.2 is entirely dedicated to this issue, precisely because these uniform developmental sequences represent the most important of the commonalities of grammatical development mentioned above. We possess solid evidence indicating that these sequences are invariable across individuals, in spite of the variable factors that can influence acquisition, learner-internal and environmental ones, alluded to earlier. In fact, they do exert influence on developmental processes, accelerating or slowing them down, but they do not alter the order of the phases within a developmental sequence.

To Sum Up: Three Crucial Properties of L1 Development

- First language acquisition is always successful.
- First language acquisition happens at a fast rate.
- Grammatical development in first language acquisition is uniform; children proceed through identical developmental phases.

Quite obviously, ultimate success, uniformity of the process, and rate of L1 acquisition require an explanation if we want to understand how infants develop into native speakers of the languages to which they are exposed. After all, if they had to discover all the grammatical properties of a language by experience, extracting them from the partly deficient and necessarily limited amount of input data encountered in communicative interactions, we would expect some learners to fare better than others, some to come up with solutions to acquisition problems different from those of others and to follow different routes towards the target system and some to require significantly more time than others.

A possible explanation of the above-mentioned characteristics of L1 development is to assume that children are equipped with a *Language Making Capacity* (LMC) that guides linguistic development. This can explain the success and the fast rate of acquisition as well as the fact that grammatical development in all languages is characterized by identical developmental phases through which all children proceed, acquiring similar grammatical phenomena in a uniform fashion. Importantly, the LMC does not relate to specific languages but contains principles and mechanisms enabling children to acquire whatever language they are exposed to. The LMC is genetically encoded and species-specific, i.e. only humans possess a faculty for language. It is innate, meaning that children are endowed with it at birth, although initially they cannot make full use of it, either because they are cognitively not yet ready or because parts of the LMC only become accessible in the course of development.

In fact, developmental changes do not affect all components of the LMC alike. Our cognitive system comprises general-purpose as well as domain-specific operations, the latter specializing in the processing of information relating to specific tasks like vision – or language. The LMC contains both kinds, but since they differ in function and in how they develop in early childhood, linguists have introduced terminological distinctions. The language-specific component is referred to as the *Language Acquisition Device* (LAD) and the subcomponent of the LAD that specifies formal properties of grammars is called *Universal Grammar* (UG) and consists of principles constraining all human grammars. In the following chapters, I will mainly refer to the LMC, but occasionally it will be necessary to focus on one of its components, especially in Chapter 7 where I will address the issue of age-related changes to our capacity to acquire languages.

To Sum Up: The Human Language Making Capacity (LMC)

- The LMC comprises general-purpose and domain-specific cognitive principles and operations.
- The Language Acquisition Device (LAD) is the component of the LMC that comprises the language-specific principles and operations.
- Universal Grammar (UG) is a subcomponent of the LAD, comprising principles that specify formal properties of human languages.

What needs to be retained during the discussions of this chapter is that children come equipped with cognitive capacities that comprise principles constraining formal properties of mental grammars and with acquisition mechanisms guiding them in the process of language development. Quite obviously, they are not aware of this acquisition capacity, and its principles and mechanisms are not accessible through introspection. The crucial point is that the language-acquiring child does not have to consider every logically possible hypothesis about properties of the target grammar when facing the task of extracting grammatical information from the input data. Rather, the LMC eliminates a large proportion of the possible options, thus reducing the number of hypotheses to be considered by the child. In sum, the fast rate, success and uniformity of grammatical development favour strongly the assumption that children can rely on the support and guidance provided by an innate capacity for language acquisition. It is the LMC that explains how mere exposure to the primary linguistic data enables them to attain native competences.

I should add that the assumption that linguistic development in monolingual and bilingual first language acquisition is guided by an innate LMC, comprising a language-specific LAD and UG, follows from a particular theory of language and of language acquisition. In my view, it is a convincing theory that can explain universals as well as particulars of acquisition. Unfortunately, however, justifying this theoretical choice would go far beyond the scope of the current discussion. I can therefore only refer to the excellent and well-written introduction by Pinker (1994) that presents and explains the theoretical framework adopted here.

Let me finally remind you that the focus of the discussions in the following chapters lies on commonalities of acquisition processes. It goes without saying, however, that successful acquisition requires more than to follow guidelines offered by universal principles. It further requires learning of properties particular to specific languages, and it even tolerates learners resorting to idiosyncratic solutions to learning problems. Consequently, acquisition processes are shaped by universal principles constraining all languages as well as by language-particular ones. Taking both types into account and leaving aside behaviour specific to individuals, it is possible to identify developmental milestones characterizing the acquisition process of all children acquiring a given language. These can serve as benchmarks when we inquire whether and how bilingual acquisition differs from monolingual acquisition and, to the extent that this is the case, whether it is a quantitative or a qualitative difference.

2.2   Developmental Sequences in the Acquisition of Grammars

Uniformity of grammatical development across languages and children is probably the most surprising and most significant property of first language acquisition, one that speaks strongly in favour of the assumption that all children share a common acquisition mechanism. We want to know whether it operates in the same fashion in bilingual and in monolingual children. Let us therefore look at some commonalities characterizing acquisition processes in early childhood in order to understand the implications of the claim that children follow the same path towards a native competence in the language of their social environment – a narrow path marked by gradually emerging abilities concerning perception, comprehension, and production of linguistic expressions.

The most important observation is that children developing grammatical competences in their ambient languages proceed through invariant developmental sequences characterizing the acquisition of core properties of these grammars. These sequences consist of a number of developmental phases, each defined by a grammatical phenomenon that emerges in children's speech during this phase. The sequences are invariant in that the order in which children attain these phases is not reversible. Some children will take longer than others before advancing to the next phase, but they will never acquire the phenomenon characterizing phase Y before the one defining phase X if these phases are strictly ordered in an X – Y sequence.

The fact that all children follow the same developmental logic is an important insight. It suggests that they are indeed guided by common acquisition mechanisms, rather than by individual preferences shaped by personal characteristics (intelligence, personality, etc.) or by their environment. Such developmental commonalities are observed from early on, as can be illustrated by the chronology of emergence of linguistic skills characterizing the first two years of a child; see the following two boxes. The first one summarizes the development of language perception and comprehension, the second one the production of language. Note that the ages mentioned here are approximate because the rate of development can vary considerably across individuals.

Some Milestones of L1 Development: Language Perception and Comprehension

- *During the first days after birth, infants*
  - recognize their mother's voice;
  - distinguish between linguistic and non-linguistic sounds;
  - distinguish between their ambient language/s and foreign ones.

- *During their first months,*
  - they discriminate a wide variety of sound contrasts that serve grammatical functions;
  - language is processed in the left hemisphere of the brain.
- *During the second half of the first year,*
  - they focus on properties of the target languages and become less successful in perceiving contrasts that have no functional values in these languages.
- *At around 10 months,*
  - they begin to comprehend words.
- *At 14 months,*
  - they react differently to function words as compared to content words.

As mentioned earlier, the onset of phonetic acquisition happens before birth. Intra-uterine recordings have shown that speech sounds are perceived distinctly, and although not much is known about what kind of use is made of this input, infants of only a few days old recognize the voices of their mothers. Moreover, they distinguish between linguistic and non-linguistic sounds. Infants are also able, within the first days and weeks, to discriminate the languages of their environment from foreign languages and they distinguish between (some) foreign languages. It is thus obvious that newborns are neurologically and cognitively predisposed to language processing and that prenatal exposure to language does have a learning effect.

This conclusion is confirmed by what we know about perception of speech sounds during the subsequent weeks and months. Importantly, speech is already processed in those designated areas of the brain where language is processed in adult brains. This shows that the sounds of language are distinguished from other kinds of acoustic input. Speech is special; it is not just another kind of noise. In fact, children show early sensitivity to acoustic features that form the basic building blocks of sound systems (tone, intonation, consonants, vowels, etc.) of human languages, increasingly focusing on properties of the languages to which they are exposed.

Moreover, continuous changes in certain acoustic properties of sounds are not perceived as continuous but as categorically distinct. What this means is that physical differences between similar sounds, such as for example *b* and *p*, are gradual rather than abrupt, and their pronunciation varies across languages and even across varieties of one and the same language. Thus, *p*, as it is pronounced in one language, sounds more like *b* in another one. Yet native speakers of each of these languages perceive the two sounds as categorically distinct. Interestingly, children at this early age, too, perceive acoustically gradual changes as categorically distinct. This is crucial for their acquisition process because categorical perception enables them to get into the linguistic system of their target language. It is not a coincidence that this happens at a time when infants increasingly attend to properties that serve functional purposes in the systems of their ambient languages. In other words, although this may at first seem paradoxical, progress towards the phonological system of the target language means that learners become less successful in perceiving contrasts which have no functional value in their language. What may appear as a loss of learning abilities is really a prerequisite for the development of a specific linguistic system, because it means that the focus has shifted to what is most relevant for the acquisition of the target language.

At the age of approximately 10 months, children begin to comprehend words, i.e. they are able to relate sound sequences to meanings. Soon afterwards, at around 14 months, they begin to react differently to function words as compared to content words. Function words are elements like conjunctions (e.g. *and*, *that*) or articles (e.g. *the*, *a*), primarily serving to encode structural relationships, whereas content word like nouns, verbs or adjectives express complex concepts. The fact that children perceive these types of words as distinct is a first indication that they are about to develop grammatical knowledge. Note that this happens at a time when they are not yet able to use functional elements in their own speech.

Some Milestones of L1 Development: Language Production

- *During the first four months,*
    - sounds resembling vowels (V) and consonants (C) are produced;
    - there is a rapid change of vowels.
- *As of approximately the sixth month,*
    - babbling takes place, preferring CV sequences with frequent reduplications;
    - they produce sequences of syllable-like units and sentence intonation;
    - deaf children's production decreases;
    - increasing accommodation to ambient language/s.
- *At 12 months,*
    - first 'words' emerge, preferably combining front C and back V;
    - sound–meaning relations emerge;
    - holophrastic utterances emerge.
- *At 18 months,*
    - there is a rapid increase in the number of lexical elements;
    - multi-word utterances emerge.
- *At 24 months,*
    - grammatical morphemes emerge.

Similar milestones have been observed in infants' early speech production. During the first four months they produce a range of vowel-like sounds and a limited set of consonant-like ones, with the vowels changing rapidly. After approximately five months, *babbling* begins, i.e. children produce units that look like syllables; however, these do not yet express meaning. Consonant-vowel combinations (CV) are preferred and reduplications are frequent, e.g. *baba, dada.* One can also detect sentence intonation patterns in this early production. This is to say that children produce sequences of units that sound like questions or commands, although they do not yet contain anything that resembles words of the target languages. Note that the range of sounds which infants produce is initially not limited to the inventory of the respective target languages, i.e. to what occurs in parental input. Progressively, however, the kind of sounds that occur in their production is reduced to what is encountered in their linguistic environment. In fact, some researchers claim that this already happens before the age of six months. Interestingly, even the crying of babies exhibits characteristic melodic patterns influenced by the target language.

Another important fact is that the frequency of speech-like production of deaf children decreases during this period. This too indicates that children increasingly focus on and react to the properties of their ambient languages. It certainly confirms what I mentioned in the preceding paragraph: during the second half of their first year of life, children tune in to the characteristics of the languages to which they are exposed, and they develop the ability to perceive formal properties of these languages.

At around 12 months, children typically produce their first words. This represents a major step in their cognitive development because it means that they are able to establish more or less stable sound–meaning relations. In fact, comprehension studies demonstrate that they are able to do so as of approximately 10 months. However, early 'words' are not yet identical to the corresponding words of the adult languages. Initially, the sound parts of the sound–meaning pairings are approximations, frequently consisting of CV sequences that encode marked articulatory contrasts. What this means is that an 'optimal' syllable consists of a consonant produced at the front of the mouth (or rather: the articulatory organ), like a bilabial, e.g. *p*, *b*, *m* or a dental, e.g. *d*, *t*, combined with a back vowel, e.g. *a*. It is hardly a coincidence that in many languages adult or baby talk words exist that refer to mother or father and that exhibit this shape, e.g. *mama*, *papa*, *dada*, etc. Target words can also be remodelled according to the articulatory preferences. In German child language, for example, *Ball* 'ball' frequently emerges as *ba*.

As for the meanings of the sound–meaning pairings, they, too, differ from those of the corresponding adult words. Initially, they may be used like proper names. The word 'ball', for example, can refer to one specific object, e.g. the child's red ball with white stripes, until its meaning is extended to all 'ball' objects, whatever their size or colour. Once this is achieved, one frequently finds overextensions, e.g. the child's word for 'ball' is used for an orange or the one for 'dog' refers to all four-legged beings. In fact, one of the children who we studied used the French word *auto* 'car' to refer to all four-legged entities that move: dogs, cats, cows – and cars.

During the first half of the second year, the size of the lexicon increases steadily, lexical items becoming more and more adult-like in form and meaning. Initially, lexical development is relatively slow, with one or perhaps two words being added every other day. Parents who like to keep track of their children's linguistic development in a diary can easily do so. However, once the lexicon attains a size of approximately 50 words, one can observe a developmental spurt in the lexicon, with new words emerging so rapidly that most parents concede defeat and abandon the diary.

Early vocabulary items differ from adult words not only in that their meanings may be wider or narrower, they actually function like entire adult sentences. This is why linguists call these expressions *holophrastic* or *one-word utterances*. When a child says *cookie*, for example, it is rather unlikely that the intention is simply to name the object to which the word refers. Instead, the meaning of this utterance probably amounts to something like 'I can see that there is a cookie jar up there on the shelf, and I want you to give me one immediately'.

In the course of the following months, i.e. during the second half of the second year, children's utterances unfold into two- or multi-word utterances. This ability to combine words represents a huge new developmental achievement. Crucially, these sequences are combined productively; they are not formulaic expressions. Rather, a word appears together with a variety of other words, and it does not necessarily occupy the same position all the time, e.g. *want cookie, cookie gone*. These word concatenations are early sentences, exhibiting the first signs of syntax. Recall that already at about 14 months, children begin to react differently to content and to function words. This is a prerequisite for the development of syntax. A few months later, multi-word combinations emerge that can be regarded as simple syntactic units.

Shortly before or after their second birthday, children start using grammatical *morphemes*, like inflectional suffixes, e.g. German *Auto fährt* 'car runs' (3rd person singular suffix *-t*), or *du fährst* 'you drive' (2nd person singular *-st*). Morphemes are the smallest meaningful units of a language. They can be *free*, like 'dog' or 'the', or *bound* like suffixes, i.e. the latter must be attached to others. Bound grammatical morphemes are of particular interest for this summary of linguistic development, because they are a new kind of animal. Their meanings do not refer to objects, actions or events like nouns and verbs, and they cannot stand alone. Children's early lexicons consist almost exclusively of words modelled on adult nouns and verbs, with some adjective- or adverb-like elements added to them – all of them independent elements. Not long after they begin to be assembled in simple syntactic concatenations, grammatical morphemes are attached to them – unmistakable signs that the children now have access to grammatical knowledge.

Interestingly, in acquiring grammatical morphemes, children behave uniformly in yet another way. They not only proceed through ordered developmental sequences, they also exhibit striking resemblances across individuals and across languages in that they produce the same kinds of errors, and they even resemble each other in the kind of errors that they do *not* make. For example, it is not uncommon for L1 learners to overextend the use of regular morphology to irregular items, e.g. French *batté* instead of *battu* 'beaten' or English *wented* or *goed*. In other words, they do not merely imitate what they encounter in the speech of adults or peers. They rather use newly acquired forms productively, attaching, for example, the suffix *-ed* to verbs in order to produce past tense forms. In most cases, this yields the correct form; only with a small number of irregular verbs does it result in an error. They do not, however, attach grammatical morphemes inappropriately across syntactic categories. Verbal markers for person agreement, for example, are not attached to nouns, e.g. German *die Blume* 'the flower' does not yield *es blumt* 'it flowers' (verb + 3rd sg marking). The fact that this type of error never occurs in children's speech suggests that they implicitly know that nouns and verbs are distinct categories. Note that in English we do find *the flower* – *it flowers*, because 'flower' can be a noun 'a flower' or a verb 'to flower'; the 3rd sg *–s* is thus correctly attached to a verb, not to a noun. These kinds of observations allow us to conclude that children indeed follow a narrow path towards L1 knowledge, i.e. they make the same kinds of errors and they avoid other types.

The more general conclusion that we can draw from the observed changes in children's language use is that no later than during the second half of the second year they have acquired an at least basic grammatical competence. The presence of multi-word utterances and grammatical morphemes in their speech are unambiguous signs that they organize it according to morphosyntactic principles. During the third year, a wealth of further grammatical markings appear, many of which emerge in a fixed order, indicating that they have made further progress in their grammatical development. The new forms and constructions can be interpreted as milestones characterizing developmental phases, each of them defined in terms of newly available grammatical knowledge. This is of particular interest for our purposes because we can refer to the ordered sequences of milestones when comparing bilingual and monolingual acquisition. If the sequences are identical in both acquisition situations (monolingual vs. bilingual), we can conclude that bilingual children differentiate their two grammars early on and that each grammar in the bilingual child develops in the same way as in monolingual children. Both these points address crucial issues to be discussed in more detail in the following chapters. At this point, it must suffice to look briefly at an example illustrating what such sequences look like.

One of the earliest properties on which developing and mature languages converge, usually before age 2;0, is the position of the verb with respect to its complements, i.e. either preceding objects, as in English and in Romance languages, or following them, as in German and other Germanic languages (VO/OV). Thus, early child utterances look like the following examples: French *mange gâteau* 'eat cake' (VO), but German *Kuchen essen* 'cake eat' (OV). Linguists assume that in every language there exists a basic or neutral position for each constituent in sentence structures, e.g. verbs being placed clause-finally in German or to the left of objects in French or English. If a language allows an element to appear in more than one position, additional orders are derived from the basic one. To give an example, in many languages the verb that normally follows the subject can be placed in a position to the left of the subject in interrogative constructions, as in French *il vient – vient-il?* or German *er kommt – kommt er?* 'he comes – comes he/does he come?'. When there are two verbal elements, as in constructions with auxiliaries (*she has come*) or with modals (*she must come*), it is the *finite* one that leaves the basic position. Finite verbs are the ones that can carry subject and object agreement or tense and aspect markers, as opposed to non-finite verbal elements like past participles, infinitives, etc.

Concerning the acquisition of these phenomena, it is remarkable that from very early on children prefer their language's basic VO or OV order in their own speech, even if it is not the one most frequently encountered in the input data. It is equally remarkable that children correctly place finite verbs in the position required by the target grammar as soon as they use verb inflection productively. This, too, happens very early, since subject–verb agreement markers, as in our German example above (*Auto fährt* 'car runs', *du fährst* 'you drive', etc.), are the first instances of verb morphology to appear in children's speech, arguably the earliest uses of grammatical morphology altogether. An example of the correct placement of verbs during early developmental phases is the French negative construction. In this context, the finite element precedes and the non-finite one follows the negative element *pas*, as in *il ne mange pas* 'he doesn't eat' as opposed to *il ne veut pas manger* 'he doesn't want to eat'. As soon as French children begin to use finite verb forms, they place them correctly in preverbal position. A similar situation applies in so-called V2 constructions in German where the finite verb occupies the second position (V2 position) of the sentence, thus preceding the subject if an element other than the subject occupies the first position (*sie kommt morgen – morgen kommt sie* 'she comes tomorrow – tomorrow comes she'). German children, too, place the finite verb in the required position, as soon as they use finite verb forms.

In sum, children initially prefer the basic word order of the target language. Once they are able to use finite verb forms, they immediately place them in the position required by the target grammar, and they never mistakenly put a non-finite element in this position. Shortly afterwards, verbs in child language carry not only subject agreement but also aspectual and temporal markers, and auxiliaries, modals, and copulas emerge at this point of acquisition. All this happens within a few months, beginning at around age 2:0. A similar sequence has been documented for nominal elements, starting with the first occurrences of articles and of nominal inflection, followed by a developmental phase, during the second half of the second year, when case, gender, and number markings come in. Soon afterwards, at around 2;6, subordinate clauses emerge, introduced, where appropriate, by subordinating conjunctions. Interrogation, which up to then appeared exclusively in the form of intonation questions, is now expressed by different syntactic means, including sentence-initial placement of question words. Other parts of grammar develop in much the same fashion, and at around 3;0, children are able to use a substantial part of the inventory of grammatical devices offered by the target languages. At around 4;0, most of the grammar is in place. Importantly, for our present interests, monolingual children reach this state by proceeding along a largely invariant developmental path.

2.3   An Endowment for Bilingualism

The crucial question now is: Are bilinguals special? It goes without saying that they are indeed special in that they develop mental representations of two languages and are able to communicate in both of them, alternating between them. Yet what this question is really asking is whether bilinguals who are exposed to their two languages from birth can acquire both of them in basically the same way as the corresponding monolinguals. More specifically, is it possible in simultaneous acquisition to advance in each language at a rate characteristic of L1 learners, to proceed through identical developmental sequences and to attain a native competence in both? A detailed treatment of these issues will have to wait until later chapters. But it would be useful to give an at least tentative answer to this question at this point in order to make explicit the general line of argument that will be followed throughout this book. After all, this is not a whodunit where readers must be kept in suspense until the very end. Rather, it should be clear from the start that grammatical development in bilingual children need not differ substantially from that of monolinguals. In fact, research on child bilingualism revealed that the human Language Making Capacity is an endowment for bilingualism. In this section, I present a brief summary of some of the research results that justify this conclusion. Specific issues, especially the ones related to concerns expressed by parents, will be discussed in the following chapters, backed up, where necessary, by references to further research results.

Let us first address the questions of whether grammatical development in bilinguals, too, is characterized by invariant developmental sequences and, provided this is the case, whether the sequences are identical to the ones observed in monolingual acquisition. The first problem that arises here actually concerns the question of whether the two languages are differentiated from early on or whether they are merged, at least temporarily, into a single system. Early differentiation is a necessary precondition for L1-like grammatical development. Should it not be feasible, the point of departure of the acquisition process in the two languages would necessarily be different for bilinguals, as compared to their monolingual counterparts. Consequently, the subsequent developmental phases, too, would be different or at least be ordered differently, even if they ultimately led to the same final point, i.e. if it was still possible to reach L1-like native competences.

In other words, the first crucial task that the bilingual child faces is to initiate the development of two distinct mental grammars rather than to incorporate all the acquired knowledge into a single system. From a monolingual perspective, this may seem like a formidable challenge. Yet studies analysing a variety of linguistic phenomena in the speech of children acquiring different language pairs have shown that bilinguals do not have to proceed through such a unitary system phase. In fact, analyses of various longitudinal corpora demonstrated that early differentiation is not only possible but characteristic of the developmental pattern through which simultaneous bilinguals typically proceed. This is what the *Dual System Hypothesis* states, a hypothesis widely accepted today on the basis of findings obtained by a steadily increasing number of case studies carried out over the past 30 years. The case studies investigated an impressive variety of language combinations, including non-Indo-European languages like Basque, Hebrew, Inuktitut, Korean, Mandarin, and Quechua.

Importantly, this research established beyond reasonable doubt that grammatical systems are differentiated during the earliest phases of productive use of particular constructions. I will return to this claim immediately. Let me first mention that we have good reasons to believe that grammatical differentiation actually sets in earlier, because differentiation of phonological knowledge precedes the separation of syntactic systems. It is therefore plausible to assume that language differentiation is initiated and enhanced by prosodic bootstrapping. Recall that newborns are able to distinguish between languages with different prosodic or rhythmic properties. This suggests that prosodic information facilitates the differentiation of systems, certainly of phonological systems, but probably also of morphosyntactic ones. In consideration of these discriminating capacities, which bilinguals display already in the prelexical phase of linguistic development, it is not at all surprising to find that they are able to distinguish the lexical and grammatical systems of the ambient languages from very early on, quite probably even before they actively use the corresponding linguistic devices in their speech production.

Returning to the evidence for early grammatical differentiation based on children's linguistic production, it primarily refers to the fact that bilingual children, from very early on, use different word order patterns in their two languages. What does 'very early' mean in this case? Differences in word order begin to appear as soon as children start using multi-word utterances, typically at around age 1;10, i.e. just before their second birthday. However, as mentioned earlier, individuals differ considerably in their rate of development. Already at this age, shortly before or after their second birthday, some children are several months ahead of others. Age is therefore not always a reliable yardstick when it comes to assessing the period during which a particular phenomenon is acquired. For this reason, child language studies prefer to refer to *mean length of utterances* (MLU) as a means of indicating specific points of grammatical development. MLU values are obtained by computing the number of words or morphemes per utterance, based on approximately 100 utterances produced by an individual at a given time. The underlying idea is that longer utterances are likely to be more complex than shorter ones, and that higher MLU values will therefore indicate more advanced stages of grammatical development. Although this is not necessarily the case, MLU has indeed proven to be a more reliable criterion than age when it comes to assessing grammatical acquisition.

As it turns out, distinct word order patterns in the two languages of bilingual learners are attested during a period when they attain an MLU of approximately 1.75. In other words, the average utterance, at this point of development, contains less than two words. For obvious reasons, it is not possible to establish an earlier point in linguistic development at which generalizations can be made concerning the acquisition of syntax. We can thus conclude that the differentiation of grammatical systems does happen very early, namely as soon as children use multi-word utterances, at approximately age 1;10 or at a calculated MLU of 1.75.

What kind of distinct word order patterns may we expect to find in the two languages of bilinguals? The ones mentioned in the preceding section 2.2 can serve as examples again. As mentioned there, languages differ in the kind of basic order of verbs and objects, e.g. VO or OV. Children acquiring simultaneously an OV language like Basque or German and a VO language like Spanish or French, use OV order from early on in the OV but not in the VO language. Moreover, other word order patterns which are specific to these Romance languages, and which are commonly attested in monolingual corpora, are never used in Basque or German, e.g. VOS order appears in French utterances of French-German bilinguals, but not in their use of German, neither during this early period nor later. This unmistakably indicates that these children indeed differentiate the two languages during the phase of grammatical development during which they are using the first two- or multi-word combinations.

The next phase is the one where the finite verb is placed in different positions, depending on what is required by the target grammar. Recall that this means that, in V2 languages, it must precede the subject when the clause is introduced by a con-stituent other than the subject. If, for example, an adverb appears in initial position, subject–verb order is reversed: *Dort geht er* (adverb – finite V – subject), as opposed to *Er geht dort* 'there goes he – there he goes'. Given that young children frequently use constructions beginning with deictic *there* or with some other type of adverbial, examples of this sort appear early and fairly frequently in recordings. In the speech of monolinguals acquiring V2 languages, this phenomenon is attested as soon as they begin to use finite verb forms. Yet it is never found in recordings of those acquiring a non-V2 language. It is therefore interesting to see how bilinguals behave who are simultaneously exposed to a V2 and a non-V2 language. A number of studies investigated this phenomenon in bilinguals acquiring German simultaneously with French, Italian, Portuguese, or English. The results unambiguously show that children place the finite verb in such constructions in second position when using German main clauses and in third position in the various other languages. This can be illustrated by examples from a French-German child, uttered at ages 2;2 and 2;4.

Da in Tasche musst du das
(there in bag must you that)
'You must put that there, into the bag'

Un petit peu ça pique
(a little bit this itches)
'It's a little bit itchy'

Findings like these confirm the Dual System Hypothesis and allow us to conclude that simultaneous acquisition does qualify as an instance of dual first language acquisition because it exhibits no qualitative differences as compared to monolingual L1 development, at least not during early phases of grammatical development. This amounts to saying that, due to the early differentiation of grammatical systems, bilingual grammars exhibit the same properties as monolingual ones. I should hasten to add that what these research findings show is that children exposed to two languages from birth are able to distinguish them in their mental representations of lexical and grammatical knowledge. However, this does not necessarily mean that language differentiation will always be successful, with all individuals and in all acquisition settings. These questions need to be dealt with in more detail, and this is why Chapter 3 is entirely dedicated to the problem of differentiation and related issues.

There still remain a few other questions, however, that should be addressed first. The first one concerns the linguistic development after early differentiation of languages: once the two languages have been separated successfully, can they be kept apart in the course of development? This amounts to asking whether bilinguals proceed through the same developmental sequences as monolinguals, and it leads to the question of whether they will attain grammatical competences indistinct from those of monolinguals. Last but not least, we also need to know whether all this happens at more or less the same rate as in monolinguals.

The first issue thus is whether the two grammars of bilinguals develop independently, following the same trajectories as in the corresponding monolinguals, or whether the course of development is altered as a result of interaction between the two systems. In other words, we need to know whether cross-linguistic interaction affects the grammatical *competence* of bilinguals. If this was the case, simultaneous bilingualism would not qualify as an instance of dual first language acquisition. Consequently, parents might decide against a bilingual education if it was likely to lead to non-native linguistic competences. If, on the other hand, cross-linguistic interaction merely affects the kind of *use* children make of their languages, this should not lead to such a serious concern. Either way, it should be useful to obtain more information about cross-linguistic influence. Even if it is limited to the linguistic behaviour of bilinguals, understanding linguistic interdependence can help us to understand the strategies of bilingual speech organization, and it can provide insights into the mechanisms of bilingual production. In Chapter 4, I will therefore deal at length with various forms of cross-linguistic interaction, including effects of transfer from another language, mixing of languages, and the like. We will see that interdependence can result in acceleration or delay of grammatical acquisition, as well as in transfer from one language to another one. Yet only the latter of these three possible effects would arguably result in qualitative changes of linguistic knowledge, because transfer implies that a construction proper to one grammar is incorporated into the other one, resulting in a grammar qualitatively distinct from that of monolinguals. Acceleration or delay, on the other hand, can be regarded as quantitative changes of the course of acquisition – unless they are of such a kind that they alter the ordering of developmental phases in otherwise invariant sequences. If this happened, it would certainly have to count as a qualitative change although no alien property is incorporated into a given grammar. These topics will all be discussed in Chapter 4.

But we also need to know what causes cross-linguistic interaction to occur and whether it can be triggered by the kind of
input bilingual children receive. It has indeed been claimed that
interaction occurs primarily in settings where one language is
dominant and the other one weak, either in the social context or
in the mind of speakers. Possible causes of cross-linguistic interaction will therefore be discussed in Chapters 5 and 6, together
with problems related to the role of quantitative and qualitative
differences in the kind of input that bilinguals receive. At this point,
I can already say that most effects of language dominance and of
varying types of input concern the on-line activation of the two
languages rather than the underlying grammatical knowledge. We
know that both languages of bilinguals are normally active simultaneously, even if individuals interact in predominantly monolingual contexts. Hence, the one currently not used needs to be
inhibited during this kind of interaction – it needs to be confined
to stand-by modus, so to say. When inhibition of the other language is not entirely successful, this can lead to cross-linguistic
interaction in language use. Cross-linguistic effects that can be
explained as resulting from insufficient inhibition of the inactive
language do not, however, indicate alterations of the underlying
grammatical knowledge. Rather, as I will explain in Chapters 4
and 5, cross-linguistic interaction does not prevent bilinguals
from proceeding through the same developmental sequences as
their monolingual counterparts. I will nevertheless make a few
recommendations as to how parents can provide a multilingual
setting favouring this kind of development.

Turning now to the second question, whether bilinguals can
attain two competences indistinct from those of monolinguals,
it is much more difficult to offer a satisfying answer. This probably comes as a surprise, but research on bilingualism has not yet
presented overwhelming support for the claim that bilinguals do
not differ from monolinguals in their ultimately attained grammatical knowledge. This is not to say, however, that arguments or
empirical evidence *against* this claim were available – and this is
the crucial point because we are dealing here with a hypothesis for

which it is difficult to present positive evidence. The reason is that even monolinguals exhibit considerable variation in their grammatical knowledge. As I explained in the first chapter (section 1.2), monolinguals are multilectal. They thus exhibit considerable variability in their language use. We must therefore rely on properties of the grammatical core shared by members of a speech community in order to decide whether an individual is a fully competent speaker. Although defining this core is a controversial matter, it is not difficult to identify at least some properties that belong to it. If one could show that bilingual grammars lack some of them, this would constitute decisive evidence against the claim that ultimate attainment in simultaneous language acquisition is identical to that of monolinguals. Yet no such evidence has as yet been presented. In other words, if we do not have positive support for the claim that bilinguals are able to develop grammatical competences that are qualitatively equivalent to those of monolinguals, this does not imply that this assumption is incorrect, nor does it mean that evidence in its support could not be obtained. Surprisingly, perhaps, researchers do not seem to consider this as an issue worth pursuing. In fact, early grammatical differentiation and autonomous development speak very strongly in favour of the assumption that bilinguals are on their way to native competences in both languages. We can thus assume with reasonable confidence that bilingual children are able to attain this goal.

There is, nevertheless, one crucial condition that must be met in order for successful acquisition to be possible: sufficient exposure to the target language. In other words, if the amount of input from the language to be acquired is drastically reduced, the possibility of acquiring a native competence, too, is reduced. Unfortunately, we only have an approximate idea of what constitutes 'sufficient' exposure to the primary linguistic data, i.e. the utterances directed to children by adults and peers. We do know, though, that children raised in bilingual settings are able to develop two native competences in spite of the fact that they normally receive less input than those growing up monolingually. As we will see in Chapter 6, it may well be that some parents raising their children bilingually produce more speech within a given amount of time than parents of monolinguals. Still, the relative time of exposure to each of the languages of bilinguals amounts at best to 50 per cent of the amount of child-directed speech for monolinguals. In most cases this entails that the quantity of input in each language is significantly reduced for bilinguals. Nevertheless, it suffices for the acquisition of native competences. In fact, even when the two languages are not balanced with respect to their availability to the child, bilinguals can attain two native competences. Yet although the LMC is obviously a robust enough device to enable children to acquire native grammars in spite of reduced input, there can be no doubt that a minimum amount of exposure to the input data is necessary for them to be able to achieve this because, trivially, zero input will result in acquisition failure. The challenge thus is to determine how decreasing amounts of input affect grammatical development and to quantify the minimum threshold for successful acquisition. This issue is of particular relevance for children acquiring more than two languages simultaneously. Quite obviously, their exposure either to all their languages or to at least one of them is even more limited. Chapter 6 deals with trilingual and quadrilingual acquisition, and this will be an occasion to inquire whether it is possible to define the minimum amount of input required for successful acquisition of a native competence.

To conclude this section and this chapter, let us finally address the question of whether language acquisition in bilinguals happens at more or less the same rate as in monolinguals. If this was not the case, i.e. if grammatical development in bilinguals was delayed in comparison to monolinguals, as has been claimed occasionally, it might indeed be a reason for concern if the delay exceeded the range of what is considered normal in monolingual acquisition.

The possibility of a risk of this type can, however, be discarded. Although some studies found that bilinguals tend to begin to speak later than monolinguals, the reported delays are well within the range of what counts as a normal rate of language development for monolingual children. As for the more principled question of whether bilingual acquisition progresses at a slower rate than

sometimes two is better than one.

Sometimes two is better than one

monolingual acquisition, a conclusive answer cannot be given. This is mainly due to the fact that a reliable yardstick against which to measure the pace of linguistic development does not exist. Among the criteria used in child language research are MLUs, as explained above, the emergence of specific structures at a specific age, and the number of words produced at a given age. Irrespective of which of these criteria is applied, one finds a considerable amount of variation across individuals, among monolinguals as well as bilinguals. It is worth noting that up to 20 per cent of monolingual children have been qualified as late talkers, based on the criterion of number of words (= less than 50) produced at age 2;0. Yet although there may indeed be an overall tendency for a slower acquisition rate in bilinguals, this is not an indication that bilingual children fall outside the norms established for monolingual acquisition. Rather, they resemble slower monolinguals.

In sum, bilinguals are special, but there are excellent reasons to believe that they can acquire each of their languages in much the same way as the corresponding monolinguals. Simultaneous acquisition of two languages can justly be regarded as an instance of dual first language development. This is the idea guiding the discussions in the following chapters.

2.4 Reading Suggestions

Readers who wish to know more about monolingual acquisition will probably find the following book to be of some interest. The author follows a quite different approach to first language acquisition than the one advocated here, focusing on adult–child interaction rather than on the Language Making Capacity or the child's innate faculties. However, such a complementary view on acquisition may be useful for those interested in getting a broader view on the issues at stake.

Clark, E. V. (2017). *Language in children*. London: Routledge.

3 Two Languages in One Mind

Differentiating Linguistic Systems

3.1 Confused by a Multilingual Environment?

For adults who are perhaps struggling with the learning of foreign languages in school, it is difficult to imagine that small children who can barely walk should be able to acquire two or even more languages simultaneously without apparent effort. Will they not get confused? How do they figure out which word or which grammatical construction belongs to which language? Will they not end up with a macaronic mix of languages that could have negative effects on their ability to think clearly?

Differentiating two or more languages without instruction or some other kind of explicit help must indeed appear to be a formidable challenge for monolinguals or those who grew up monolingually until they learned a foreign language in school. It is therefore not surprising that the fear is quite widespread that children might not succeed in differentiating languages to which they are exposed at an early age or, if they do accomplish this, that they will not be able to keep them apart in their young minds. These concerns figure prominently on the list of possible risks attributed to child bilingualism that I gave in Chapter 1 (section 1.1), and I repeat three of the most threatening ones in the following box.

Alleged Risks of Early Child Bilingualism

- Children exposed to more than one language at an early age cannot keep them apart. They fuse the two linguistic systems into a single one.

- Rather than becoming native speakers in two languages, they end up as semilinguals in two languages, with incomplete competences in each of them.
- The task of acquiring two languages simultaneously puts excessive strain on the mental capacities of young children.

If these risks were real, the suspicion that exposing young children to two languages could be disadvantageous for their linguistic and cognitive development would indeed be justified. This explains why children's ability to differentiate their ambient languages is the most frequently addressed issue in counselling sessions with parents who raise their children bilingually or who are considering doing so. Quite understandably, they want to be sure that there is no risk of fusion of linguistic systems and subsequent confusion in language use. Fortunately, language differentiation is probably the most thoroughly studied issue in research on child bilingualism, and it is today the least controversial problem among researchers. This means that virtually all questions on this topic can be answered with full confidence. In fact, already in the 1980s, it was demonstrated beyond reasonable doubt that bilingual children are able to differentiate the linguistic systems of their languages from very early on. Contrary to what had been claimed earlier, every child possesses the capacity to do so. All that is required is sufficient exposure to both languages. Bilingualism in early childhood is thus not only for the happy few, individuals specially gifted for language learning and/or growing up in social environments particularly favourable for a bilingual upbringing. Unfortunately, these insights have not become common knowledge, because they have not been widely disseminated outside academia.

The evidence on which these claims are based is manifold. In the next section, 3.2, I will present a little more detailed summaries of some of the relevant studies. But in order to get an idea of how one can decide whether children successfully differentiate the systems of their languages, it would be useful to now have a brief look at syntactic differentiation. Investigating syntactic phenomena becomes possible once children's grammatical knowledge and their linguistic skills have developed sufficiently to enable them to use multi-word utterances. From this point of development onwards, one can hope to be able to determine whether they rely on one unitary syntactic system or on two distinct ones. Examinations of word order patterns in early multi-word utterances can reveal whether the young bilinguals have differentiated the grammars of their languages at this early age, at around 2;0, as I have claimed above and also in Chapter 2 (section 2.2). To decide on this issue, we must examine syntactic properties in which the two languages of bilinguals differ, either in that particular constructions exist only in one of the languages, or because constructions with similar grammatical functions exist in both languages but differ in their formal properties.

This search for evidence of differentiation of linguistic systems must choose carefully the constructions on which comparisons are based, because not every instance of apparent fusion or interference is actually a reason to be alarmed. These uses may simply reflect the variability of patterns that exist in a language. Not to forget the fact that children are exposed to and acquire the colloquial variety of their target language. Comparisons of constructions in which the languages of bilinguals differ must therefore refer to these colloquial varieties, rather than to standard norms prescribed in grammar books. Moreover, they must also refer to properties of early *child* language, because constructions in which bilinguals differ from those encountered in adult speech may also appear in monolingual children's language use, at least temporarily.

The relevance of this comment becomes apparent when we consider so-called *null-subjects*. The languages of the world differ in that some, like English, require the subject position of every sentence to be filled by a lexical item, a noun or a pronoun. For the sake of simplicity, let us ignore elliptic subject omissions in casual speech, like *don't know* instead of *I don't know*, which are only apparent exceptions to this rule. In other languages, like Spanish, the subject position may be lexically empty. Linguists talk here of 'null-subjects', because the subject is not really missing; it is implied and understood, yet not expressed explicitly. The Spanish sentence *conozco este libro* 'know+1st $_{sg}$ this book' can only mean 'I know this book' although the subject pronoun referring to the first person singular is omitted. Depending on the linguistic context and on speaker intentions, subjects can be filled in or left out. Only if the subject does not refer to a specific entity or event, e.g. *it is raining* or *it seems*, is the so-called expletive pronoun (English *it*) obligatorily omitted in null-subject languages.

These differences between languages where null-subjects are a grammatically licensed option and others where this is not the case offer the possibility to decide whether bilinguals differentiate the grammatical systems of their languages, using null-subjects in one but not in the other language. In reality, it is not quite so easy to decide on this issue because all children, monolinguals as well as bilinguals, initially omit subjects in many or all their utterances. In other words, many utterances of early monolinguals acquiring languages that require the use of lexical subjects in every sentence resemble those of speakers of null-subject languages. This does not mean that all early child languages are null-subject languages. In fact, other elements, too, are omitted initially, articles for example, and even verbs. In all likelihood, these omissions indicate a need for simplification, facilitating language production at this early stage.

What matters in the present context is that omissions of subjects by bilingual children are not necessarily an indication of failed differentiation of non-null-subject and null-subject language systems. Whether or not this is the case can only be decided once the children have advanced beyond the initial phase during which they all omit subjects. As it turns out, bilinguals exhibit different patterns of usage in the two-language types as soon as they begin to use lexical subjects more or less consistently. Whereas in the non-null-subject language, subjects now appear in all required contexts, lexical subjects alternate with empty subjects in null-subject languages. Bilinguals thus behave in each of their languages exactly like monolinguals.

In other words, later developments show very clearly that bilinguals normally succeed in differentiating the grammars of their languages from very early on, even when this is not immediately apparent in early utterances. This confirms the observation that constructions in the speech of bilingual children that deviate from those encountered in adult speech need not indicate confusion. Cases like the acquisition of null-subject properties demonstrate that it is not sufficient to compare bilingual speech with adult colloquial varieties. Rather, the benchmark of comparison is the language use of other children, including monolinguals.

There is indeed abundant evidence indicating that bilinguals are able to differentiate the grammars of their languages without having to proceed through a phase during which they fuse the grammars of their target languages into one unitary system. They are not confused by the bilingual input. The clearest evidence supporting this claim refers to word order patterns reflecting syntactic properties in which the two languages differ. If children who acquire two languages simultaneously use the same constructions as monolinguals acquiring these languages, there can be no doubt that the task of grammatical differentiation has been accomplished successfully. In Chapter 2, I already claimed this to be the case, referring to different word orders, like the target-conforming use of VO versus OV order in the earliest multi-word utterances, or the placement of finite verbs (the ones carrying agreement, tense or aspect markers) before and of non-finite verbs after the negative element, if the adult norm requires this order, as in French or German. Let me add that children also follow the target order when it requires that both finite and non-finite verbs follow the negative element, and they are able to do so as soon as they use finite verbs. This is illustrated by the following Spanish example from a Spanish-Basque child at age 2;3:

Quique no ha traído nada
(Q (=name) not has brought anything)
'Quique has not brought anything'

Crucially, when speaking Basque, Spanish-Basque bilinguals use the correct Basque word order from early on. In this language, the finite verb is typically placed in clause-final position (SOV). In negative sentences, however, it appears towards the beginning of the clause, immediately after the negative element. And this is where young bilinguals place it, as can be seen in the example from a Spanish-Basque boy at age 2;8:

Ez daukat titiak
(Not I have breasts)
'I don't have breasts'

To Sum Up: Early Differentiation of Linguistic Systems

- Simultaneous bilinguals are able to differentiate linguistic systems from early on. There is no evidence of an initial phase of grammatical fusion.
- Simultaneous bilinguals are able to acquire native competences in both languages. They do not develop a non-native, incomplete grammar in both or in one of their languages.
- The simultaneous acquisition of more than one language does not exceed children's mental capacity. The Language Making Capacity is an endowment for bilingualism.

In view of these unambiguous research findings demonstrating that language differentiation is not a serious challenge for children exposed to two or more languages from birth, one may wonder whatever led researchers and parents to suspect that not all or perhaps not even most children could succeed in separating two languages or that they had to go through an initial phase during which they develop a single linguistic system comprising properties of both language systems.

I believe that the idea that bilinguals might require a certain amount of time in order to be able to sort out the relevant facts in an apparently confusing linguistic situation is primarily motivated by the observation that children sometimes mix their languages. It persuaded many observers to adopt the hypothesis of an initial unitary system. Parents almost inevitably view this as a serious problem, because it implies the risk of getting stuck in this phase, ending up with a permanently mixed language system rather than advancing to a phase during which systems are differentiated. Let us therefore have a closer look at *language mixing* in the speech of young bilinguals.

Talking about mixing, one probably thinks at first of cases where bilinguals insert one or more words from language B in an utterance consisting otherwise of lexical material from language A. This is indeed the typical manifestation of mixing, and the one that is most relevant for the discussion of whether or not children initially develop a unitary system. It can obviously only occur when children are able to produce multi-word utterances, i.e. not before the second half of their second year of life; cf. section 2.2. I will have more to say on mixing in multi-word utterances in the following section, 3.2.

Yet the term 'mixing' has also been applied to situations where children use language B in contexts where they are expected to use language A. In these cases, the child's utterances may consist of single words; they can therefore occur at an earlier age than mixed multi-word utterances. However, it is unlikely that these uses are really instances of mixing, indicating a possible failure to differentiate languages. Rather, they may result from a choice of language that is not the one expected by adult observers. Note that bilingual contexts necessarily oblige bilingual speakers to decide which language to use. *Language choice* is a normally unconscious process, influenced by a network of factors, such as for example the interlocutor, the topic of conversation, the social context, and so forth. A more detailed discussion of language choice in bilingual interactions must wait until Chapter 4. At this point I merely want to mention that for very young children the interlocutor plays a decisive role in determining and selecting the appropriate language in a given situation. If, then, a child addressed in language A responds in language B, we may conclude with reasonable certainty that we are indeed looking at a language A context and that the child made the wrong choice. Yet this does not solve our problem because it is not possible to decide whether the use of language B indicates that the child has not differentiated the two lexical systems or whether it results from a failure to choose the language required in this situation. Doubts therefore remain as to whether early 'mixes' really reflect a mix of languages, and they certainly do not represent strong evidence for a unitary system.

Moreover, apparent errors of language choice may not be errors at all. After all, a number of factors can influence language choice, even with very young children. It is therefore not always quite so easy to understand a child's choice. For example, if a child usually speaks language B with children at the playground, s/he may also choose this language with other interlocutors in this context, e.g. when responding at the playground to a family member with whom s/he normally speaks language A. In other words, the underlying logic of children's linguistic behaviour reveals itself only to those acquainted with their daily activities and the world in which they move.

Apparent mixes may also be the result of the child's switching into the other language. A two-year-old French-German boy explained this quite succinctly to a research assistant. In a recording session with a German-speaking person whom he normally addressed in German, he repeatedly switched to French. Eventually he explained that *nounours*, his teddy bear, does not understand German and that he therefore had to explain things to him in French. This made perfect sense because the bear was a gift from his French grandparents. Thus, what we might have interpreted as a case of confusion turned out to be an instance of well-motivated bilingual behaviour: switching languages to accommodate to the needs of a monolingual interlocutor.

Returning to the problem of deciding whether very young bilingual children differentiate languages, the least one can say is that the linguistic confusion noticed by some observers of bilingual speech does not necessarily indicate confusion on the part of the children. Rather, it may well be that adult observers misinterpret the children's linguistic behaviour. A number of empirical findings support the suspicion that language mixing is less of a problem in early bilingual development than one might have expected. First, not all children mix languages. It is thus not a kind of linguistic behaviour that is characteristic of an early developmental phase common to all bilinguals. However, those who do mix tend to do so more frequently during early phases, at around age 2;0. Yet mixing rates are very low for most children, even during these early phases. All these findings speak against the assumption that children raised bilingually struggle through a confusing linguistic situation. In the worst case, they need a bit of time to sort out the facts.

A conclusive answer to the question of what induces many young bilinguals to mix languages may be impossible to find. However, one plausible assumption is that they need to practise bilingual language use for some time until they are able to choose the adequate language consistently. After all, being bilingual is the normal state of affairs for bilingual children, especially if family members speak two languages. Figuring out that one should stick to one specific language in certain situations may therefore require some communicative experience. Secondly, as already mentioned, bilingual adults also switch between languages, even within utterances; cf. Chapter 4. Children's language mixing could thus be triggered by the linguistic behaviour of adults.

At any rate, one possible explanation, namely that mixing is mainly caused by gaps in children's lexical knowledge, can be ruled out. In most cases, they do know the word in language A that is replaced by one of language B. In fact, one finds a surprisingly high number of frequently used and early learned words in early mixes, e.g. those corresponding to English 'no/yes', 'there/that/

this', or 'all gone'. Finally, linguistic confusion can also be ruled out as an explanation of early mixing because these mixes tend to be systematic rather than chaotic. The vast majority of mixes consist of *nouns* inserted into utterances containing otherwise only lexical material of the other language. Let me give you a few French-German examples: *ça ça Sonne* 'this this sun' (age 1;11), *sent Füße* 'smells feet' (2;4), *nounours wach* 'bear awake' (2;2). Moreover, as already mentioned, from very early on children are mostly successful in choosing languages according to the interlocutor.

Thus, there is no reason to believe that early mixes indicate confusion or failure to separate the two languages. Quite to the contrary, we know that language differentiation happens very early on and that bilingual children are able to achieve this without apparent effort. Occasional language mixing does not even justify the idea of an *initial* phase during which bilinguals first develop a single lexicon and a single grammar that are differentiated later on. We know this for a fact because careful observations have revealed that, already well before their second birthday, bilinguals use different words for the same object or activity, attaching thus two-language-specific labels to one concept. These cross-linguistic synonyms do not occur very frequently. Yet this should not surprise us, since, as we have already seen, languages are not used indiscriminately in the various communicative situations experienced by a young bilingual child. Rather, depending on the various factors constituting these situations, e.g. the kind of activity, the persons interacting with the child, and so forth, one of the languages tends to be strongly preferred. Consequently, occasions to talk about the same topic in both languages tend to be rare. Nevertheless, one does find such synonyms among the first 50 words produced by bilinguals. This is illustrated by the following examples, encountered in the recordings of a French-German girl during the age period from 1;4 to 1;8: *oui/ja* 'yes', *non/nein* 'no', *chaussons/Schuhe* 'shoes', *fleur/Blume* 'flower' or *encore/mehr* 'more', *parti/ weg* 'all gone'. She even distinguishes between *maman* and *Mama* 'mommy', depending on whether she refers to her mother in French or in German contexts.

In sum, the use of cross-linguistic synonyms leaves no doubt that by age 18 months, bilinguals have begun to develop two lexical systems. In fact, the situation-appropriate use of one-word utterances during the first half of the children's second year of life already indicates that they are acquiring two distinct mental lexicons. In reality, differentiation of languages in bilingual development sets in even earlier. The pieces of evidence mentioned so far all refer to the production of words. We know, however, that language perception precedes production in the course of linguistic development; see section 2.3 of the preceding chapter. This suggests that bilinguals are already able to discriminate languages in the prelexical phase of language acquisition, during the second half of their first year of life, thus laying the foundations for the development of separate linguistic systems in the children's minds.

The only possible conclusion to be drawn from these and similar observations is that no empirical evidence supports the idea of a phase of fusion of linguistic systems in bilingual children's linguistic development or of confusion in their use of the languages that they are acquiring. The fact that many though not all of them tend to mix languages in their speech, sometimes even within an utterance, does not stand in conflict with this statement. Most instances of mixing simply reflect linguistic behaviour typical of bilinguals, children and adults alike, as we will see in more detail in Chapter 4. Yet even in cases in which children deviate in their mixing from what is commonly encountered in the speech of adult bilinguals, they show no sign of linguistic confusion. Rather, we find that they systematically distinguish the two languages and develop different systems from very early on.

To Sum Up: Early Mixing Does Not Indicate Fusion or Confusion

- Mixing during early developmental phases is not a reliable indication of a failure to differentiate languages. Closer examination reveals that it does not constitute evidence of grammatical or lexical fusion.

- Some apparent mixes are really switches into the other language. They may also be due to a choice of language not expected by adults.
- Language choice is a kind of bilingual behaviour that requires experience. Children need to practise bilingual language use for some time until they are able to choose the adequate language consistently.

3.2   Separating Languages in a Child's Mind

At the beginning of this chapter, I listed some possible risks attributed to early childhood bilingualism by critics as well as by concerned parents. The reason why I emphasized that they need to be taken seriously is that they refer to phenomena that do occur in the speech of young bilinguals, such as language mixing or constructions that are non-existent in the target language, as it is used by parents and peers. This observation inevitably leads to the question of whether these kinds of usage indicate that bilingual environments confuse children if exposure to more than one language happens at an early age. In the preceding section, I gave a negative answer to this question, based on arguments provided by a wealth of research investigating this issue. The findings of these studies suggest that bilingual children develop mental representations of two lexical and grammatical systems from very early on. In other words, they are not confused by the multilingual input to which they are exposed; rather, they keep the languages separate in their minds. In fact, their competences do not seem to differ from those of the corresponding monolinguals, given that the structural properties of early multi-word utterances are the same for both learner types. All this amounts to is saying that bilinguals who differentiate languages during early acquisition phases are off to a good start towards the goal of developing native competences in two languages.

This is a very positive and optimistic picture of early child bilingualism, and sceptical readers may wonder whether the claims and conclusions are indeed well founded and how reliable the research findings are on which they are based. However, optimism is justified in this case because this problem is indeed the least controversial one in current child bilingualism research. Consequently, questions raised by parents and other caregivers can be answered with full confidence. Nevertheless, it would be useful for them and for all readers to learn about the research that allows us to adopt such a positive attitude towards early child bilingualism. After all, research results are obtained by hypothesis-testing: hypotheses are formulated to account for the known facts concerning a specific issue, and as more facts become available, they serve to test the initial hypothesis that is considered to be correct as long as no disconfirming evidence is found. In the latter case, the hypothesis is modified or replaced by one that accounts more satisfactorily for the available empirical evidence. Scientific 'proof' must thus be regarded as truth with an expiration date.

In studies of child bilingualism, the predominant view until the 1980s was that young bilinguals initially develop a single lexical and grammatical system comprising elements of both languages. This idea is commonly referred to as the *Unitary System Hypothesis*. In view of the fact that early studies of bilingual children focused mainly on language mixing, it is not surprising that this hypothesis was favoured. Note that child bilingualism was a marginal topic in linguistics and psychology during the first half of the twentieth century. Many early studies were carried out by non-professionals such as missionaries reporting on their own children growing up in foreign countries where they acquired the local language in addition to the language of their parents. In fact, most of the linguists or psychologists among the early authors were not specialists in language development either. It is probably for these reasons that they were primarily interested in sociolinguistic or pedagogical issues. Not to be misunderstood: we owe them a wealth of pertinent observations about bilingual children, but they passed over grammatical problems rather superficially.

Whereas language mixing caught their attention, they were less interested in developmental issues and hardly at all in the acquisition of grammatical knowledge. This did not change significantly until the 1970s, although this line of research had started very well with the first systematic investigation of bilingual development by Ronjat (1913), studying the simultaneous acquisition of French and German by his son. Yet in spite of a few notable exceptions, such as Pavlovitch (1920) (Serbian-French) or Leopold (1939–1949) (English-German), the studies that were carried out and published during the following 50 years did not enhance significantly our understanding of child bilingualism.

This only changed when researchers began to ask what kind of linguistic *knowledge* children develop in the process of acquiring two languages simultaneously. Language mixing continued to be interpreted as an indication that bilinguals encounter difficulties in separating the lexicons and the grammatical systems of their languages. However, already in the 1970s researchers agreed that children growing up with more than one language eventually succeed in separating their languages, without much effort or specific pedagogical support. This was a significant insight, since confusion was now regarded as only a temporary phenomenon.

Nevertheless, the possibility of fusion of lexical and grammatical systems during an early developmental phase was justly considered to be a potentially serious problem. After all, if such a phase of undifferentiated linguistic knowledge did exist, it might last through later age periods or result in deficiencies in subparts of the competence of one or both languages. The essential questions therefore seemed to be how and when bilinguals manage to emerge from the unitary system phase. However, this issue was not pursued in much detail. Later research revealed that language mixing and the use of constructions apparently transferred from the other language do not, in fact, justify the assumption that the underlying linguistic competences of bilingual children consisted of undifferentiated unitary systems. In what follows, I will report on some of the findings that led to the abandonment of the Unitary System Hypothesis in favour of the

Dual System Hypothesis in the late 1980s. This idea of early differentiation of linguistic systems soon gained vast support. Over the subsequent 30 years, it has been confirmed by a multitude of studies investigating a large number of grammatical phenomena in numerous languages.

Concerning language mixing, the following summary can be very brief, since some of these findings have already been mentioned in the preceding section, and code-switching, the ability to select languages according to interlocutor, situational context, topic of conversation, etc., is the topic of section 4.1 in the next chapter. Code-switching is of particular importance because it includes the possibility of changing languages within an interactional sequence or even a sentence. In the latter case, switching is not only constrained by sociolinguistic principles, but also by grammatical ones. Crucially, for the present discussion, at least some early instances of mixing are already cases of such rule-governed behaviour. Yet even when mixes do not follow these patterns, early mixing is not an indication of linguistic confusion and certainly not evidence supporting the idea of an early phase of a unitary language system through which bilingual children must proceed before becoming able to differentiate their languages.

Some arguments leading to this conclusion have already been alluded to in section 3.1. First of all, remember that not all children mix languages. It is also not generally the case that mixing frequency decreases with increasing competence; in fact, for some children the frequency increases over time. Furthermore, self-corrections in cases when the child addresses someone in the wrong language are observed quite early on, between the age of 2;0 and 2;6. During the same age period, children begin to repeat their own utterances in the other language in order to attract both their parents' attention or to ensure that the content of their utterance is understood. These observations strongly suggest that children distinguish their languages functionally, i.e. they are sensitive to their linguistic environment when choosing the language they are about to use.

With respect to the properties of the switched elements, one finds that very early mixes are reminiscent of what has been referred to as *tag* switches in adult bilingual speech. They consist of the insertion of elements with loose or no grammatical links to the rest of the sentence, such as the German negative element *nein* 'no'. Switches of this sort typically appear before age 2;4–2;6, and they then disappear abruptly. Moreover, up to age 3;0, bilinguals tend to insert single lexical items from one language into the other one, mostly nouns.

Yet whereas before age 2;6, these nouns are bare, i.e. not accompanied by articles, during the second half of the third year they are accompanied by articles or other elements, and switches regularly occur between these elements and the noun, as in the following examples from a French-German boy at age 3;1.

> Moi je va à la **Küche**
> (Me I goes to the kitchen)
> 'I go to the kitchen'

> Il y a beaucoup de **Berge**
> 'There are many mountains'

These changes clearly reflect children's grammatical development. After all, in the case of sentence-internal switching, the well-formedness of a sentence depends on the grammatical properties of both languages. In other words, code-switching is constrained by grammatical principles; it requires a certain amount of grammatical knowledge in both languages to be able to switch like adults. Consequently, language mixing by young children, who are still in the process of acquiring the grammars of their target languages, differs necessarily in its formal properties from code-switching by adults. This explains why early mixes lack the full set of functional and formal properties of adult code-switching. Children have not yet acquired the full sociolinguistic knowledge and the grammatical competence of adults. Quite obviously, their language use, including their language mixing, reflects the knowledge attained so far. Importantly, their speech already exhibits sufficient evidence of language differentiation. This allows us to conclude that these mixes are early forms of code-switching, in spite of the fact that they still differ in some respects from those of adults. At any rate, these differences do not justify the assumption that bilingual children rely on unitary language systems.

The same conclusion can be drawn from analyses of young bilinguals' use of lexical elements and early syntactic constructions. This is what I claimed in the preceding section and in Chapter 2 (section 2.3). In what follows, I want to support this claim with some more information about the arguments presented in the 1980s against the Unitary System Hypothesis. Although this may at first seem paradoxical, it is due to the efforts of scholars who defended an updated and explicitly formulated version of this hypothesis that it became possible to attain conclusive evidence against it. Previously, it had been a vague idea that could be interpreted in different ways, and it is precisely for this reason that it was difficult to find counterevidence against it. Volterra & Taeschner (1978) then presented their *three-stage model of bilingual development* that was soon widely accepted and referred to in textbooks and guides for parents as the standard view on child bilingualism. The basic idea is that bilingual acquisition proceeds through an initial period during which children develop only one system before they succeed in differentiating first the lexical and then the grammatical systems of their languages.

I. The child has only one lexical system comprising words from both languages.
II. Development of two distinct lexical systems, although the child still applies 'the same syntactic rules to both languages'.
III. Differentiation of two linguistic systems, lexical as well as syntactic.

However, this scenario turned out not to capture the developmental pattern of bilingual children: early differentiation of systems has been shown not to be the exception but the rule in simultaneous language acquisition. During the phase when children use mostly one-word utterances, one can already find cross-linguistic synonyms, as shown in section 3.1. Volterra and Taeschner had noticed this too, but they argued that the meanings of the alleged synonyms were not actually identical. Take, for example, the lexical pair *lo specchio – der Spiegel* 'the mirror', as used by an Italian-German child. The words might refer to a hand mirror in one language and to a full-length mirror in the other one. This is indeed possible if language use within a bilingual family follows a complementary distribution of languages across everyday situations, where one kind of mirror is talked about in conversations with the Italian-speaking father and the other one when interacting with the German-speaking mother. Yet this is not consistently the case with all potential cross-linguistic synonyms and certainly not with all children. In fact, subsequent studies showed that true synonyms across the two languages of bilingual children occur from early on. This constitutes unambiguous evidence that bilinguals develop two distinct lexicons, contrary to the claim that they initially proceed through a one lexical system stage.

As for the proposed stage II, during which children allegedly rely on one grammatical system, this hypothesis must be tested by contrasting constructions exhibiting clearly distinct properties in the language pair of a bilingual. Remember that they can only serve as evidence confirming or disconfirming the assumption of a unitary syntactic system if they meet certain requirements, e.g. the differences must occur consistently, and they must be detectable in the speech of young children, not only in that of adults. The arguments by Volterra and Taeschner in support of stage II are based on three construction types, adjective–noun order, possessor–possession patterns ('John's car'), and placement of the negative element. Unfortunately, these three constructions do not meet the criteria in the language pair investigated, Italian and German.

As just mentioned, one can only make a convincing case in favour or against the claim that languages are differentiated if the cross-language differences appear consistently. This is clearly not what we find when we look at adjective–noun order in Germanic and in Romance languages. In English, German and other Germanic languages, adjectives must precede the noun, as in *an unknown person, eine unbekannte Person*, whereas in French, Spanish and other Romance languages, adjectives typically follow the noun, as in *une personne inconnue, una persona desconocida.* However, some adjectives may appear before or after the noun in Romance languages, and some can only be placed prenominally, as in French *une petite fille* 'a little girl'. If, then, English-French or German-Italian children place adjectives in the Romance language before nouns in cases where the adult language does not allow this order, a plausible explanation is that they have not yet figured out which adjectives may appear in this position. It does not, however, indicate that they are developing a unitary system for both languages or that the Germanic language interferes with the Romance language. If, on the other hand, English or German adjectives appeared consistently after the noun, this would indeed support the hypothesis that a property of the Romance language has been integrated into the Germanic system, provided the same patterns are attested in both languages. However, to my knowledge, such a case has never been encountered in studies of bilingual acquisition. Not surprisingly, the Italian-German child studied by Volterra and Taeschner did not use adjective–noun ordering that would have supported the unitary system assumption.

Concerning noun + noun sequences expressing possessor–possession, a similar problem arises because the allegedly Italian order, as in *la macchina di Giovanni* 'the car of Giovanni', also exists in colloquial German, *das Auto von Hans* 'the car of Hans'. Finally, the placement of the negative element in final position in Italian sentences, supposedly due to cross-linguistic influence from German, also occurs in the speech of monolingual Italian children. At any rate, none of the three constructions is used in the same fashion in both languages, as one would expect if they were generated by one and the same grammar. Consequently, the evidence provided in support of a unitary system at stage II is not convincing. Ultimately, the three-stage model had to be rejected.

If, then, the available empirical evidence leads us to reject the Unitary System Hypothesis, the question remains as to whether it supports the Dual System Hypothesis. Or do we find evidence against this approach as well? We have already seen (sections 2.3 and 3.1) that phenomena meeting the selection criteria do exist, i.e. they qualify as potential empirical evidence enabling us to decide between the two hypotheses. Word order, for example, distinguishes Germanic and Romance languages, and differentiating constructions occur in children's speech as early as at around age 2;0. As mentioned earlier, children acquiring an OV (object–verb) language like Basque or German simultaneously with a VO (verb–object) language like Spanish or French use OV order only in the OV language. French-German bilinguals, for example, use OV only in German, never in French. Similarly, word order patterns specific to Romance languages are not attested in Basque or German, e.g. VOS order appears in French but not in German utterances of French-German bilinguals.

Moreover, once children have acquired the distinction between finite and non-finite verbs, finite verbs appear in the position required by the target grammar. In verb-second languages like German they precede subjects when a constituent other than the subject introduces the clause. If, for example, an adverb appears in initial position, the usual subject–verb order is reversed. This is indeed what we observe in the speech of early bilinguals. They place finite verbs in such constructions in second position when using German main clauses and in third position in the other languages. In Chapter 2 (section 2.3), I have already given examples of how verbs are placed in the required positions by bilingual children. Here is another example of this word order contrast from the recordings of a French-German boy at around age 3;0. The finite verb (in second position in German, in third position in French) appears in italics.

> Da *ist* 'n Loch
> 'There is a hole'

> Maintenant le cochon il *saute* la kangourou
> 'Now the pig it jumps (over) the kangaroo'

This kind of contrast across languages is a reliable indication of language differentiation. Note that distinct target word orders as in these examples are easy to detect. One does not need training in linguistics to make observations of this kind. This is to say that you can be sure that a bilingual child has developed two distinct grammars when you find cross-language differences of this sort.

Another grammatical domain that reveals unambiguously whether or not the grammars of bilinguals have been differentiated is inflectional morphology, e.g. verb endings. English is not the best language to test this because it does not have a large repertoire of verb endings. In languages with a rich verb morphology, however, the situation is quite different, and bilinguals use verb inflection as soon as they are able to use grammatical morphology productively. Importantly, they do not randomly attach inflectional morphemes of one language to lexical material of the other language. In other words, language mixing within words is a rare phenomenon, and the acquisition of distinct target morphologies constitutes strong support for the Dual System Hypothesis.

Subject–verb agreement is an example that can illustrate this point. In many languages, finite verbs agree with subjects in person and number; in others, verbs also agree in gender with subjects, or verbs agree with direct and indirect objects in person and number. For the sake of simplicity, let us focus on person and number agreement with the subject. Whereas English merely marks the third person singular (3rd sg) on the verb (*he speaks*), other languages mark each person differently and distinguish between singular and plural forms, e.g. Spanish *hablar* 'to speak': *hablo* (1st sg), *hablas* (2nd sg), *habla* (3rd sg), *hablamos* (1st pl), *habláis* (2nd pl), *hablan* (3rd pl). Interestingly, these markers are the first instances of verb morphology to appear in children's speech, mostly as of approximately age 2;0. Moreover, children make virtually no errors in person agreement and very few in number agreement.

The question here is how bilingual children fare with respect to this acquisition task. The short answer is: They do just as well as monolinguals, and they succeed with this task equally well in both languages. In fact, even Basque-Spanish bilinguals perform like this, although Basque verbs represent a particularly complex learning task because they agree not only with the subject but also with direct and indirect objects in person and number.

In sum, the development of verb morphology, a well-studied phenomenon across a large number of languages, confirms strongly the claims based on facts concerning word order acquisition and on careful examinations of early instances of language mixing. They all provide clear evidence supporting the Dual System Hypothesis. We can thus conclude that, due to the early differentiation of linguistic systems, the emerging grammars of young bilinguals exhibit the same properties as those of monolingual children. In other words, simultaneous acquisition of bilingualism has justly been referred to as an instance of *dual first language acquisition*, given that it does not exhibit qualitative differences compared to monolingual first language development; see Meisel (1989).

To Sum Up: The Available Evidence Supports the *Dual System Hypothesis*

- Mixing during later developmental phases is *code-switching*. It is not chaotic; it is constrained by the children's grammatical and sociolinguistic knowledge.
- Lexical as well as syntactic and morphological properties of bilingual children's speech show that their language use does not differ from that of monolingual learners of the same languages.
- Children exposed to two languages from birth acquire two first language competences.

Importantly, the effects of language differentiation are manifest in bilingual children's speech. In fact, they become perceptible in two ways: either by contrasting properties of an individual's two languages, or by comparing properties of one of the languages with those of the same language as it is used by monolinguals.

1. In cases where the languages of bilinguals exhibit different properties of equivalent constructions, these differences become visible in cross-linguistic comparisons within individuals. This is to say that their speech exhibits different realizations of equivalent constructions, for example finite verbs placed before or after the subject in sentences introduced by adverbs, or finite verbs placed before or after the negative element.

2. Independently of whether an individual's two languages exhibit identical or distinct realizations of specific grammatical concepts, comparisons of developmental patterns in each of the languages with those of the corresponding monolingual peers show identical properties and identical developmental sequences. Subject–verb agreement, for example, emerges before object–verb agreement in languages that require both agreement types, and the markers for each kind of agreement appear in the same order as in monolingual children.

Before concluding this section, let me remind you that these developments set in very early. But what does 'very early' mean in this case? The answer to this question depends on the phenomena investigated. Almost all the examples mentioned above refer to children's speech production, primarily in multi-word utterances. Based on these data, the answer would have to be: early differentiation happens at around age 2;0, shortly before or after the second birthday. This is when most children start using multi-word utterances. In other words, we find evidence supporting the Dual System Hypothesis as soon as this is technically possible, since it is obviously not possible to test this hypothesis in the domain of syntax when children do not yet produce multi-word utterances. However, as briefly mentioned in Chapter 2 (section 2.3), there are good reasons to assume that grammatical differentiation actually sets in earlier. This is because we know that speech perception precedes production, and phonological development, at least some aspects of it, happens earlier than the acquisition of morphosyntactic knowledge. We may therefore expect to find that language differentiation begins well before it can be detected in multi-word utterances.

And this is indeed the case. Recall that newborns are able to distinguish between languages with different prosodic or rhythmic properties. This undoubtedly facilitates the differentiation of systems. It is therefore not surprising that some studies arrived at the conclusion that bilinguals are able to distinguish the lexical and grammatical systems of the ambient languages well before they use the corresponding linguistic devices in their speech production. In fact, investigations carried out more recently have confirmed this finding. They have shown that speech perception processes subserving language differentiation are already at work during the first six months of age. It seems that the development of phonetic perception is accelerated and acoustic sensitivity is heightened in bilinguals, as compared to monolinguals. Note that if it is true that bilinguals' heightened acoustic sensitivity is due to their richer linguistic experience, we may conclude that exposure to more than one language from birth is an advantage, rather than a reason for linguistic or cognitive confusion.

Not only are these processes activated as early as during the first half of the first year of life, but they seem to have long-lasting effects on bilinguals' language acquisition abilities. This is suggested, for example, by a study investigating the acquisition of Korean phonology by Dutch native speakers and Korean-born Dutch speakers adopted by Dutch families, some of them at age 17 months or older, others before they were 6 months old (Choi, Cutler & Broersma, 2017). The Korean-born learners, even the ones who had been 3–5 months old at the time of adoption, outperformed the Dutch group in perception and production of Korean sounds. This suggests that focusing on language-specific sounds already happens before age 6 months, possibly prenatally.

The suspicion that the foundations of bilinguals' language differentiation capacity are already laid prenatally has indeed been confirmed by recent biomagnetometric investigations. The biomagnetometer detects the beat-to-beat changes in foetal heart rate, and these studies revealed that the heart rates of foetuses changed when they heard an unfamiliar, rhythmically distinct language after having been exposed to the language usually spoken in their environment, English. Importantly, their heart rates did not change when they heard another passage of English speech. This prenatal sensitivity to rhythmic properties of languages not only provides children with crucial means that enable them to discover the properties characterizing their target languages; it can also help them to distinguish languages in a multilingual environment.

Why is this important? Does it really matter at which age children begin to perceive language-specific properties? I think that it is indeed a relevant piece of information, especially for parents who intend to raise children bilingually. After all, bilinguals who succeed with this task are off to a good start towards the goal of developing native competences in two languages. There is no need to disentangle an initial unitary system. If differentiation failed, not only would the starting point of the acquisition process differ from monolingual acquisition, bilinguals would also have to proceed through different developmental sequences, and it is questionable whether native competences could be attained under such conditions. Thus, although it is only during the second half of the second year of a bilingual child's life that we can begin to observe the results of the ongoing process of language differentiation, we should know that the foundations of this amazing capacity are laid much earlier, during the first weeks and months or perhaps even prenatally. It is therefore advisable to address children in both languages right from the first day of their lives. Bilingual families sometimes wonder at what age they should begin to do so, since infants initially do not understand what is said to them. Now that we know that they perceive properties specific to the ambient languages well before they understand words and sentences, we can say that it is never too early to expose the future bilinguals to both their languages.

The Bilinguist

3.3 One Person, One Language? Talk, Talk, Talk!

There can be no doubt that children bring to the task of first language acquisition an amazing capacity that enables them to develop a native competence in their target language – and all they need is exposure to the language in communicative contexts. Yet how does this capacity fare when it needs to deal with more than one language simultaneously? From what we have seen so far, children are well equipped to deal with this situation. At least during early developmental phases, it does not seem to represent too big a challenge for the language-learning child. Rather, it looks like the Language Making Capacity is indeed an endowment for bilingualism, as suggested in Chapter 2 (section 2.3). Language differentiation is a crucial first step towards the goal of becoming a native speaker of two languages – a step that is taken without much apparent effort by most bilingual children. It is thus not implausible to assume that the LMC provides the necessary means for the child to cope with this task.

Yet does this mean that differentiation will always be successful, independently of the linguistic or sociolinguistic environment of children? Or does the linguistic behaviour of parents, peers or other persons interacting with them enhance or hinder differentiation and ultimately the acquisition process? These are questions frequently asked by parents and other family members, as in this email by the mother of a German-Turkish boy living in Germany.

One Person – One Language

We are a binational German-Turkish couple with an 18-month-old son who we want to raise bilingually. About two months ago, he started using his first words. So far, I mainly used Turkish when talking to him, and his father only talked German with him. Moreover, one afternoon per week, each of his grandparents take care of him. They speak German or Turkish, respectively. In addition, for seven months now, he has been attending a bilingual daycare where care workers of Turkish origin also speak Turkish to him.

We hope that, in this way, he will succeed in becoming bilingual, but we are not sure, because mother and father do not always stick to the strict separation of languages that is frequently regarded as indispensable. This happens especially in situations where my son and I are in company of people who do not understand Turkish. Unfortunately, my husband also speaks very little Turkish, and I therefore speak occasionally German to our son, when my husband is present.

(Translated from German, JMM)

These parents know that they must see to it that their son has sufficient opportunities to use both languages. Their arrangements concerning the distribution of languages across various contexts of the life of a young child are exemplary in that the boy interacts in the two languages with his parents, other family members, and outside the family where he also meets other bilingual children. Nevertheless, they are disconcerted, wondering whether the language distribution within the family – the mother speaks Turkish to the child, the father German – is optimal, given that it is not always possible to adhere to it strictly.

The language distribution in this family follows the *one person, one language* method (OPOL). It is the language strategy most frequently adopted in bilingual families, and it has probably been followed ever since parents with different mother tongues wondered how to go about raising their children bilingually. It is certainly the one recommended most consistently since the publication of the first longitudinal study of bilingual development by Jules Ronjat (1913). The author's wife was German, and when their son Louis was born in 1908, they decided to bring him up bilingually. Up to then, Ronjat himself, a French lawyer and linguist known for his work on the history of Occitan, had not studied language acquisition nor child bilingualism and apparently did not pursue this topic in later years either. This is probably why he asked his colleague and friend Maurice Grammont for advice, who had published on child language. Ronjat (1913: 3) quotes from Grammont's letter of advice:

> Il n'y a rien à lui apprendre ou à lui enseigner. Il suffit que lorsqu'on a quelque chose à lui dire on le lui dise dans l'une des langues qu'on veut qu'il sache. Mais voici le point important: *que chaque langue soit représentée par une personne différente.* Que vous par exemple vous lui parliez toujours français, sa mère allemand. *N'invertissez jamais les rôles!* De cette façon, quand il commencera à parler, il parlera deux langues sans s'en douter et sans avoir fait aucun effort spécial pour les apprendre.

Let me summarize the main points: The child does not need language instruction. All that is required is exposure to both languages in daily interactions. Bilingual acquisition will then happen quite naturally. However, everyone interacting with the child must adhere to one language and should never switch to the other one. The first recommendation is totally in line with today's understanding of language acquisition, monolingual or bilingual. Grammont implicitly attributes to children a language acquisition faculty that merely requires exposure to the target languages to succeed. More surprisingly, he assumes that they will succeed equally well in bilingual settings, a view that coincides entirely with our current understanding of bilingual acquisition but that was certainly not common knowledge at the beginning of the twentieth century.

Grammont's second piece of advice is that each language in the child's environment be represented by one person and consistently by the same one. He thus recommends adopting what Ronjat (1913: 4) called the *one person, one language* method. Interestingly, Grammont insisted on exposing the child to both languages from birth and to adhere to the *one person, one language* (OPOL) method from the start. This, he explained, enables children to assimilate vocabulary and pronunciation of both languages, also a view supported by modern acquisition research, as we have seen in the preceding section. In Louis' case, everyone interacting with the child was instructed to follow the OPOL principle: other family members and friends as well as the German-speaking nanny. The family language, the one used between Ronjat and his wife, was German, the minority language in a French-speaking environment.

Does this mean that we should give a positive answer to the question at the beginning of this section and affirm that parents can enhance or perhaps hinder language differentiation and subsequent developmental processes in the simultaneous acquisition of two languages? Probably. A more definitive answer is, however, difficult to give. This uncertainty may come as a surprise, in view of the fact that so many families have followed the OPOL method over more than 100 years. We do know that it led to the desired results in a huge number of cases, including Louis Ronjat, whose linguistic development from birth until the age of almost five years is documented in his father's book.

Yet would these children have been less successful if their parents had not followed this principle or followed it less strictly? This we do not know for certain. After all, Ronjat did not mention what motivated him, or Grammont for that matter, to suggest the OPOL method. It is highly unlikely that this recommendation was based on some previous observations of bilingual children. You may come across references to a book by Grammont, published in 1902, in which he allegedly introduced the OPOL method. In reality, no such book exists. Rather, the bibliographical reference (Grammont, 1902) refers to an article reporting on the early language use of two children, mostly on phonetic particularities. It is an interesting study demonstrating that children are quite systematic in the way in which they deviate from adult word forms. However, it does not address issues related to bilingualism and it does not mention the OPOL method that he later recommended in a letter to Ronjat. It thus seems that this principle or method is based on common-sense considerations rather than reflecting insights into mechanisms underlying bilingual acquisition. As pointed out by Ronjat (1913: 3), its purpose is to help the child to avoid linguistic confusion and to facilitate differentiation. In this respect, it has undoubtedly been successful – for over 100 years.

Still, we do not know to what extent this success depends on the OPOL method because the distribution of languages in the family is definitely not the only factor influencing early bilingual development. I can affirm this, because we have reports on children who were equally successful in their simultaneous acquisition of two languages, although the people interacting with them in early childhood did not adhere to the OPOL principle. Multiple factors are at work here, and I will address some of them later in the book. At this point, let me merely mention one of the most crucial ones, namely quantity and quality of child-directed speech. The amount of speech addressed to children varies enormously across parents, in monolingual as well as in bilingual settings; see also Chapters 5 and 6. This has important effects on the children's linguistic development. For children to become bilingual, talking to them frequently is probably as important as following the OPOL strategy.

Let me nevertheless remind you that children differ quite significantly in personality, communicative behaviour, learning capacities, etc., and internal factors of this sort can either attenuate or reinforce external ones that can be influenced by parents and other caregivers. We should therefore not expect all individuals to make the same use of opportunities offered by identical settings. This point can be illustrated by the observation that children whose parents normally adhere to the OPOL method react quite differently when a parent uses the 'wrong' language. Whereas some do not mind at all, others are manifestly upset. Some even demand violently that mother or father use the 'good' language.

In sum, considering the fact that so many children have succeeded in becoming bilingual who have been exposed to two languages according to the OPOL principle, I recommend adopting it in binational families or wherever parents can speak different languages to their children. Importantly, as already emphasized by Grammont, no teaching is required: mere exposure to the two languages suffices. It may well be that some or perhaps even many of these bilinguals would have been equally successful if this principle had not been followed. It is also possible that similar results could be obtained if the family languages were not distributed according to persons but by adopting other criteria, e.g. using one language during meals and the other one when playing with the child. However, I strongly advise against experimenting with children, especially in this case where we can rely on a method that has led to the desired result so many times in the past.

I thus recommend the OPOL principle, but I want to emphasize that it is a very useful strategy, not a dogma that needs to be followed to the letter. First of all, I know of no reason why one should stick to it categorically and at all times. Despite Grammont's admonition never to diverge from it, my recommendation is to remain flexible and follow one's common sense, as did the parents of the Turkish-German boy whose letter I cited at the beginning of this section. Remember that the OPOL principle is supposed to help children to not be confused by a linguistically complex environment and to facilitate their task of separating two linguistic systems. This means that it plays a crucial role during the first three years of the child's life and that it becomes less relevant once language separation is well established. Other factors will then be more important. For example, whether children become actively bilingual, i.e. whether they not only understand but also speak both languages, depends more on the choice of the language that parents use among themselves than on the OPOL principle; see section 5.1. Yet even during earlier phases, the purpose of adopting this principle is not to hide from children the fact that a parent can understand and speak the language he or she does not use when addressing them. After all, young bilinguals expect other people to be bilingual like themselves. And switching to the other language when addressing monolingual friends or family members, or simply in their presence, is not a source of confusion. Rather, it offers an opportunity to learn how to adapt one's language choice to the communicative environment. My advice thus is: follow the OPOL method, but be flexible and feel free to diverge from it occasionally, if the situation requires it. Most importantly, talk to your child. Or rather: talk *with* your child, engaging in meaningful interactions. Talk, talk, talk!

As has certainly become obvious, the foregoing discussion and my recommendations concern primarily the distribution of languages in binational families or in families where one parent has decided to speak a different language to the child, regardless of whether or not it is the parent's mother tongue (the latter case is discussed in Chapter 6, section 6.2). My assumption is that the rationale for this decision is to enable the child to acquire two first languages simultaneously. This not only implies the development of two native competences. As I will show in Chapter 8, language acquisition also means acculturation, and bilinguals can or should become bicultural individuals, at home in different value systems, familiar with two educational styles, etc.

However, not all readers will subscribe to these goals. Some might set more modest ones, aiming, for example, at a knowledge of the other language that allows the child to understand family members who speak only that language. At any rate, the choice of strategy depends on what the parents want to achieve. And what can be achieved depends on the context within and outside the family. Is one of the family languages the majority language, the dominant language outside the family? Is neither of the family languages the majority language? Does the family live in a bi- or multilingual society or in a predominantly monolingual environment? In the following chapters, I will refer to these different contexts, although I will continue to focus on the possibility of achieving a native competence in both languages and becoming bicultural as well as bilingual.

Before concluding this chapter, I want to draw your attention to one further aspect of the OPOL method and similar strategies. It does not concern the children but the parents who adopt it. As is explained in the following email from the mother of a boy raised bilingually, the consistent use of another language by one parent can result in a situation where the other one feels excluded from an important part of the interaction within the family.

Excluding One Parent by the Adopted Language Strategy?

My husband grew up in a Swedish-speaking family in a Swiss-German environment. He is thus bilingual and speaks both Swiss-German and Swedish fluently. In his family, it is common practice to switch to German when persons are present who do not understand Swedish. Switching is thus an act of politeness and happens automatically and smoothly. He has decided to raise our son (1;6) in Swedish.

I, myself, grew up monolingually (German) and have a passive knowledge of Swedish, sufficient for contexts that are not too complex. My problem is an emotional one – I feel excluded when my husband speaks to our son in a special language in which I am not able to participate actively in a conversation. As a passive listener in Swedish, I miss badly a language that connects the THREE of us.

My husband insists on holding on to the one-person-one-language method, speaking exclusively in Swedish to our son. I would want to have a family language in which all three of us were able to interact – I believe I would then feel equal and integrated.

(Translated from German, JMM)

This is undoubtedly a serious issue. It has the potential to negatively affect relationships within the family and especially between husband and wife. However, from the perspective of someone commenting on bilingual children's linguistic development – the only perspective I am qualified to adopt – I cannot advise the father to refrain from using Swedish consistently when speaking to his son. In fact, using it in intimate and emotionally loaded contexts is particularly important for the parent as well as for the child. Note that this offers the bilingual child the opportunity to become familiar with the linguistic variety that is appropriate in such situations. This is, of course, one of the qualities of a true native speaker. Admittedly, it is also a kind of knowledge that second language speakers are likely to lack. In this particular case, the second language speaker is the mother who may thus feel excluded from some of the interactions in the family. Quite obviously, the problem is even more urgent in families where one parent has no knowledge at all of the other's language. The only advice I have to offer is to encourage parents and, in fact, all family members to learn the other language spoken in the family. If children are expected to become native speakers in two languages, it should not be unreasonable to expect other family members to learn a second language. They need not become native-like, but they can acquire enough of the other family language not to feel excluded in most situations of everyday communication. And remember that the OPOL principle is not a dogma. It is a strategy that promises the best results if it is put to practice with flexibility.

3.4 Reading Suggestions

Readers who wish to know more about the *one person, one language* method or other strategies for the distribution of languages within the family will find more detailed information in the following book and may want to read Chapter 7:

Barron-Hauwaert, S. (2004). *Language strategies for bilingual families: The one-parent-one-language approach.* Clevedon: Multilingual Matters.

A summary of recent research on bilingual acquisition is presented in the following book chapter:

Meisel, J. M. (2017). Bilingual acquisition: A morphosyntactic perspective on simultaneous and early successive language development. In H. Cairns & E. M. Fernández (Eds.), *Handbook of psycholinguistics*, pp. 635–52. New York: Wiley Blackwell.

4 Keeping Languages Apart

Mixing, Interference and Interaction
of Languages

4.1 Children's Mixing and Switching of Languages

No confusion, no fusion, no sign of excessive mental strain – children exposed to two languages from birth are able to differentiate the two linguistic systems, and are thus off to a good start on their way to becoming native speakers of two languages. Is this tantamount to saying that they are two monolinguals in one person? Certainly not. Bilinguals are more than the sum of two monolinguals because knowing two languages implies, among many other things, knowing how to choose the adequate one in monolingual as well as in bilingual situations and how to alternate between them in bilingual contexts. This is only possible if the one currently not used is not totally switched off. Rather, it needs to be set to 'sleeping mode', like electronic devices that are temporarily not in use but should remain ready for use at any moment. This constant low-level activation makes it possible to access rapidly the language currently not in use whenever the situation or a person's communicative needs or intentions require it. However, just as your 'sleeping' laptop or TV set continues to consume energy, bilinguals need to make additional efforts, as compared to monolinguals, when handling two languages, activating one and inhibiting the other. This is not necessarily a disadvantage. On the contrary, it provides bilinguals with opportunities to practice cognitive control mechanisms, and they seem to be able to carry over these skills to other cognitive domains; see Chapter 8 (section 8.2).

Nevertheless, since both languages are at least partially activated in bilingual settings, one may wonder whether constant interaction between them does not result in alterations of the linguistic systems that were initially separated. In other words, is it possible for young bilinguals to keep the two systems apart in the course of development? Do they proceed through the same acquisition sequences as monolinguals, and does this development happen at approximately the same rate? These questions will be addressed in the next section, 4.2, because they can only be answered by examining children's underlying linguistic knowledge. In this section, let us first take a closer look at how bilinguals alternate between languages and how children learn how to do this.

Alternating between languages is, in fact, not such a strange phenomenon. Remember that monolinguals also switch between varieties of their language, as we have seen in Chapter 1 (section 1.2). We all, monolinguals and bilinguals alike, accommodate our speech to the communicative context, using, for example, different registers, depending on the formality of the situation, whether we speak to strangers or friends, to adults or children, and so forth. Although the required changes can concern all aspects of language, vocabulary, pronunciation, and even grammar, the transition normally happens smoothly and unconsciously. We rarely need to reflect on how to behave linguistically. The same is true for the way in which bilinguals accommodate their use of language to different communicative contexts, in spite of the fact that they are dealing with a more complex task, since it involves the choice of the appropriate language in addition to the choice of the adequate variety.

The most obvious and also easiest case is the change between different monolingual situations where everything indicates the need to alternate between languages. In potentially bilingual contexts, on the other hand, it is necessary to first decide which language to start out with, i.e. to choose what has been called the *base language*. Subsequently, it may be the case that at some point of the conversation the most adequate variety is actually a variety of the other language, thus requiring language switching, or *code-switching*, as it has been termed in sociolinguistics. What will be perceived as an adequate choice depends on a number of factors. Importantly, speakers are rarely aware of the fact that their linguistic behaviour is guided by external and internal factors – switching is mostly not a conscious but an intuitive choice. The factors in question can be contextual or structural ones, or they result from the speakers' communicative intentions. In what follows, I will briefly explain what this means.

Not surprisingly, one finds that language choice and switching reflect the social and, more specifically, the communicative experiences of bilingual individuals. Typically, they do not use both languages equally often in all situations of everyday life. Rather, one language tends to be preferred or to be used even exclusively in specific *domains*: family, school, work, religion, sport, etc. Consequently, the two languages are more or less strongly tied to these domains, and the degree to which one of them is preferred over the other one depends on the factors that characterize the domains, e.g. particular interlocutors, situational contexts, topics of conversation. The ability to select languages according to such factors and to code-switch when these contextual variables or the communicative intentions of the speaker require it is part of the pragmatic competence of bilinguals.

Imagine, for example, a bilingual individual, speaker of a minority language in a predominantly monolingual society, entering a government office in order to file a request or a complaint. Almost certainly, the community language will be the base language. If, however, this person discovers that the government official behind the counter is a childhood acquaintance and a speaker of the minority language, it is quite likely that they will switch to this language – and back to the community language when dealing with their official business. In this case, the situational context requires the choice of the majority language as the base language. However, the social relationship between the interlocutors is complex. They can therefore focus on one or the other role, shifting between relationships, either as official and citizen or as childhood acquaintances, favouring either the community or the minority language. Similarly, the change of topic of the conversation, shifting from official business to shared childhood memories and back, can trigger language switching.

Thus, social domains are not homogeneous entities but are characterized by networks of factors that favour the use of either language A or language B. The choice of a base language and the decision to switch to another one are therefore the results of usually unconscious and subtle processes that depend on the intuitive weighting of the determining factors. Not surprisingly, not all individuals engaged in an interaction will always arrive at the same conclusion. In this case, they must negotiate which language is to be used. In sum, rather than indicating a fusion of linguistic systems or confusion in language use, code-switching is an indication of elaborate linguistic and social competences.

Quite obviously, during early phases of language acquisition children do not yet possess the necessary linguistic and sociolinguistic competences that would allow them to perform like adults in bilingual interactions. This explains why early instances of language mixing sometimes differ from adult switching, as we have seen in section 3.1. Nevertheless, as mentioned earlier, situational factors do already play an important role in children's language choice at an early age. Initially, the language spoken by the interlocutor is the decisive factor, as is evidenced by the fact that bilingual children switch languages according to the interlocutor as of age 2 years. Not only that, as early as around age 2;3, they correct themselves after having addressed someone in the wrong language. Soon afterwards, they are able to make rather subtle adjustments in their interactions with bilingual interlocutors. They understand, for example, that some people prefer to be addressed consistently in the same language whereas others accept the use of both languages. This means that the interlocutor is not the only decisive factor any more. Rather, they have learned that code-switching can serve a number of communicative functions in interactions with other bilinguals.

For instance, already during the first half of the third year, children whose parents follow the one person, one language strategy (OPOL; see section 3.3) sometimes repeat their own utterances in the other language in order to attract the attention of both parents or to make sure that both parents have understood what they said. In this kind of setting, children also begin to use switching to indicate who their addressee is or to reject the language choice of an interlocutor who addressed the child in the 'wrong' language.

Further possibilities are to switch by quoting people in the language they used when uttering what is quoted, or in metalinguistic remarks, i.e. commenting on one's own or someone else's language use.

The latter functions of code-switching reveal that children of that young age are aware of their own and others' bilingualism. In fact, *bilingual awareness* increases during the third year, and children not only comment on their own language use but also ask their parents for translations. Incidentally, such metalinguistic awareness represents another strong piece of evidence indicating separation of the two languages as well as the ability to switch between these linguistic systems in a fashion that does not differ fundamentally any more from that of adult bilinguals. This conclusion is confirmed by the observation that during the same age period, i.e. approximately as of 2;6, children switch between languages in role-play. Since they regard toys or animals as bilingual interlocutors, these too are involved in role-play or are offered translations of what other toys say. The francophone teddy bear, for example, may not be able to follow the conversation of the bilingual dolls when these speak German, a situation not unlike the one encountered by the child's French grandparents, the ones who brought the bear to Germany.

In children's fourth and fifth years, code-switching serves these as well as an array of further conversational and sociolinguistic functions. In other words, while new functions emerge, the ones observed earlier are now used in more subtle ways and in a wider variety of contexts, attesting to bilingual competences much like those of adults. For example, children report on what happened in the daycare centre, quoting other people's utterances in the original language. Or they switch when reporting a conversation to mark their own utterances in contrast to those of other speakers. From approximately 4;0 onwards, children also switch languages to amuse or tease interlocutors, to produce stylistic effects or to assert their identity, either as bilinguals or as members of a distinct linguistic or cultural group. In fact, code-switching can serve to deliberately exclude a third person from a conversation.

This is illustrated by the following example where a French-German boy speaks German with his French-speaking mother in the presence of a French research assistant and switches back to French to let the research assistant know that he does not care whether or not she understands what he is saying.

> **Child to mother:** Böse kleine Männchen und dann haben sie aber bestimmt Angst.
> 'Wicked little men and then they are surely afraid.'

> **Assistant:** Moi je comprends pas, oui mais ça c'est de l'allemand dis donc.
> 'I don't understand, yes but that's German, you know.'

> **M:** Elle comprend pas Marie-Claude, tu sais.
> 'Marie-Claude doesn't understand, you know.'

> **C to M:** Ça fait rien.
> 'That doesn't matter.'

In sum, the possibility of alternating between languages offers communicative means that are not available to monolinguals, and a substantial part of the necessary pragmatic and sociolinguistic knowledge is acquired by children between ages two and five years.

Yet although young bilinguals already possess such impressive capacities, switching is also triggered by more obvious and perhaps even trivial factors, such as the lack of the appropriate word. Since bilinguals do not necessarily use both languages equally often in all domains, the lexicon of one language can exhibit gaps in the domain in which they interact predominantly in the other language. This is, of course, not a problem specific to bilinguals. Monolinguals, too, lack vocabulary specific to less-familiar topics, as one discovers when dealing with legal matters or reading a technical manual. Bilinguals may encounter such problems more frequently and with less specialized linguistic varieties. However, they have the advantage of being able to resort to their other language to fill gaps.

A similar situation applies in cases where the lexical problem is not due to a lack of knowledge but to a temporary difficulty in accessing lexical material. This, too, having trouble finding the right word at the right moment, happens to monolinguals as well as to bilinguals, but the latter can solve the temporary problem by switching to the other language, at least when communicating with other bilinguals.

Moreover, inserting a word from the other language is a means to express subtle cultural differences or semantic nuances. In this case, switching is a possible solution to the problem of finding *le mot juste*, an expression that conveys just the right message intended by the speaker. A word from the other language will be preferable if its meaning differs in precisely the desired way from that in the base language. For example, when Spanish immigrants in Germany refer in Spanish contexts to the public health insurance scheme by the German word *Krankenkasse* 'health insurance company', or jokingly *la gran casa*, the reason is not that they lack the Spanish word. Rather, these Spanish-German bilinguals feel that the German expression is better suited to refer to the German institution and that it conveys immigrant workers' experience with this institution.

Note that in the latter cases (filling a lexical gap, replacing a word temporarily not accessible, choice of a culturally adequate expression) code-switching consists primarily of single words, mostly nouns that are inserted into utterances otherwise containing lexical items exclusively from the base language. In fact, what is intended as a single-word insertion sometimes results in an unintended change of the base language, i.e. the speaker finishes the sentence in the other language without even noticing it. The reason why this happens is that inserted words function as trigger elements, causing a stronger activation of the dormant language.

Importantly, in both cases, with single-word insertions and with language switching triggered by insertions, the result is a *sentence-internal* switch, just as in the title of an early publication by Poplack (1980): Sometimes I'll start a sentence in Spanish *y termino en español*. This is crucial, as Poplack and many others have since demonstrated, because bilinguals do not switch just anywhere within sentences. Rather, they prefer certain switch points that are defined by structural properties. This is why I said above that code-switching is guided by structural as well as contextual factors. In other words, adequate bilingual language use requires not only pragmatic and sociolinguistic but also grammatical knowledge, as I will explain in more detail below. What I mean by 'adequate' bilingual language use is that the switch is inconspicuous, other bilinguals accept it as normal linguistic behaviour, and they may not even notice it. It does not, however, require a conscious choice. Quite to the contrary, bilingual speakers are rarely aware of the fact that they rely on such complex knowledge when switching between languages.

To Sum Up: Competent and Skilled Bilinguals Mix Languages

- Both mental grammars of bilinguals are constantly activated. In monolingual contexts, the one currently not used is activated at a low level; in bilingual settings, the one not in use is activated at a higher level. This enables bilinguals to switch between languages. Code-switching is a particular communicative skill of bilinguals.
- As bilingual children acquire the grammatical and sociolinguistic principles that constrain code-switching, their mixed utterances increasingly resemble those of bilingual adults.

Keeping all this in mind, let us look at sentence-internal mixing by young bilingual children in order to see whether their linguistic behaviour can indeed be qualified as adult-like code-switching or whether it is less systematic or even chaotic. Quite obviously, sentence-internal switching can only occur once children are able to produce multi-word utterances, i.e. not before the second half of their second year of life; cf. Chapter 3 where I gave some early examples of mixing in two-word utterances in section 3.1. The vast majority of these early sentence-internal mixes consist of single noun insertions, a finding that should not come as a surprise, considering what we know about factors favouring this kind of language mixing. In fact, empirical studies of switching revealed that nouns are the most frequently inserted syntactic category, not only in the earliest instances of language mixing, but also in the speech of older children and adults. They account for as much as 75 per cent of mixing by children between ages three and six, according to some studies.

This amounts to saying that insertions of single words, especially nouns, seem to be acceptable in virtually all contexts. The transition between articles and nouns is thus a possible switch point, and the structural relationship between these two categories within nominal groups (noun phrases) is clearly not preventing bilinguals from switching languages here. The following examples from French-German children should illustrate this. The first two are from recordings with a boy, the third one from the recordings of a girl.

> Das **bateau**   I 2;0
> 'the ship'
>
> Tu veux que je te donne des **Datteln**?   I 4;2
> 'Do you want me to give you dates?'
>
> Ja und ein **ceinture** ein ein -   A 2;8
> 'Yes and a belt a a –' [interrupts her utterance]

A rather different picture emerges when we look at structurally more complex cases. The fact that switches occur almost exclusively at particular transition points between two elements of a sentence and virtually never at others confirms the claim that code-switching is systematic, not chaotic. In fact, the identification of transition points as possible or impossible switch points refers to structural criteria. Linguists have tried to capture these facts by proposing grammatical constraints on code-switching.

A thorough description of these attempts would lead us too far into technical details of morphosyntactic analyses of language switching. It should suffice to say that structural relations define different degrees of cohesion between elements of a sentence and that cohesion plays a crucial role in language processing. One implication of this insight is that in speaking and listening to speech, we try to avoid interruptions at points where the structural cohesion between elements is tight. From this, it again follows that code-switching is most unlikely to happen at points of strong cohesion. Importantly, constraints are not strict rules whose violation would lead to a rejection of that mixed utterance. Rather, violations result in decreasing degrees of acceptability and arguably in higher degrees of cognitive processing costs. In other words, it is preferable to observe the restrictions on switching that are captured by these constraints. It facilitates language use.

Let us briefly look at two of the proposed constraints. One example is the *equivalence constraint* according to which switches are acceptable if the resulting mixed sentence does not violate syntactic rules of either language. Just think of an English-German bilingual. Switching after a subordinating conjunction would be awkward because subordinate clauses exhibit different word orders in these two languages: subject–verb-object order in English and subject–object–verb order in German. Consequently, in the intended sentence *I know that daddy has cooked dinner*, switching after *that* leads to a conflict between English *daddy has cooked dinner* and German 'daddy dinner cooked has'. However, if the switch occurs before the conjunction, the result is much better: *I know dass Papa das Abendessen gekocht hat*. The reason is that the conjunction is part of the subordinate clause and determines the order of the words in this clause.

Another example is the *free morpheme constraint*. It states that switching should not happen between a bound morpheme and its preceding element. Recall from Chapter 2 (section 2.2) that morphemes are the smallest meaningful units of language and that there exist free and bound morphemes. Whereas the former are independent words, the latter are parts of words, e.g. inflectional suffixes. Switches involving bound morphemes would thus be instances of word-internal switching. This in itself does not rule out switching; word-internal switches do occur in bilingual speech, though quite infrequently. Whether switching is tolerated depends crucially on how tight the cohesion between the elements at the intended switch point is – and the cohesion between bound morphemes and the ones to which they are attached is normally very tight, by definition, so to say.

A similar argument can be made for so-called *clitic* pronouns, elements that must be attached to others and cannot stand alone, much like bound morphemes. Take French subject and object pronouns like *je* 'I' or *le* 'him, it'. They must be attached to the verb. It is therefore not possible to reply *je* when answering a question like *who is there?* Rather, one must use a strong pronoun instead, like *moi*. Not surprisingly, switches between clitics and finite verbs are excluded.

More examples could be listed here, but they would merely confirm what is already sufficiently clear, namely that language mixing in bilingual speech is not unsystematic. It is not a macaronic mix but is constrained by pragmatic as well as grammatical factors and serves multiple conversational and sociolinguistic purposes. What matters in the context of our discussion of the linguistic development of bilingual children is that they, too, switch between languages in accordance with the constraints to which adult language mixing is subject. Their language mixing thus also qualifies as code-switching and must not be interpreted as a failure in keeping languages apart. Where their linguistic behaviour differs from that of adults, this can be explained as a temporary phenomenon reflecting an ongoing acquisition process. Just as is the case with pragmatic and sociolinguistic knowledge, the grammatical knowledge that constrains sentence-internal code-switching is not yet fully available when children begin to use multi-word utterances. Rather, most of the required morphosyntactic knowledge develops during the third year. As of this age, children's language mixing is increasingly non-distinct from that of adults.

"GINA IS *BY LINGAL* ... THAT MEANS SHE CAN SAY
THE SAME THING *TWICE*, BUT YOU CAN ONLY
UNDERSTAND IT *ONCE*."

Dennis the Menace
© King Features Syndicate, Inc./Distr. Bulls.

Empirical studies of children's bilingual behaviour reveal that at
around age 2;4–2;6 sentence-internal switching is constrained by
the grammatical knowledge available at that age and that, from
then on, they rarely violate morphosyntactic constraints.

Interestingly, sociolinguistic studies of Spanish-English adult
bilinguals in the United States have shown that individuals who
acquired the second language early, i.e. before age 6;0, code-switch
most frequently. In particular, intrasentential switching, which
requires specific grammatical knowledge, is used significantly
more often by early bilinguals than by learners who acquired the
second language after the age of 13. This confirms an insight of
other studies of language use by adult bilinguals according to
which the better the competence in both languages, the more
frequently they use code-switching. In sum, what from a monolingual perspective appeared to be a deficiency of bilingualism,

language mixing, is frequently an indication of highly developed skills of bilingual language use.

4.2 Interaction of Languages in Children's Minds

As we have seen, the ability to choose the appropriate language in multilingual settings and to alternate between languages is at the core of what defines bilinguals; it distinguishes them from monolinguals. Quite obviously, choosing and switching between languages presupposes that there exist two distinct systems. However, it also means that they are both activated in the minds of the interlocutors, though to different degrees. Deciding on which one is more appropriate in a specific context or on whether intrasentential switching will lead to conflicting grammatical constructions (cf. the equivalence constraint) requires access to information about both systems. If one of them were switched off entirely, it would not be possible to weigh up pros and cons in favour or against these decisions. Thus, the two systems definitely interact.

This observation leads to the question raised at the beginning of this chapter as to whether the interaction between simultaneously activated languages can lead to alterations of the linguistic systems or whether it is possible for bilingual children to keep them apart in the course of development. The answer to this question is an indispensable piece of information for anybody interested in child bilingualism. After all, early differentiation of grammars has been a major topic of research on bilingual acquisition, not least because it relates to the probably most serious concern of parents who consider raising their children bilingually. Now that we know that interaction between languages in a bilingual's mind is the rule rather than the exception, the question is whether the important achievement of having established mental representations of two separate knowledge systems is at risk. Considering the fact that this knowledge is still developing and has not yet been consolidated, the idea that one or both systems could be altered under the continued influence of the respective other one is certainly not far-fetched. The main issue is whether cross-linguistic interaction affects the grammars of bilinguals in such a way that they end up being *qualitatively* different from those of monolinguals, possibly even exhibiting properties that might qualify them as non-native competences. If this were the case, it would doubtless be a reason not to opt for a bilingual upbringing of children.

To cut a very long story short, in my view the most plausible answer to this question is that cross-linguistic interaction does not result in qualitative differences in bilinguals' linguistic competences. However, I must hasten to add that there is no broad consensus on this issue among researchers. I will therefore explain my answer, but only briefly and without going into much detail because this would require a technical discussion of structural properties of the bilinguals' languages, a debate of only marginal interest for our present purposes.

Since we are primarily interested in *qualitative* alterations of children's linguistic knowledge, let me state explicitly what should be obvious, namely that a construction used by bilinguals can only count as a qualitative difference if it never occurs in monolingual speech. Moreover, we must distinguish between the acquisition process and the ultimately attained knowledge. If, for example, the course of development were altered because of interactions between the systems, this would certainly count as a qualitative difference indicating that grammars of bilinguals do not develop independently. Yet qualitative difference in the course of development will not necessarily lead to differences in the ultimately attained knowledge. Even if they proceed through partially different developmental sequences, principled reasons do not exist for why children could not attain native competences indistinct of those of monolinguals.

As for *quantitative* differences, these must certainly be taken into account as well because they can provide insights into the mechanisms of bilingual language use, although they do not reflect differences in the underlying knowledge. If bilinguals use particular constructions significantly more frequently or, on the contrary, less often, in comparison to monolingual children, or if they take more (or less) time to acquire them, this counts as a quantitative difference. After all, the constructions in question all reflect the same grammatical knowledge, even if it emerges at a faster or slower rate, or if it is activated more or less frequently.

It is time to inquire about what kind of differences between monolingual and bilingual acquisition are actually attested and whether they are indeed effects of cross-linguistic interaction. In principle, effects of interdependent developments can manifest themselves in the *acceleration* or *delay* of grammatical acquisition, or in the *transfer* of grammatical properties from one language to the other one. The latter clearly represents an instance of qualitative change of linguistic knowledge, because transfer means that a construction proper to one grammar is incorporated into the other one, resulting in a grammar qualitatively distinct from that of monolinguals. Acceleration or delay, on the other hand, would only count as qualitative changes if they led to alterations of the ordering of developmental phases.

As for possibly qualitative changes, not all components of linguistic knowledge are suspected to be affected by cross-linguistic interaction of this sort. In morphosyntax, for example, the most frequently reported effects of language interdependence concern the overuse of subjects or objects. Overuse can occur in so-called null-subject (or null-object) languages. Remember (see section 3.1) that in many languages, including most Romance languages, subjects may be lexically empty; in others, the same is true for objects, in Basque, for example. Importantly, this is a grammatically tolerated *option*. Whether an element is actually dropped or not depends on grammar-external factors, e.g. context or speaker intentions. This is not all that different from the choice between nominal and pronominal elements in non-null-subject languages like English. Just imagine how strange it would be to repeat nouns again and again, rather than using pronouns when referring repeatedly to the same object or person, as in the following example: *My car broke down. My car is old. I should sell my car* rather than *My car broke down, it is old, I should sell it.*

In null-subject languages, the identical element can be dropped altogether if it were to appear in the subject position again, though omission is not obligatory. One can use pronouns instead, similarly as in non-null-subject (pronominal) languages, if one wants to put emphasis on the element or in order to avoid ambiguity.

It is in these contexts that bilinguals have been observed to use a higher rate of overt subjects, as compared to monolinguals. Unfortunately, this observation raises more questions than it answers. At first sight, it seems to support the idea of monolingual–bilingual differences. Yet one may wonder whether it is a grammatical phenomenon or one that indicates a particular kind of language use. More importantly, the question is whether overuse of pronouns is indeed an interdependence effect triggered by the fact that the overt use of subjects or objects is obligatory in the other language. The answer is that this is almost certainly not the case. As it turns out, bilinguals who speak *two* null-subject languages also use overt subjects where monolinguals prefer empty subjects. Whatever the explanation of this linguistic behaviour may be, transfer from a non-null-subject language can definitely be ruled out in this case. Moreover, if it were an instance of cross-linguistic interaction, we should expect it to operate in both directions. This is to say that null-subject properties should occasionally occur in pronominal languages, e.g. if the null-subject language is the dominant one in the children's environment. However, none of the many studies investigating this phenomenon found that null-subject properties are transferred to pronominal languages. It is therefore safe to conclude that we are not looking at an instance of cross-linguistic interaction and that, moreover, overuse of lexical subjects is hardly a grammatical phenomenon. After all, we know that the choice between null, pronominal or nominal subjects is determined by pragmatic factors. It is therefore plausible to assume that these are also at play here, resulting in quantitative shifts between various instantiations of subjects, although the preference for one of these may well be determined by an interaction of pragmatic and syntactic information.

This latter observation is of particular interest, because we are looking for a generalized definition of vulnerable grammatical domains, rather than testing one specific case after the other, as in for example subject overuse in null-subject languages. Interestingly, one such generalizing proposal is that cross-linguistic interaction is most likely to affect constructions that involve grammar-internal as well as grammar-external principles. Vulnerable grammatical domains would thus primarily consist of so-called *interface* phenomena. They require access to and processing of different kinds of information, e.g. grammatical and grammar-external information, or information pertaining to different subcomponents of grammar, especially if the construction in question is structurally complex.

Complexity is defined in terms of the number of grammatical operations required to generate functionally similar expressions. In interrogatives, for example, question words referring to syntactic objects are either moved to clause-initial position, or they remain in object position. In most languages, one of these options is obligatory; in others, both positions are possible, as in colloquial French: *tu as appelé qui?*, *qui tu as appelé?* 'who did you call?'. Since the one with the question word in initial position requires at least one more operation (fronting), it can be regarded as structurally more complex. The idea, then, is that if the languages of a bilingual differ in that one exhibits a more complex option than the other one, the less complex one will be transferred and replace the more complex construction.

The crucial question is whether predictions are valid that are based on considerations of this sort. Do structural criteria (interface phenomena, structural ambiguity, or complexity) define vulnerable grammatical domains that are affected by cross-linguistic interaction? The somewhat disappointing answer is: yes and no. Child bilingualism researchers investigated these issues in much detail, in numerous studies on many different language pairs. They concluded that a majority of the cases in which effects of interdependence were detected indeed involve interface phenomena. However, such effects also emerged with constructions not located at an interface level, and, vice versa, not all interface phenomena exhibited these effects, not even when additional conditions (ambiguity, complexity) were met. Thus, the proposed structural properties are neither necessary nor sufficient conditions for effects of interdependence to occur. They merely seem to favour it to happen.

Moreover, virtually all studies show that cross-linguistic interaction between linguistic systems does not occur in the speech of *all* children. Rather, it is attested in the speech of only *some* individuals – and even there it does not happen in all cases that meet the structural requirements. The latter observation is a crucial one because it shows that interdependence or cross-linguistic interaction does not mean that constructions of one languages replace corresponding ones in the other language. Instead, the symptoms of interdependence are quantitative in nature; they compete with the target expressions and substitute them occasionally in the speech of bilinguals. If the grammar of one language had been altered under the influence of one of the other language, these effects should occur consistently. The crucial message therefore is that parents need not be concerned about cross-linguistic interaction of this sort. If it happens at all, it is a temporary phenomenon, and it does not mean that bilinguals run the risk of developing grammatical knowledge qualitatively distinct of that of monolinguals.

However, an all-clear still cannot be given because we have not yet examined the role of language-external factors as causes of interdependent developments. *Dominance* of one language is most frequently mentioned as a cause of cross-linguistic interaction. However, dominance can mean different things, as we will see in Chapter 5 (section 5.1), which is dedicated entirely to the discussion of the role of dominance in bilingual acquisition. At any rate, interdependence effects commonly refer to the rate of acquisition, meaning that one language develops at a faster rate than the other one. The idea is that children who can rely on more elaborate grammatical knowledge in one language, the dominant or rather stronger one, will occasionally resort to it when speaking the other one.

This has been claimed to be most likely to happen in cases where language-internal factors like structural ambiguity or higher complexity in the weaker language favour this option. However, this is a controversial issue among researchers, and I do not want to reopen the debate on the role of structural triggers of interaction. What we do want to know is whether grammatical interference actually happens, no matter whether under the influence of language-external or internal factors. Whereas the overwhelming majority of studies give a negative answer to this question, a few do report that they find evidence of grammatical transfer. Since this is an important point for parents of bilingual children, let us take a brief look at one of these studies in order to see what its implications are.

In their study of a bilingual boy acquiring Cantonese and English simultaneously, Yip and Matthews (2000) found signs of grammatical transfer. Their strongest case concerns word order in interrogative constructions, suggesting that clause-final placement of question words is transferred from the dominant language Cantonese into English. Cantonese is one of the languages, mentioned above, where this final position is required in almost all contexts. Syntactic analyses show that it is the position where interrogative elements originate. They thus remain there (*in situ*) in these languages, whereas their appearance in initial position is the result of a displacement operation. One would therefore expect the final position to be easier to learn because it requires fewer operations.

Children acquiring *in situ* languages like Cantonese indeed acquire this word order without problems. In fact, clause-final placement also occurs in the speech of monolingual English children, though much less frequently than in the data from the Cantonese-English boy. This has led to the claim that a grammatical property of the dominant language Cantonese has been transferred to English. However, empirical facts do not actually support this assumption. The first observation contradicting it is that the first occurrence of an interrogative construction with a question word in the child's English is one with the question word in initial position. Moreover, this word order co-occurs with the *in situ* pattern during the entire developmental period on which this study reports. In other words, the English-type construction has not been replaced by the Cantonese-type alternative. Rather, the two coexist in the child's grammar. After all, *in situ* order exists in English too, in so-called echo questions where the question word is emphasized as in *you have bought* **what?**

Finally, what casts serious doubts on the claim that the *in situ* property is likely to be incorporated into non-*in situ* languages is the fact that other studies investigating the acquisition of *in situ* languages and English by bilingual children (Japanese-English, Korean-English) did not find evidence of grammatical transfer although the Asian languages were always the dominant ones. This is all the more remarkable since the clause-final position of question words represents a syntactically less complex construction than the one with fronting, as we have seen above. Moreover, Korean as well as Cantonese allow fronting in some specific contexts, and the fact that two options are available has been argued to trigger cross-linguistic interaction. Yet although dominance as well as structural properties favour cross-linguistic interaction, the Korean-English children did not use a single *in situ* construction in their spontaneous use of English, and Japanese-English simultaneous bilinguals did not show evidence of grammatical transfer either.

In sum, we can safely conclude that it is very unlikely that grammatical transfer causes bilingual children to develop linguistic knowledge qualitatively distinct from that of their monolingual counterparts. But how, then, can we account for the fact that interdependence effects do occur, if only occasionally and not in the speech of all bilinguals? In fact, this question has already been answered in Chapter 2 (section 2.3), although very briefly. The explanation is that these effects are caused by the simultaneous on-line activation of two languages rather than by an interaction of grammatical knowledge. As mentioned in the preceding section, psycholinguistic studies leave no doubt that both languages are usually activated simultaneously in the brains of bilinguals, even in predominantly monolingual contexts. From this it follows that speakers engaged in monolingual conversations must inhibit the language not selected for use, i.e. the non-selected language needs to be confined to stand-by modus, so to say. If inhibition is not entirely successful, this can lead to cross-linguistic interaction, i.e. the inhibited language is activated after all. Normally, this happens involuntarily, although it can also be a relief strategy enabling the bilingual to access compensatory information, substituting knowledge that is not or not readily available in the other language. In either case, failure to inhibit the non-selected language does not happen consistently at identical points in the course of language production. It rather depends on the demands exerted on the processing mechanisms, and this accounts for the fact that the observed effects appear only temporarily and only with some children.

For parents and all others concerned about the well-being of bilingual children, the most important insight gained from studies of linguistic interdependence is that the ultimately attained grammatical competence will not be affected by possible cross-linguistic interaction during early years of linguistic development. In fact, all or most of the proponents of interdependence agree that this is not the case. Although some studies report that children's linguistic development can be delayed or accelerated, no convincing evidence has been found as yet that would support the idea of permanent qualitative alterations of grammars. Thus, changes under the influence of the other language, to the extent that they occur at all, are temporary ones.

To Sum Up: Cross-Linguistic Interaction Does Not Result in Non-Native Competences

- As bilingual children acquire the grammatical and socio-linguistic principles that constrain code-switching, their mixed utterances increasingly resemble those of bilingual adults. Switching is a performance phenomenon that does not affect the underlying competence.

- Cross-linguistic interactions are not detected in the speech of all bilingual children. When it does happen, it concerns only some aspects of grammar, and it is typically a temporary phenomenon.
- Although mental grammars of bilinguals interact, this does not lead to interference. Development of grammatical knowledge may be delayed or accelerated in bilinguals, but it is not qualitatively different from that attained by the respective monolinguals.

To conclude, my answer to the question of whether one finds cross-linguistic interaction in early bilingual development is *no* in that there is no developmental phase during which bilingual children systematically use devices of the other language. The answer is also *no* in that there exists no convincing empirical evidence suggesting that grammatical elements from one grammar are incorporated into the other one. In fact, there is no reason to believe that interdependence affects mental representations of grammars. Nevertheless, the possibility cannot yet be excluded that some kind of 'problematic input' might lead to temporary confusion of bilinguals. I will discuss this problem in Chapters 5 and 6.

In other respects, however, I do find cross-linguistic interaction, and the answer is *yes*, in that the course of development can be accelerated or delayed, in comparison to monolinguals. It is also *yes* in that *some* children *sometimes* use constructions that appear to be the result of influence from the other language. These, however, are quantitative differences, as compared to monolingual children.

4.3 Parents' Language Choices

Children exposed to more than one language from early on are able to keep the developing linguistic systems separate in their minds. Interdependence between these systems can lead to an acceleration or retardation of the acquisition process of certain grammatical properties, but cross-linguistic interaction affects neither the course of morphosyntactic development nor the ultimately attained linguistic competence. The fact that these children sometimes mix languages does not speak against these statements. It rather means that they behave in much the same way as adult bilinguals, using language mixing as a conversational strategy in interactions with other bilinguals yet almost never when addressing monolingual interlocutors. In other words, they use code-switching, constrained by pragmatic as well as grammatical factors. This is, in short, what the research literature on bilingual children's language mixing reveals.

But what about bilingual parents and other bilinguals who communicate regularly with the children? So far, they only appeared as interlocutors who, as such, represent the most important factor determining the children's language choice, at least during the children's third year. What do we know about these adults' use of language mixing? Not much, because acquisition studies mostly rely on parents' self-reported accounts of their linguistic behaviour in adult–child interactions. Nevertheless, studies that analyse parents' child-directed speech systematically do exist, and they show that parents, too, mix languages.

This in itself is not surprising, if we keep in mind that mixing is normal bilingual behaviour and that code-switching is a valuable means of bilingual communication. What is noteworthy, however, is that adults interacting with bilingual children tend to mix languages more frequently than they are aware of themselves, as becomes obvious from discrepancies between self-reports and recorded behaviour. It is confirmed by analyses of recordings where a parent rather than a researcher interacts with a bilingual child. In fact, even the parents who adhere strictly to the one person, one language (OPOL) strategy and who reject mixing do mix and switch languages. One can thus say that language mixing is a rather common phenomenon in children's linguistic environment, although bilingual families, just like bilingual societies, differ significantly in how they view and how they practise language mixing. Whereas some accept it as a normal and even useful way of communicating among bilinguals, others regard it as inappropriate linguistic behaviour. Frequency of mixing therefore varies accordingly, across families as well as across bilingual societies.

Most children growing up bilingually are thus exposed to mixed speech, albeit to different degrees. Since this chapter is primarily concerned with the question of whether children are able to keep two linguistic systems apart, we need to ask what the possible effects are on the acquisition process. Does mixing by parents and other caregivers affect children's mixing behaviour? Does exposure to frequent mixing favour cross-linguistic interaction and perhaps even grammatical transfer? And how should parents react to their children's language mixing or to the choice of the 'wrong' language? These and similar questions are often raised in counselling sessions.

Parents' Language Mixing

I am Egyptian, and I went to a French school in Cairo where the instruction was exclusively in French. Our communication in school as well as at home was a hotchpotch of Arabic, French and English. I am now married to a German and have a seven-month-old daughter who I want to learn Arabic, so that she can communicate with my family where no one speaks German. I now have this question: Is it wise to speak in a mishmash to her, will she be able to differentiate the languages?

Nine months later

Parents' Reaction to the Choice of the 'Wrong' Language

My daughter is now one year and four months old. How should I react when she answers me in German? Should

I simply continue to speak Arabic when I answer her? I would feel sorry for her if I did not encourage her to speak German. Her father is at work all day, and she therefore speaks and understands Arabic much better than German. I therefore thought I could tell her in Arabic 'daddy says X and mommy says Y'. Is this ok or will I confuse her?

(Translated from German, JMM)

These are quotes from two emails, nine months apart, by the mother of a bilingual girl; she herself grew up trilingually. Her questions require more than a simple sentence as an answer. This is partly due to the fact that the answers depend largely on parents' educational style and on the goals that they want to achieve. The first question, whether parental mixing affects children's linguistic behaviour, is the easiest to answer. Some research evidence does indeed support the suspicion that children who hear many mixed utterances mix frequently themselves. In fact, the percentages of mixes in the children's speech sometimes mirrored exactly the frequencies detected in the speech of their parents. Although not all studies confirm this finding, it is established well enough to justify an affirmative answer to our question.

However, this does not mean that one should encourage parents to mix freely and to create a linguistic hotchpotch, as the Egyptian mother called it. After all, the reason why she asked for advice is that she wondered whether this might not make it more difficult for her daughter to differentiate her languages and to keep them apart. The fact that it apparently had no negative effects on her own linguistic development is of course not a reason to sound the all-clear. Not only can we not draw conclusions based on a single case, mixing in this particular one may not actually have been chaotic. We know that bilinguals are rarely aware of the fact that they follow pragmatic and grammatical guidelines when they code-switch (see section 4.1).

The crucial issue here is the one addressed by our second question, namely whether frequent mixing in family interactions or in child-directed speech favours grammatical transfer or cross-linguistic interaction more generally. Unfortunately, evidence that would allow us to answer this question with confidence is scarce. It goes without saying that ethical considerations do not allow us to examine this issue by adopting a research design where one would try to confuse children and compare their acquisition with children not exposed to this kind of language use. We therefore have to rely on studies investigating the simultaneous acquisition of languages in contexts where mixing is known to occur frequently.

The few existing studies of this sort suggest that children exposed to this sort of mixed speech succeed without apparent effort in differentiating the linguistic systems and in keeping them apart. Wolof-French bilingualism in Senegal is an example of this kind of situation, as code-switching is used frequently among adult bilinguals in Dakar (Baars, 2002). Nevertheless, the two bilingual children studied, one balanced, the other one with Wolof as the stronger language, succeeded very well in early differentiation of grammatical systems. The least one can say is that findings like these suggest that exposure to speech containing frequent mixes need not represent an acquisition problem for the children. The tentative answer to the second question is thus a negative one: High mixing rates in the speech of adults will probably not entail qualitative changes in developing grammars.

Nevertheless, I do not recommend mixing languages freely in child-directed speech. What we can deduce from findings such as the ones just mentioned is that children are not easily confused by a certain amount of exposure to mixed speech. What we do not know with sufficient certainty is whether there exists a critical upper limit for the amount of mixed speech that they can handle without problems. Nor do we know whether all individuals are equally successful in dealing with challenges of this sort. My advice is therefore to opt for a more conservative strategy, one that provides support for the language-learning child rather than one that is likely to test the limits of the language acquisition capacities. This is to say that adult interlocutors should make it a habit to adhere to one language in addressing the child, in accordance with the OPOL principle, keeping in mind, however, that it is a useful strategy, not a dogma. Language mixing or switching is thus not excluded, since there is no reason to be concerned about potential effects of mixed speech on bilingual acquisition. On the contrary, code-switching, inserting nouns from the other language, etc. can facilitate or even improve communication. Children exposed to these bilingual conversational practices get the opportunity to acquire the necessary pragmatic knowledge and skills that will enable them to engage in bilingual interactions in an adequate fashion. At the same time, it proscribes language mixing in monolingual settings.

This brings us to the question of how parents should react to their children's mixing or choice of the 'wrong' language. Let me begin with a perhaps self-evident comment: just like adults, children should be allowed to mix or switch to another language when they feel this to be appropriate. However, their adult interlocutors need not accept this choice; rather, they may switch back again. This kind of trade-off happens among adult bilinguals, too. A very different situation arises when children consistently stick to one language and refuse to use the other one altogether. Chapter 5 is dedicated entirely to this problem. At this point, I am concerned with an intermediate situation, where children do not switch consistently yet more than occasionally – so frequently that parents do not feel comfortable with their children's choices. This is obviously a subjective assessment that will vary considerably, depending on family norms or preferences. However, it also reflects concerns such as the one expressed by the Egyptian mother. In either case, the crucial issue at stake is whether the reaction by parents or other caregivers might influence the bilingual acquisition processes.

The picture that emerges from studies investigating how parents' linguistic norms and discourse strategies influence children's developing bilingualism is somewhat blurred. Nevertheless, it does show clearly that the linguistic behaviour of parents can enhance the simultaneous development of two competences. Whereas the nature of the grammatical knowledge remains unaffected, the progress of the acquisition process can be stimulated in cases where children's performance in one language shows signs of deterioration. This concerns primarily cases of unbalanced bilingualism where one language is markedly stronger than the other one. As we will see in Chapter 5 (section 5.3), the use and development of the weaker language can probably be enhanced if parents encourage the use of *both* languages.

Parents' reactions to children's choice of the 'wrong' language play a crucial role in this process. Apparently, children are more likely to use the 'right' language, i.e. they refrain from mixing or from switching to the other language, if parents adopt what has been called, somewhat confusingly, *monolingual discourse strategies* (Lanza, 1997). What this means is that the adult conveys to the child the message that they should both continue to use language A and that it would not be appropriate to resort to language B at this point. The strategy employed by the mother of the Arabic-German girl (*daddy says X and mommy says Y*) qualifies as a monolingual strategy in this sense. It tells the child that her message has been understood, but that it would be more appropriate to use Arabic when talking to her mother. An American father adopted a more radical monolingual strategy, as he explains in the following quote.

Parents' Reaction to the Choice of the 'Wrong' Language

I am an American who has two small children who each live with a German mother. The mothers and the court give my children little access to my family (including me). They give no support for the language of my family (English). Given these restraints, in order to give my children a chance at being able to speak the language of my family (English) with my family (via telephone), a family that does not, and never will, even understand German, much less speak it, I have had to take drastic steps. The main step I have taken was to not speak German in their presence, and even more drastic, I do not show them that I even understand German when others attempt to speak it to me in their presence.

Pretending not to understand the other language is not an option I would recommend. In fact, it is not a discourse strategy that can serve the purpose of maintaining temporarily a mono-lingual situation. It rather creates a permanently monolingual setting. If a parent really does not speak the child's other language, this is obviously the only option. However, in the present case the father could have been a bilingual role model – a missed oppor-tunity. Most importantly, the children will eventually discover that their father is bilingual – if they do not know this already – and they will probably feel deceived.

A less drastic strategy is to request explicitly the use of language A (*Say it in A!*), although this is definitely not as subtle a metalin-guistic remark as the one used by the Egyptian mother (*Daddy says X and mommy says Y*). It is also possible to encourage the child to continue using the current language without interrupting the flow of the conversation, for instance by asking for clarification (*What did you say? Sorry?*). Since it happens frequently that interlocutors do not understand an utterance in the course of an interaction, this will be perceived as a natural part of the conversation. The most subtle reaction that still qualifies as a monolingual strategy consists of repeating in language A what the child said in language B, as in the following exchange between a German-speaking research assistant and a bilingual French-German boy at age 1;9.

> **Assistant:** Das ist ein Löffel. Und das?
> 'This is a spoon. And that?'

> **Pa:** Une fourchette.
> 'A fork.'

> **Assistant:** Ne Gabel, genau.
> 'A fork, exactly.'

Repetitions do not stand out in adult–child interaction, because adults frequently repeat children's utterances anyway. Whereas these and other monolingual discourse strategies have been shown to result in lower mixing rates in the children's speech, bilingual discourse strategies can have the opposite effect. They signal to the child that the adult interlocutor tolerates mixing and switching. This is the case, for example, when the adult simply moves on with the conversation in language A and does not react to the child's switch to language B, or when the adult accepts the child's code-switching and continues the conversation in language B.

As for the choice of discourse strategies, I refrain from recommending one, although it has probably become apparent that I tend to prefer the more subtle ones that do not interrupt the flow of the adult–child conversation. The decision on what is the optimal strategy depends on the family norms on language mixing, and, most importantly, on the child. With more silent and perhaps shy children, for example, it would probably be wise to avoid unnecessary interruptions. Others do not mind occasional nudges, moving them towards a particular type of bilingual behaviour. There simply does not exist one strategy that would work best for all children. Parents know best what the needs of their children are and what will work with them. Just remember that mixing is not a deficiency that must be eradicated at all costs.

4.4   Reading Suggestions

Readers looking for more detailed information about research results on how bilingual children keep their languages apart can find this in the following state-of-the-art article. It addresses the main issues that are currently still under investigation.

Meisel, J. M. (2001). The simultaneous acquisition of two first languages: Early differentiation and subsequent development of grammars. In J. Cenoz & F. Genesee (Eds.), *Trends in bilingual acquisition*, pp. 11–41. Amsterdam: John Benjamins.

A concise summary of some parental discourse strategies aiming at the right choice of the 'right' language can be found in Chapter 4 (especially pages 132–45) of this textbook:

De Houwer, A. (2009). *Bilingual first language acquisition*. Bristol: Multilingual Matters.

5   Language Dominance
Strong and Weak Languages

5.1   When Children Refuse to Speak One of Their Languages

What if your bilingual child speaks only one language? At some point, bilingual children may stop speaking one of their languages, for several months or perhaps for years, and it is almost always the minority language that disappears. Children who succeeded easily, it seemed, in differentiating two linguistic systems and developed competences in both languages without apparent effort, use only one of them actively. For parents, this is a deeply disconcerting experience. They may feel guilty and wonder what they did wrong in their efforts to create an environment that would enhance their children's bilingual first language acquisition. It is a particularly difficult situation for the parent whose language has apparently disappeared and who experiences this as a personal rejection or as a rejection of the culture associated with this language.

However, it can also be problematic for the children, as is suggested by studies according to which adolescents who use different languages than their parents feel emotionally more distant from them than those who interact with their parents in the same language. Admittedly, we cannot be sure whether the choice of language is indeed the cause of the observed emotional reaction or whether, vice versa, emotional distance explains why the language of a parent is not used. Still, it is undoubtedly a very demanding situation for both parents and children when bilinguals do not speak one of their languages, and it is one that occurs more frequently than one might suspect. In fact, large-scale surveys claim that it concerns about 25 per cent of children raised with two or more languages. The figure varies considerably, however, depending on acquisition environments and individual properties, as we will see later in this chapter. The good news is that this variation across bilingual environments demonstrates that it is possible to influence children's behaviour, at least to some degree, by modifying acquisition settings, especially the distribution of languages in the family.

Strong and Weak Languages

My daughter is now 21 months old. Since her birth, I have been consistent in speaking French with her, my mother tongue. My wife speaks German, and I speak German with her. I now noticed – as with a number of other children who are raised bilingually French-German in Germany – that my daughter answers me only in German and prefers using German words, although she understands what I say to her in French. In the other families, whose children are already older, I also noticed a German accent when they speak French. My concern is that my daughter will follow a similar development. My explanation for the fact that she prefers German is that it is the community language, which is obviously the one spoken most frequently. I guess, furthermore, that she is answering me in German because she has noticed that I speak and understand German and that this does not offer incentives to speak the less frequently used language. However, I am not sure whether these interpretations are correct. What I would like to achieve is that my daughter answers in French when I address her in that language. I also wish she would speak it more often, to become proficient in French rather than using it like a foreign language.

(Translated from German, JMM)

This quotation from an email to a counselling service by a father of a German-French girl exemplifies how parents experience the monolingual behaviour of their bilingual children. It also explains some of their concerns resulting from such a situation. His daughter understands French but is reluctant to speak it. The concern is that she might stop speaking it altogether or that she will acquire a kind of second language knowledge rather than a native competence. The father does not specify in his letter how much time per day he speaks French with his daughter and whether he is the only one to use that language with her. But he suspects that the main reasons for the girl's preference of German is the larger amount of exposure she gets to this language and her being aware that he is bilingual, understanding and speaking German.

Three different issues are raised here, directly or indirectly, and I will address all three of them in this chapter, though not in equal detail, because, unfortunately, they are not equally well understood.

The first issue concerns the causes of children's monolingual behaviour. The father of the German-French girl mentions two possible explanations: the amount of exposure to the two languages and a kind of minimal effort attitude by the child who knows that her communicative efforts will be just as successful if she uses only one language. I will briefly discuss these and other possible causes in this section and will return to this issue in the following sections of this chapter. However, I should mention right away that *why* questions concerning human behaviour are notoriously difficult to answer, and this is also true in our present case.

The second issue concerns the linguistic *knowledge* of bilingual children who either do not use one language actively at all or who strongly prefer the other one. As I will explain in Chapter 7, the grammatical knowledge of second language (L2) learners seems to be qualitatively different from that of L1 speakers. The question thus is whether the knowledge attained in the weaker language indeed resembles that of L2 learners. These and related questions are discussed in some detail in section 5.2.

The third issue, finally, concerns the possibility of influencing the children's linguistic behaviour. The question is whether parents and caregivers can nudge them into returning to bilingual language usage and what exactly they can do to achieve this goal. This is the topic of section 5.3. Yet since intervention possibilities aim at changing the causes of monolingual behaviour, the first and the third issue are closely related. They are therefore both discussed briefly in this section and then again in section 5.3 in more detail.

Firstly, however, I want to address another potentially problematic issue. If children stop speaking one language or if they try hard to avoid speaking it, may we still refer to them as bilinguals? The answer is definitely a positive one if they understand the language that they do not speak. Had they not acquired a grammatical competence in this language, they would not be able to understand it, no matter whether or not they use it spontaneously. We are dealing here with *receptive* rather than *active* bilingualism. This is not only a terminological distinction; it rather captures a fundamental difference that becomes relevant when one attempts to change this state of affairs. After all, filling a knowledge gap and learning to use this new knowledge is a bigger challenge than merely trying to activate existing knowledge. In fact, the latter can happen spontaneously, e.g. after a stay in a country where the language is the community language. This proves that the competence had not been lost, it had perhaps not even diminished, but the children had encountered difficulties when attempting to put it to use. Let me add that this may also be the case with children who do not show clear signs of understanding the non-activated language, although this is obviously more difficult to determine. Nevertheless, we do know that linguistic knowledge once acquired does not get lost. For example, if the active use of a language fades out during the third year of life, the previously acquired grammatical knowledge will not disappear. I have more to say about this topic and will return to it in section 5.2.

Let us now tackle the difficult *why* question. It is difficult for two reasons. The first one is a methodological problem that arises in all studies of human behaviour: it is rarely possible – if ever – to determine an undisputable cause–effect relationship. People do not have to behave in a specific way under the influence of a factor that favours this behaviour; they can always make different choices. If one finds that they do behave as expected, it is plausible to assume that this factor has caused them to do so. Nevertheless, it could be a coincidence, i.e. some other factor that was not considered could be responsible for the observed result. On the other hand, if some individuals do not behave as predicted, this need not mean that the factor under investigation is not a possible cause; they may have made a different choice. The second reason that makes it difficult to answer the *why* question is that it would be unreasonable to expect that a single factor could explain people's behaviour, linguistic or other. Rather, it is undoubtedly a network of factors that determines the language choice of bilinguals, children as well as adults. Consequently, we can identify factors that enhance or inhibit the use of both languages by bilingual children, but their weight will vary across children, i.e. what influences some children very strongly, is of less importance for others.

Keeping this in mind, it is nevertheless safe to say that parental language use is a major factor, arguably the most important one that influences children's bilingual behaviour. In cases of family bilingualism in predominantly monolingual societies, it is closely related to the presence of the minority language in the children's linguistic environment. In Chapter 3 (section 3.3) I mentioned that children are able to differentiate languages when parents follow the one person, one language (OPOL) strategy, but that it depends crucially on parents' choice of languages used at home whether they will become actively bilingual. This is the conclusion at which several large-scale studies arrived. Children were most likely to speak both the minority and the majority language if both parents used the minority language at least sometimes at home. According to De Houwer (2007), more than nine out of ten children spoke both languages if the minority language was the only one spoken at home or if one parent used only the minority language and the other one both. Approximately eight out of ten spoke both languages if both parents used both languages or if one of them adhered to the minority and the other one to the majority language, i.e. if they adopted the OPOL strategy. Finally, only one-third of the children behaved bilingually if one parent spoke both languages at home and the other one only the majority language.

The latter is clearly the worst option if parents want their children to become active bilinguals, but the OPOL strategy does not fare quite as well as one might have expected. However, one should not jump to conclusions and abandon the OPOL principle, as I will explain in section 5.3.

At this point, the question is whether these findings allow us to answer the *why* question. Can they tell us what causes children to use both or only one of the languages to which they are exposed? The findings undoubtedly suggest rather strongly that children are more likely to become active bilinguals if the minority language is not just used by *one* parent. This has been interpreted as indicating that quantity of exposure to the two languages is the decisive factor and the primary cause leading to active bilingualism.

That is, of course, an intuitively plausible assumption, and it is also what the above-quoted father of the German-French girl suspected. However, the results concerning the role of parental language use are based on information obtained by surveys among families with adolescents or children who were mostly 4–10 years old. We therefore do not know whether they are also valid for younger children. Older children and adolescents interact, of course, more frequently with people outside the family home. For them, the amount of contact with the majority language is therefore much larger than for children up to age 4, and they may consequently need more exposure to the minority language at home. Moreover, these surveys by means of questionnaires only tell us which language or languages family members use at home, but they do not reveal the distribution of languages within the family. We thus do not know who speaks what language to whom and when. Yet this is crucial information when dealing with young children who are still in the process of acquiring their languages, because linguistic development depends on child-directed speech – overhearing conversations by family members does not play a significant role in acquisition.

In sum, it is by no means evident that children up to age 4 need additional parental support in the minority language when parents follow the OPOL principle. This also depends on the nature of children's linguistic and social relationships outside the family, on attitudes towards bilingualism and on whether they have opportunities to interact with other minority language speakers, especially bilingual children.

In fact, similar considerations also apply to older children. In exclusively or predominantly monolingual societies, there not only exist more opportunities outside the family to use the community language, but adopting a monolingual strategy also allows bilinguals to behave inconspicuously as compared to their interlocutors, most importantly the members of their peer groups. This is a particularly important point for children who are not only in the process of acquiring a language but who are also being socialized in their social environment and who want to become members of their peer groups. Dominance of the community language is thus not only a quantitative factor but a sociopsychological one, as well. As such, it reflects attitudes towards bilingualism in general as well as the social prestige of the speech communities of particular languages in specific contexts.

Some time ago, an Italian colleague experienced this in a rather dramatic fashion. Married to a German woman and teaching at a university in a part of the country where many Italian immigrant workers live, his daughters asked him not to attend parent–teacher meetings in school. Although their father held a prestigious university position, they were embarrassed by his foreign accent. At that time, they apparently also considered Italian to be a low-prestige language. I am not aware of any research investigating this question, but it seems plausible to assume that the social prestige of a speech community can exert an important influence on the acquisition of a minority language by bilingual children.

Let me add one more point that can highlight the necessity of considering not merely amount of exposure to languages in a search for possible causes of receptive bilingualism. So far, I have focused on the role of parental bilingual behaviour. However, the children's knowledge of their two languages needs to be taken into account, too, as studies of unbalanced bilinguals have argued that children tend to avoid the use of their weaker language or rather that they opt for the one in which they feel more at ease. This is to say that parents' use of the two languages need not be the primary cause of children's receptive bilingualism; rather, the children may feel uncomfortable speaking a language in which they are less proficient. What exactly this means, to be less proficient in one of one's languages, will be the topic of the next section (section 5.2). At this point, what matters is to not confound the amount of opportunities to communicate in a language with the ability to do so. This distinction should also be reflected by the terminology used to refer to these phenomena, rather than subsuming both under the term *dominance*, as is frequently the case in studies of unbalanced bilinguals.

In fact, some authors profess that balanced bilingualism is impossible to achieve and that one language will always be dominant. However, they do not provide empirical evidence in support of their claim, nor do they explain why this should be the case. This idea is thus not a conclusion summarizing research findings. It is at best the expression of an educated guess, but it may also reflect terminological confusion, failing to distinguish between preponderant use of one language in a given situation and acquired competence in that language. Empirical justifications for qualifying a language as 'weak' or as 'non-dominant' commonly refer to one or more of the following observations: a) The language in question is rarely or not at all used actively; b) the other language is strongly preferred; c) the development of the allegedly weak language is less advanced than that of the other language. Unfortunately, none of these criteria captures the linguistic knowledge of speakers. In fact, all three are quantitative in nature, and they can plausibly be interpreted as effects of particular acquisition settings. In other words, what is regarded as the strength of a language may actually reflect its stronger presence in the children's environment rather than qualitative differences in their linguistic knowledge.

To avoid this kind of confusion, we need to distinguish conceptually as well as terminologically between three phenomena: a) The communicative and learning environment, especially with respect to the presence and accessibility of the two languages; b) the use that bilinguals make of their languages; c) the development of linguistic knowledge in the individual.

I think it is intuitively plausible to define the term *dominance* as referring to the predominance of one of the ambient languages. If, on the other hand, bilinguals regularly resort to one of their languages and avoid using the other one, notwithstanding contextual factors that guide code-switching and language choice, this can justly be regarded as an instance of language *preference*. These two phenomena are of course closely related because dominance is likely to lead to a larger amount of exposure to the dominant language, and this can be the reason why children prefer to use it. More exposure also leads to a higher input quantity, thus possibly enhancing the learning process, which, in turn, results in a more developed knowledge system of one of the child's languages, and the better knowledge can favour the use of this language. Nevertheless, it is preferable to distinguish between *dominance* and *preference*, precisely in order to capture this kind of interdependence, but also because dominance is not the only factor motivating preference or avoidance of a language in multilingual settings.

Note that neither dominance nor preference refers to properties of the learners' linguistic knowledge. Yet they can have a considerable impact on the development of knowledge, which can therefore be stronger or weaker. In other words, it is the competence in each language that should be characterized in terms of *strength*. For example, if children can indeed fail to develop a native competence in one language, developing an incomplete knowledge of that language, as has been claimed in bilingualism research, the one whose grammar is incomplete could justly be qualified as a *weak* language. If, on the other hand, the rate of acquisition is significantly slower in one language than in the other one, this may merely be a temporary effect. Nevertheless, such situations, too, have been described as cases of unbalanced bilingualism where one language is *weaker* and the other one *stronger*. I adopt this terminology, although it is by no means evident that this distinction also applies to the ultimately attained knowledge. For all we know, children can acquire a native competence in their temporarily weaker language as well as in the stronger one.

To Sum Up: Different Terminological Labels for Different Facts

- *Dominance* is an environmental factor. The dominant language is the one most strongly present in the child's communicative and social environment. Consequently, the amount of exposure is larger in the dominant than in the non-dominant language.
- *Strength* refers to the acquired competence. A language can be temporarily *weaker* if it is acquired at a slower rate. If the ultimately acquired knowledge of one language is incomplete, it can be regarded as a permanently weaker language.
- *Preferences*. Bilinguals tend to prefer using one of their languages, even if this is not the one favoured in a bilingual setting. Dominance and strength play a role here, but other factors can override their influence, e.g. attitudes towards a language or the culture it represents, emotional ties to speakers of a language, etc.

Let me add two remarks concerning these terminological choices. Firstly, it is of little importance which terms one favours. What is crucial, however, is to make sure not to refer to different things by identical terms or vice versa. In this spirit, I insist on keeping three phenomena apart, irrespective of whether one adopts the terms that I am using when referring to them: *dominance*, *preference*, and *strength* (weak/strong). Secondly, now that we have established these terminological distinctions, it is indeed possible to agree with the claim that one language will typically be dominant and that bilinguals tend to prefer one of their languages at any given moment. In this sense, balanced bilingualism may well be the exception. Importantly, however, unbalanced bilingualism does not necessarily entail that one language is weaker than the other one, and if it is, this may only be a temporary phenomenon. Even more importantly, the grammar of the temporarily weaker language need not exhibit qualitative differences, as compared to that of the stronger one.

I will discuss this issue in more detail in the following section (section 5.2). At this point, I want to add that dominance as well as preference can change repeatedly over the lifespan of a multilingual individual, as has frequently been observed by studies of unbalanced bilinguals. Just think of so-called *heritage language speakers*, raised as simultaneous bilinguals with the family language as the dominant one, although it is the societal minority language. In contexts where the majority society predominantly entertains negative attitudes towards bilingualism in general or against specific languages or cultures in particular, the initially dominant language is likely to eventually become the weaker one for these individuals, especially if they cannot count on support from the educational system. In fact, even for successive bilinguals the first language does not always remain dominant for their entire lives. For example, for monolingual emigrants to countries where they have no opportunity to speak their native languages any more, the later-acquired second language will end up being the dominant one.

In sum, as I have tried to show, it is difficult to give a straightforward answer to the question of why some bilingual children do not actively use one of their languages or why they try to avoid using it. Nevertheless, it is possible to identify several factors that interact in a causal network in these cases. Socio-psychological factors exert an important influence, and children who aspire to behave like the members of their peer groups can be enticed to use exclusively the dominant language. A developmental delay or a lower proficiency in one language, real or imagined, can result in the avoidance of this language and a preference for the other one. Yet the most crucial factor is the bilingual behaviour of parents and other family members, especially during early years when they are the children's principal interlocutors.

I would like to add at this point that the person–language link that develops during these early years is of particular importance and should not be underestimated. This is why parents themselves should not stop speaking one of the family languages. I strongly advise them not to change easily the language used in child-directed speech. At some point during the first years of their children's bilingual upbringing, they may find it demanding to continue with this experience, especially if the language in which they interact with the children is not their native tongue. Although children differ considerably in this respect, they may react very negatively to such a change. It is important to take into account the above-mentioned person–language link. The language is not merely a means of communication. It is also an expression of the personality of the speaker. A change of language in child-directed speech can be experienced as a drastic change, because the person speaking seems not to be the same any more, at least not in the perception of the child.

5.2 The Weaker Language: Deficient or Delayed?

Balanced bilingualism may well be less common than unbalanced bilingualism. After all, the dominance of one language is a reflection of a speaker's environment, and this is rarely balanced with respect to the presence of the two languages. If bilingualism is confined to the family home, the majority language is likely to become the dominant one, even if the minority language played this role initially. Once the amount and frequency of social interactions outside the family increase, a shift of dominance can be expected to happen, and it can change again repeatedly, over a person's lifespan. Meeting a new partner who speaks the minority language, moving to a place where it is the majority language – many kinds of changes in a person's social environment can trigger such a shift. In contexts of social bilingualism, language dominance can also change repeatedly, of course. Here too, the languages are normally present to variable degrees in different social domains. Consequently, they will be of variable importance over time, depending on an individual's changing network of social interactions. Language dominance is thus a highly variable factor, within individuals over time as well as across individuals.

The question that I want to pursue in this section is how a long-lasting period of dominance of one language affects the development of the linguistic knowledge of the language that is used infrequently or not at all. Since dominance determines a bilingual's opportunities to use both languages, it also influences the motivation to speak them, possibly resulting in a preference for the dominant language. As argued in the preceding section, this is not merely a quantitative but also a socio-psychological effect. A reduced amount of opportunities to hear and speak a language, together with a lack of positive attitudes towards it or minimal motivations to use it actively, can plausibly be expected to affect the acquisition process, as is evidenced by heritage language learners. The non-dominant language might thus develop as the weaker language, as compared to the dominant and stronger one. What remains to be seen is whether this manifests itself in a slower acquisition rate of the weak language or in qualitative deficiencies of the attained knowledge. Delay or deficiency? That is the question.

Two scenarios have been reported in research on child bilingualism to allegedly result in only partial success in grammatical development, namely *successive acquisition* of two or more languages and settings in which one of the languages of bilinguals is a *weak language* (WL). In both cases, it has been argued that the course and result of acquisition resemble adult L2 acquisition. Successive acquisition of languages in childhood will be the topic of Chapter 7, and I will show there that it indeed exhibits major differences, as compared to monolingual or bilingual first language acquisition. It is therefore plausible to assume that age of onset of acquisition is an important cause of this type of development. If, however, similar effects are found in the weaker languages of children acquiring two languages simultaneously from birth, age of onset of acquisition cannot be the only cause of allegedly incomplete acquisition by heritage language learners and others. Rather, it suggests that exposure to the language must not only happen early, it must also reach a certain quantitative threshold, an idea that I discuss in the next chapter (section 6.2). I mention it here because it illustrates how important it is to find an answer to the question of whether the weaker language exhibits competence deficiencies.

Some studies indeed report that the weaker languages of bilinguals contain properties that differ from what one typically finds in first language development. Several of these unusual constructions resemble the ones that have been claimed to result from cross-linguistic interaction; see Chapter 4 (section 4.2). This is not really surprising because one can expect the stronger language to influence the weaker one, although transfer should not be the main and certainly not the only property characterizing the WL, if it is the outcome of acquisition failure. Empirical studies mention several grammatical phenomena that appear in weaker languages, most importantly deviant word order patterns and deficiencies in inflectional morphology. Crucially, the WLs are claimed to exhibit considerable variation in this respect, ranging from complete absence of the grammatical phenomena to a lower occurrence, in comparison to the frequency of occurrence in the stronger language. WLs supposedly share these properties with L2 acquisition. If this can be confirmed, we will have to conclude that simultaneous bilinguals run a risk of not being able to become native speakers in both languages, if one language is weaker than the other one.

Let us therefore have a closer look at constructions that might indicate acquisition failure, paying special attention to word order phenomena with which we are already familiar; see Chapters 2 (section 2.3) and 3 (section 3.2). I will not deal at length with others discussed in the research literature, because they represent quantitative differences between the WL and the stronger language. This is the case, for example, with the omission of obligatory elements, e.g. subjects, objects or articles, because omission is a phenomenon that does not reliably indicate qualitative grammatical differences, as we already saw in Chapters 3 (section 3.1) and 4 (section 4.2.). Most importantly, these elements are never omitted consistently. This shows that the necessary grammatical know-ledge has been acquired, yet children encounter problems when putting it to use. Moreover, omissions of this kind also occur in the speech of monolingual and balanced bilingual children, although at a lower frequency and over a shorter period. A similar argument can be made concerning apparent problems with the acquisition of inflectional morphology, e.g. verb inflection. The non-target uses attested in the WL of bilingual children occur in the speech of monolinguals as well as of balanced bilinguals. What is unusual is only the rather long period during which these phe-nomena are used. This suggests that grammatical development in the WL is delayed, but it does not mean that it is deficient.

Word order is thus one of the domains that are most likely to suffer from deficient acquisition in weaker languages. Once again, it is the placement of finite verbs in second position that seems to be a vulnerable domain of grammar. Recall (section 2.3) that, in V2 languages, the verb must precede the subject when the clause is introduced by a constituent other than the subject. If, for example, an adverb appears in initial position, subject–verb order is reversed: *Dort geht er* (Adverb – finite V – subject), as opposed to *Er geht dort* 'there goes he – there he goes'. Bilingual children have been reported to occasionally fail to place the finite verb in second position when using a V2 language that is their WL. The verb then appears in third position, following an adverb or some other initialized element and the subject.

This is what Schlyter and Håkansson (1994) found in a study of Swedish-French bilinguals. They analysed the use of word order in the speech of four types of learners: (i) Swedish monolinguals, (ii) child L2 learners of Swedish, (iii) Swedish-French simultan-eous bilinguals with Swedish as the stronger language, and (iv) simultaneous bilinguals with Swedish as the weaker language. Focusing on constructions where the finite verb either precedes or follows the subject (SV/VS), they observed different patterns of usage in L1 as compared to child L2 learners. The L1 learners used target-like V2 constructions in which the subject is placed after the verb when an element other than the subject appears in clause-initial position. The L2 learners, on the other hand, sometimes used SV order in this context, thus exhibiting ungrammatical XSV (*V3) order. The bilingual children for whom Swedish was the weaker language behaved more or less like L2 learners whereas those with Swedish as the stronger language resembled L1 children. The authors concluded that the weaker language is in some cases acquired as a second language.

However, a closer look at the facts on which this conclusion is based reveals that the WL children actually differ from L2 learners in their use of these constructions. The main feature distinguishing the four learner types is the number of occurrences of ungrammatical *V3 patterns. Although these also occur in the speech of monolingual L1 children, this happened only rarely. The L2 children, on the other hand, used *V3 in virtually every recording and with a higher frequency. The bilinguals with Swedish as the stronger language behaved like the monolinguals; they rarely failed to place the verb in pre-subject position, and the frequency of *V3 never exceeded 2 per cent, just as with monolinguals. The picture was less clear for the children for whom Swedish was the weaker language. Their use of word order patterns was much more variable, across children as well as for each of them across time. The incriminating L2-like constructions, including *V3, occur in only some, not in all, recordings. Most importantly, this longitudinal study does not reveal a chronological pattern that could be interpreted as reflecting learning progress, e.g. if L2-like constructions were only used during early phases of acquisition. Rather, L2 properties disappeared and reappeared repeatedly over time. It is thus not possible to argue that they are due to deficient grammars, unless one wanted to argue that acquired knowledge is lost and re-acquired repeatedly – a developmental pattern never attested in any type of language acquisition.

Rather than representing evidence for alterations of the children's grammatical knowledge, these patterns of usage indicate that unbalanced bilinguals encounter performance problems.

We are indeed looking at a similar phenomenon as the one we examined in Chapter 4 (section 4.2) in the discussion of cross-linguistic interaction. In both cases, it is not a lack of grammatical knowledge that causes target-deviant patterns to appear. In fact, neither in the WL nor in the one affected by cross-linguistic interaction does one find empirical evidence of possible alterations of developmental sequences or other kinds of qualitative changes in grammatical competences. What studies such as the one mentioned above have demonstrated is that one of the languages of bilinguals can develop more slowly in terms of MLU values (mean length of utterance, see section 2.3 in Chapter 2). Moreover, they have shown that the WL may exhibit types of usage that are uncommon in the speech of monolinguals or bilinguals who acquire the language as the stronger one. Note, however, that these unusual constructions do occur occasionally in the speech of monolinguals and balanced simultaneous bilinguals. On the other hand, many though not all WL speakers use them; those who do, use them more frequently and over longer developmental periods than monolinguals or balanced bilinguals.

In sum, we can conclude with reasonable certainty that the occasional use of unusual constructions does not indicate acquisition failure in the WL. Nevertheless, this still leaves us without a satisfactory account of what causes them to emerge in bilingual child language. The observed variability of use of these constructions at different moments in the course of development and in different contexts favours an explanation in terms of processing mechanisms. The crucial insight to be retained here is that there is no reason to assume that the knowledge of the weaker language represents a deficient or incomplete version of the target grammar.

This conclusion has been reached by examining unusual constructions that occurred in the speech of unbalanced bilinguals. The language in which they used them was classified as their weaker language, precisely because of their occurrence. In order to test whether this line of argument is valid, let us adopt the reverse perspective and examine the non-preferred and arguably weaker language of bilingual children who refuse to speak one language for an extended period.

The necessary data are available. In one of the longitudinal studies that I directed at the University of Hamburg, for example, two of the German-French children did not speak French for some time. The children in this study were videotaped every second week. Their linguistic development was assessed in terms of MLU values (see section 2.3 in Chapter 2) and according to the size of their verb lexicon. This revealed that the acquisition of French by two boys, Chr and Fr, lagged well behind that of German. Let me briefly introduce the two children.

Chr is the second child of a French mother and a German father, growing up bilingually in Germany. His mother consistently addressed him in French. With his brother and his father he interacted in German. Up to age 2;4, French was his stronger language, but at approximately age 2;6 he began to respond mostly in German, and at around age 3;0 his mother gave up speaking French to him because he hardly responded in that language any more. Three months later, after visits to his grandparents in France, he started to use French again. When, at approximately age 3;10, he began to avoid speaking French once again, the frequency of the recordings was reduced to one every three months. Interestingly, French MLU values in the recordings immediately after he began to speak French again were higher than before the period during which he spoke virtually no French. In other words, his MLU values had not decreased during his period of silence in French, although they were consistently lower than in German. His development in French had thus not come to a halt or deteriorated; it had merely slowed down.

Fr is also his parents' second child. His mother addressed him in French. With his sister he spoke mostly German, and with his father he interacted only in German. As with Chr, French was initially his stronger language, yet during the age period ranging from 2;8 to 4;0, he spoke very little French any more, and his mother gradually gave up addressing him in this language. As of approximately age 4;0, after he had started to attend a monolingual

German kindergarten, he refused to speak French altogether. During the period from 3;8 to 4;0, his MLU values stayed below 3.0 in French, whereas they steadily increased in German, reaching 6.0 at the age of 3;10. However, at age 4;3, after a stay in France, Fr resumed speaking French again, and his French MLU values remained consistently above 3.0 from then on. Several later visits to France had similar effects, and the development of his French continued to improve.

As their MLU values show and as also becomes evident from these short biographical notes, French was the stronger and preferred language for both children during an initial period, ending for Chr at around age 2;4 and for Fr at approximately age 2;6. From then on, German was not only the preferred but soon also the stronger language of these boys. The question now is how this preference and the strength, assessed in terms of MLU values, is reflected in the grammatical competence of both these children's two languages – if at all.

Let us first check whether we can find unusual word order patterns, since this is the grammatical domain that has been claimed to exhibit the most salient differences between the weaker and the stronger language of unbalanced bilinguals. Surprisingly, perhaps, neither Chr nor Fr used any French word order constructions that differed significantly from what one finds in the language use of monolinguals or balanced bilinguals. There was no evidence, for example, of German V2 patterns transferred into French. Rather, both children correctly used French V3 constructions in contexts where German requires V2. Similarly, they both placed French finite verbs before and non-finite verbs after the negative element *pas*, as required by the target norm. The same is true for three further phenomena that have been argued to reveal differences between L1 and L2 acquisition (see section 7.1), namely, morphosyntactic properties of French subject clitics, omission rates of subjects, and the use of tense and aspect markers.

In sum, the speech of the two boys did not contain systematic deviations from French norms (Bonnesen, 2009). Most importantly, Chr and Fr proceeded through exactly the same acquisition phases in their grammatical development as monolingual children. The only difference, as compared to French monolinguals, was that their grammatical development was delayed in some domains. Yet nothing in the acquisition process of the weaker language could be interpreted as qualitative differences, as compared to monolingual or balanced bilingual children. In other words, their speech contained no evidence suggesting that the weaker language was acquired as a second language or that unbalanced bilinguals might attain only an incomplete or deficient competence in their weaker language. Note that this amounts to saying that the acquisition of French, the language that the two children avoided speaking during an extended period, proceeded more slowly than habitually is the case, but it continued to develop during the silent period. This is a remarkable finding because it has led to new insights into the nature of acquisition mechanisms. It demonstrates that the passive use of language in receptive bilingualism can be sufficient to keep the developmental process going. It proceeded slower than normally but it did not deteriorate, as one might have expected.

To Sum Up: The Weaker Language is Delayed, Not Deficient

- In cases of unbalanced bilingualism, one language can be weaker than the other one. For simultaneous bilinguals, this normally means that it develops at a slower rate.
- If 'unusual constructions' appear temporarily in the weaker language, i.e. constructions that do not occur when the language is stronger, this is likely to be due to limited skills of language use. They do not indicate incomplete acquisition.
- Language acquisition does not come to a halt in case of receptive bilingualism, when one language is not used actively or only rarely.

We have thus seen that preference and strength of a language are related. Admittedly, it is difficult to determine what is cause and effect in this case: whether one of a bilingual's languages becomes weaker when the other one is preferred or whether it is avoided because it is weaker and the child is less at ease using it actively. Moreover, being weak means first of all that the rate of development of the language will be delayed, sometimes quite significantly.

Both types of approaches to the study of weak languages coincide in this result: the analysis of unusual constructions that arguably indicate that a language is weaker than the other one, as well as the search for signs of acquisition deficiency in the non-preferred language of unbalanced bilinguals. They both show that the rate of development can be delayed but do not provide evidence of incomplete acquisition. Since delay is undoubtedly a quantitative effect, the only possible conclusion is that the weaker language is not acquired as a second language. Rather, even in cases of unbalanced bilingualism, children exposed to two languages from birth are able to develop two native competences. However, these children occasionally encounter problems in putting their knowledge to use. In acquisition settings where one language is strongly dominant, it appears to be difficult for some children to cope with the task of establishing and developing the sets of mechanisms required for bilingual language use. The latter include the ability to switch into the other language or, conversely, to inhibit inappropriate switches. As we have seen in Chapter 4 (section 4.2), both languages are normally activated but only one is put to use, the other one being temporarily inhibited. Failure to inhibit activation of the stronger language could thus account for the unusual constructions. However, they do not constitute evidence for the hypothesis postulating partial acquisition failure in the weaker language.

Nevertheless, this possibility cannot be ruled out altogether. In fact, one can plausibly expect acquisition failure to happen in at least some domains of grammar if acquisition conditions deteriorate significantly. For example, if the amount of exposure to one

Speaking two languages at home

language is drastically reduced, this will inevitably lead to a situation where the quantity of input to which the learner has access falls below the necessary minimum. Language dominance does not necessarily lead to such a situation. Children have been shown to be able to differentiate languages and to proceed through the same developmental phases as balanced bilinguals or monolinguals, even if they receive a reduced amount of input in the non-dominant language. However, it is not impossible that in situations where one language is dominant, the children themselves further reduce the quantity of input if they avoid interaction in that language. This, in turn, can induce parents to address the children less frequently in the weak language or abandon its use altogether. There could thus be a risk that the amount of exposure to one of the languages drops below the required minimum – a scenario that I will discuss in more detail in the next chapter (section 6.2). However, the risk can be minimized if parents and other caregivers follow the advice given in Chapter 3 (section 3.3): talk, talk, and talk to and with your children! In the following section, I will offer some more detailed and more discriminating recommendations.

5.3 Making the Weaker Language Strong Again

When bilingual children try to avoid speaking one of their languages or simply refuse to speak it at all, the parents as well as the children themselves find themselves in a trying situation that is frequently experienced as an instance of failure and perhaps of rejection. In reality, the reasons that can lead to such a situation are manifold, as we have seen. It is therefore not possible to point to a single factor that would explain children's linguistic behaviour. It is not even possible to identify a bundle of factors that could account for the behaviour of most or all bilinguals who do not actively use both languages. Individual differences play an important role in this and make it difficult to predict how children will react.

However, if it is correct that 25 per cent of the children raised bilingually strongly prefer to use only one of their languages, as mentioned at the beginning of this chapter, this means that three out of four do become active bilinguals, and they succeed in this without apparent problems. This is all the more puzzling since learning environments of active and receptive bilinguals do not necessarily differ in obvious ways; they are, in fact, very similar, if not identical, at least in many cases. The resulting uncertainty about the causes of monolingual behaviour makes it difficult to make recommendations that might help to change it. Nevertheless, it is not impossible to find ways to strengthen the weak language and to entice children to use it. Individual differences across children certainly represent additional challenges in that learners do not respond uniformly to specific measures. This calls for finely tuned operations, adjusted to the needs of individuals – and who would be in a better position to choose and implement them than parents and other close family members? We know by now that parental language use is not the only factor influencing bilingual children's linguistic behaviour but it is a crucial, probably the most crucial, one. Changes, sometimes only minor ones, in the patterns of language use by parents and caregivers thus constitute the most promising measure to make a language strong again.

In what follows, I will, of course, make some suggestions as to how one can achieve this goal. Firstly, however, a few general remarks are in order. They merely state or even repeat the obvious, but it should be useful to remember it at this point. Most importantly, the choices to be made depend on the goals that are to be reached, in this case the kind of bilingualism parents want their children to acquire. Should they become native speakers of two languages or native speakers of one language with a competence and proficiency sufficient to enable them to communicate with monolingual family members? Quite obviously, educational goals depend not only on the needs and desires of the parents but also on the future needs of the children. Where will they go to school and look for jobs? Is it foreseeable where they will spend their adult life? Which language or languages will they have to use then?

Not to forget the trivial fact that even the best plans and intentions must meet the reality check of what is feasible under the given circumstances. For example, it is undoubtedly useful for children to spend time in environments where their minority language is the majority language. However, financial or other practical considerations may not allow for such trips, as desirable as they may be. Similarly, it may be helpful if parents spoke the minority language at home, at least among themselves. Yet if one parent does not know the language, it is not possible to choose this option.

In my recommendations, I ignore such limitations. I am assuming that the goal is to develop a balanced bilingualism with native competences in both languages. This should allow parents and other readers to choose the measures that best fit the needs and possibilities of their specific situations. The goal is to help them make the right choices by providing information about research results that show what worked for other children, not only for one or two but for a larger number of individuals. My counselling experience has taught me that they are often fully aware of what the options are but that they hesitate which one to choose. The following email by the mother of a boy growing up trilingually can illustrate this point. It summarizes succinctly the linguistic setting and the possible choices concerning the distribution of languages. The questions are all very much to the point – so much so that I can answer them with yes or no.

A Weak Language?

I am Spanish from the Basque Country, and my husband is German. We live in the Basque Country, in Spain. Our child is four months old. I speak Basque with him, and my husband speaks German with him. Our question is which language we should use when talking to each other. On the one hand, we thought we should continue using German, since we met in Germany and have always been speaking German to each other, and this will be the 'weak' language for the child. Moreover, my German is better than my husband's Spanish. On the other hand, we thought it might be a good idea to speak Spanish to each other, because my husband has been living in Spain for four years now and has not yet mastered this language. Spanish and Basque are the community languages where we live, and although our child would not grow up with Spanish, I am not afraid that he will not master this language. I myself grew up with Basque, yet my Spanish is better today than my Basque. Here are our questions:

- whether it is important which language my husband and I speak to each other;
- whether it matters that we sometimes speak Spanish and sometimes German (in addressing the child, we would strictly follow the one person – one language principle);
- whether the fact that my husband does not speak Spanish very well could be bad for the child;
- whether it would be better to speak German to each other, since this language is only spoken by daddy and is thus the weak language.

(Translated from German, JMM)

The core issue of this email is the status of the weak language or rather the language that is expected to develop as the weak one because it is the minority language, only spoken by one parent, whereas Spanish and Basque are the dominant languages outside the family context. The fact that we are dealing here with a trilingual situation certainly complicates matters but the questions addressing the possibly weaker language apply to bilingual settings too. Problems particular to multilingual acquisition where three or more languages are acquired simultaneously will be discussed in the next chapter (Chapter 6).

These parents suggest using German, the minority language, as the family language to be spoken between themselves. They mention several reasons why they tend to prefer this option. German is the language they have used so far between themselves and it is thus emotionally the right choice; the mother is more proficient in German than the father is in Spanish; finally, and most importantly, the father will otherwise be the only person in the child's environment to speak German, i.e. the language needs support. I think these are all good reasons to choose German as the family language.

As for the questions formulated in this email, my short answers are the following: Yes, it does matter which language is used among the parents. And yes, it is good to strengthen the minority language. No, no harm will be done if the parents sometimes switch to Spanish when talking to each other, and no, it is not a problem that the father does not speak native Spanish. I will come back to the latter question, whether non-native input leads to acquisition problems, in the next chapter (section 6.2). The reasons why I answer the other questions in the way I do will become clear in the remainder of this section.

The first point is that parental language use does matter. This is good news, I believe. It does not mean that parents should be blamed if the result of the bilingual upbringing of their children is not what they or other family members had hoped for. I can only emphasize that their support for the children's bilingual development is of inestimable value but they cannot, or rather should not, force them into using both languages actively. The second point is, as we have seen earlier, that the grammatical competence in a language used rarely or not at all can nevertheless develop further during the period when it is not used actively. This is also good news because it means that parents need not search for compensatory measures to repair deficient knowledge; rather, the goal must be to entice and encourage children to use the languages that they know.

However, before I address the *what to do?* question, I must mention a few things that one should *not* do. First of all: do not start a linguistic war! I already warned against forcing children into using a language actively. Putting undue pressure on children is likely to lead to the opposite result of what is intended. It may sound trivial but children are most likely to practise active bilingualism if they experience bilingualism as an entirely normal and natural situation. This is why the solution cannot be to resort to monolingualism when they are reluctant to speak one of their languages. Pretending to not understand the child's preferred language is therefore not a good idea, as I already pointed out in Chapter 4 (section 4.3). How could children possibly accept bilingualism as something natural and positive, if parents pretend to be monolinguals? On the other hand, if children are allowed to use their preferred language, parents should have the same privilege. Do not give up too easily! Not even if your paediatrician recommends addressing children in the language that they understand best, unless your child has been tested for proficiency or comprehension in both languages. The assumption that unbalanced bilinguals avoid using the weaker language because of comprehension problems is in conflict with a wealth of studies that have shown that children refuse to speak a language although they do understand it well.

In sum, when young bilinguals do not actively use one of their languages for weeks or months, this need not be a reason to abandon the idea of raising them bilingually. It may be only a temporary phenomenon, as we have seen in the preceding section (section 5.2), and if the family home is a communicative setting that favours bilingualism, changes can happen. Undue pressure on the children is to be avoided – but parents may, of course, make offers that children cannot refuse! For example, if activities that are of particular interest to them happen in contexts where the weaker language is the only option, if their favourite games require the use of the disfavoured language, and so forth. The claim that parental language use does matter refers primarily to the choice of language in various communicative situations in the family context. In the preceding chapters, I recommended the well-known OPOL principle, presented and discussed in Chapter 3 (section 3.3). However, the fact that some children refuse to speak one language might raise doubts over whether this is indeed the optimal solution. In the remainder of this chapter, I will argue that the OPOL strategy is indeed valid, provided it is adapted to specific demands that arise in different social and linguistic contexts and with children's increasing age.

First of all, recall that according to large-scale surveys the OPOL strategy works for approximately 80 per cent of children. Secondly, flexibility is not a problem, as emphasized repeatedly. In other words, if parents sometimes switch between languages, as mentioned by the Spanish-Basque mother, this normal bilingual behaviour has no negative effects on children's linguistic development. Thirdly, parental code-switching when talking to children is also unproblematic. As we have seen, young bilinguals themselves switch languages, mostly triggered by sociolinguistic domains, and already during their third year of life, the interlocutor is no longer the only factor that determines their choice of language. Parents can thus behave accordingly. In fact, as pointed out in section 4.3, they do mix, and they tend to do so more frequently than they are aware of themselves. Yet although children exposed to frequent mixes mix more often themselves, this does not have negative effects on their linguistic development, as far as we can tell. Nevertheless, I recommended not to mix freely, and I want to emphasize this point in the present context of dealing with unbalanced bilinguals. When interacting with children who avoid speaking one language, subtle monolingual discourse strategies can encourage the use of this language whereas switching into the dominant language may well have the opposite effect.

In sum, the OPOL principle has been shown to be useful in that it enables most children to become active bilinguals, even when it is not applied very strictly – or perhaps especially when it is applied with some flexibility. Nevertheless, the question remains as to whether it is also an adequate procedure in situations where one language is the minority language and children interact in this language with only a single person. In other words, we must ask whether it would not be better for the Spanish-German family in the Basque Country to speak German to each other, or to establish German as the only language used at home. In fact, according to the findings of the large-scale studies mentioned at the beginning of this chapter, these options seem to be the ones that promise the best results.

Let us thus consider briefly some alternative strategies to the OPOL principle and ask what the chances are that they will enhance children's bilingual development and enable them to become active bilinguals. Remember that the studies informing us about the success rates of various approaches all investigated bilingual families in predominantly monolingual societies. Parents filled out questionnaires that asked who in the family speaks what language at home. 'Success' means that children and adolescents speak the minority language at home that is spoken by at least one parent. The, in this sense, most successful approaches are the mL@H and the mL/2L strategies. The former, the minority language (mL) at home strategy, requires that both parents speak only the minority language at home. In other words, they create a monolingual environment at home and rely on the children's exposure to the majority language outside the home, assuming that it will suffice for the acquisition of that language. mL/2L means that one parent speaks the minority language and the other one uses both languages at home. Annick De Houwer (2007) computed success rates of approximately 97 per cent (mL@H) and 94 per cent (mL/2L) for these strategies, a statistically not significant difference. The runners-up were 2P2L (79 per cent) and OPOL (75 per cent), this difference not being significant either. 2P2L means that both parents speak both languages at home. By far the least successful approach (36 per cent) is ML/2L, a variant of mL/2L in that one parent uses both languages, yet the one who uses only one language speaks the majority rather than the minority language.

These studies are extremely useful because they involve thousands of bilingual children and adolescents, whereas so far in this chapter and in the previous ones, I discussed mostly case studies investigating small numbers of children. The large-scale studies provide a solid basis for generalizations, whereas the case studies offer insights into details of the children's linguistic knowledge and proficiency. By merging the results of both types of research, we gain a reliable source of information that should allow parents to choose the bilingual strategy that best fits their goals and needs.

What emerges clearly from the surveys is that in contexts where there exist few or no opportunities to use the minority language outside the home, support for the mL in the family is useful if not necessary. This means that ML/2L is not really an option since it does not provide sufficient exposure to the minority language. The other four strategies are all possible choices, depending on what matters most to parents and on whether they speak and understand both languages in cases where this is required. Nevertheless, I do not find all four strategies equally recommendable, and I will explain this briefly in order to help you, parents and caregivers, with your choice, being fully aware, of course, that the ultimate decision is yours.

From a bilingual acquisition perspective, the least attractive of the four choices under discussion is the mL@H strategy. This may come as a surprise, because it is frequently adopted by immigrant families, and it is the one credited with the highest success rate with respect to transmission of minority languages. However, success has a high price here because it requires a monolingual environment in the family. This is not only problematic because it deprives children of the opportunity to acquire bilingual skills of language use, it also means that exposure to the majority language must happen entirely outside the home. The large-scale surveys show that children raised in mL@H environments speak both languages at home, but they do not provide information about the level of competence and proficiency attained in the majority language. If children are to acquire two native competences, they must be exposed to *both* languages in early childhood; cf. Chapter 7 for information about the importance of an early age of onset of acquisition. In other words, it is essential that they be offered opportunities to speak and hear the majority language during their first years. This is certainly not impossible to manage in an mL@H context but it does require special arrangements, since the number of occasions to interact with the world outside the family is normally quite limited for toddlers and young children. Keep in mind that watching television or videos has been shown to be of virtually no effect for language acquisition. A comforting insight, in my opinion.

As should have become apparent, my advice is not to try to increase the success rate for the transmission of the minority language at the expense of bilingualism. Rather, the minority language can and should be supported by parental language use *within* the family. The three remaining strategies are all suited to achieving this goal. Unfortunately, the questionnaire-based surveys are not really helpful when it comes to deciding between the three because they only tell us who speaks which languages at home, but we do not know who the addressees are of the parents or siblings who use the community and/or the minority language at home. Since child-directed speech is of considerable importance for children's linguistic development, it is crucial to know whether parents who speak both languages at home actually address children in both languages. If parents adopt the OPOL principle but use the minority language between themselves, is this a case of OPOL or of mL/2L? If we do not distinguish between child-directed speech and interaction between other family members, both definitions apply here, as the one who addresses the child in the majority language also speaks the minority language at home.

Interestingly, this is exactly how Ronjat and his wife proceeded; they adopted a rigid one person German, one person French principle and spoke German between themselves; cf. Ronjat (1913). It is also what I recommended the Spanish-Basque family to do, i.e. to use German as their family language. In fact, it is what I recommend whenever there is only a single interlocutor for the child in the minority language and occasions to use this language outside the family are scarce or non-existent. The distribution of languages according to the OPOL principle creates a bilingual environment at home. In fact, it was first suggested to help children cope with linguistically complex environments and to facilitate their task of separating two linguistic systems. We now know that most children may not need this kind of support for language differentiation. But why abandon something that works and that may very well be of crucial importance for some children who might otherwise not become active bilinguals?

Remember that the language differentiation problem concerns primarily the first three years of the child's life. Later on, the OPOL principle becomes less relevant because language separation is well established by then. Instead, support for the minority language becomes the more crucial issue. If it is used as the family language among the parents, as I suggested for families where both parents speak and understand it, the minority language already plays an important role in the bilingual environment within the family. As the children are growing up and interact more frequently with majority language speakers, additional support for the minority language will be useful and even necessary in those cases where children begin to refuse speaking it. We have seen in the two preceding sections of this chapter that receptive bilingualism is typically a later development. These children differentiated languages from early on and proceeded through the same acquisition sequences as monolinguals. Attributing an increasingly more important role to the minority language can entice them to use it actively rather than preferring the dominant language.

In sum, my recommendation is to follow the OPOL principle during early phases of language development and to increase, later on, the presence of the minority language in the family context, in the spirit of the mL/2L strategy. There is no reason why one should not change strategies over time, adapting parental language behaviour to the changing needs of the children. Nevertheless, as emphasized repeatedly, changing the language used in child-directed speech is only recommended if the children accept it, and abrupt changes are to be avoided in any case. Parents know best how to measure out the dosage of the measurements intended to foster active bilingualism by their children. Let me add that the 2P2L strategy, where both parents address the child in both languages, amounts to free language mixing. It is not a type of parental language use likely to enhance bilingual development in preschool children.

5.4 Reading Suggestions

Since the focus of this book is on preschool bilingualism, the following study may be of interest to readers who are looking for information about later developments. The author reports on the linguistic development of his three English-French children. At about 10 years of age, the oldest boy begins to refuse to speak French, and his sisters follow his example. Eventually, however, all three become bilingual and biliterate. This report is not so much about specific properties of the children's grammatical competence or language use. It rather highlights the role of peer group relationships, how they determine attitudes and preferences in language use, and how they change over time.

Caldas, S. J. (2006). *Raising bilingual-biliterate children in monolingual cultures*. Clevedon: Multilingual Matters.

6 Trilingual and More

The Role of Input

6.1 Native Speakers of More Than Two Languages

Multilingualism is not as exotic a phenomenon as it may appear from a European or North American perspective. In some parts of the world, especially in Africa and Asia, interacting in three or more languages in everyday dealings is not uncommon. However, where monolingualism is the norm or the idea of raising children bilingually meets with reservations, an education in three or more languages is likely to be considered an extravagance. In reality, multilingualism is today no less than a necessity for many bi- or multinational families, e.g. for parents with different first languages, neither of which is a community language in the region where they live. In fact, over the last ten years, more than half of the requests for counselling that I received referred to such situations.

Are three languages too much? And what about acquiring four languages in early childhood? If the question is whether the children's cognitive system allows for the acquisition for three or more languages, one can give an affirmative answer, without reservations. In Chapter 2 (section 2.3), I emphasized that children are equipped with a Language Making Capacity that is an endowment for bilingualism, and we have seen in the subsequent chapters that bilinguals can indeed acquire two *first* languages. In reality, this LMC is an endowment for multilingualism. No principled reasons are known that would impose an upper limit on the number of languages that the LMC allows us to acquire. In fact, some polyglot individuals apparently speak dozens of languages, though perhaps not native-like. Still, native competences in three or four languages are definitely attainable. We know this from research reports studying multilingual individuals. Just as in monolingual and bilingual first language acquisition, the only requirement is that children be exposed to the target languages from birth or from very early on and that this happens in meaningful social interaction.

Nevertheless, although children have the capacity to acquire more than two languages simultaneously and can become native speakers of these languages, we know regrettably little about how this happens and about what enhances or impedes multilingual acquisition. The reason for this unsatisfactory state of affairs is that studies dealing with the simultaneous acquisition of three or more languages are scarce compared to the wealth of research on bilingual first language acquisition. However, the ones available leave no doubt that it is possible to acquire three or four languages. If this is what you want to know, you need not worry; this question can be answered with much confidence. However, answering some of the more specific questions concerning, for example, parental language use or dominance and strength of the children's languages, requires consideration of a number of factors, not all of which are equally well studied.

Are Three Languages Too Many?

I am half-Italian and my husband is half-French; we both grew up in Germany. My Italian is very fluent, though not quite as good as my German. We have two daughters who we raise trilingually, because many of our relatives live in other countries and in other cultures. However, this can be difficult to manage. This is why I sometimes speak German rather than Italian with the children. They attend a German daycare and have been going to an Italian playgroup over the last three years. My husband wants them to go to the nursery school at the Lycée Français, this autumn. Once they go to the Lycée where they only speak French, should I continue to speak Italian with them or would their German suffer then? Or will all this be too much for them? So far, their development is entirely normal.

(Translated from German, JMM)

This is a quote from an email by a mother of two trilingual daughters. The children have been exposed to Italian, French and German from very early on. The parents adhere to the one person, one language principle, speaking Italian and French with their children, but they occasionally switch to the community language, German. They thus follow the OPOL strategy in a non-dogmatic fashion, maybe because they grew up bilingually themselves. In this way, they succeeded in creating a trilingual environment for their daughters. In family interactions, German is apparently not sufficiently represented, but it is strengthened by the attendance at the German-language daycare. In fact, as the societal language, it was probably already the children's dominant language at the time when this email was written. It is therefore a good idea to strengthen the minority languages, Italian (playgroup) and French (nursery school). Negative repercussions on German are not to be expected. This is a point I can make with much confidence because this potential problem has been studied extensively. In fact, German, as the societal language that is also present in the children's environment, is likely to become the strongest language, anyway. In other words, adding opportunities for the children to speak and hear French will not be too much for them. Rather, supporting the language that might otherwise be at risk to develop as a weak language should help to continue the normal development in all three languages.

Thus, there can be no doubt that it is possible to acquire three or four languages simultaneously. What is more difficult to affirm with certainty is whether, or rather under which circumstances, multilingual development will result in *trilingual* or *quadrilingual first language acquisition*. Only case studies performing in-depth analyses of linguistic development can answer this question. Unfortunately, a mere handful of publications provide information of a sort that can reveal whether these multilingual children have acquired a native competence in all or at least more than one of their languages. Most of the already small number of studies of trilingual children focus on language mixing and code-switching. They show that potentially problematic aspects of *multi*lingualism are the same as the ones frequently attributed to *bi*lingual first language acquisition: cross-linguistic interaction, dominance of one language, and the possibility that one of the three languages develops as a weak language. These are, of course, precisely the issues discussed in the preceding chapters. The results obtained by research on trilinguals demonstrate that multilingual acquisition is not fundamentally distinct from 2L1, in this respect, although the problems are apparently more acute when more than two languages are involved. This does not really come as a surprise since the dominance or strength of languages depends crucially on the amount of exposure to each language during early developmental phases, and adequate amounts of exposure are obviously more difficult to attain, the more languages are to be acquired.

The problem remains that only very few studies of multilingual individuals provide any kind of information that might inform us about the conditions necessary for trilingual first language acquisition to be possible. Nevertheless, the available research results demonstrate that trilinguals, too, can differentiate their languages from early on and proceed through the same developmental sequences as monolinguals and simultaneous bilinguals. It is therefore reasonable to assume that trilingual acquisition need not be qualitatively distinct from bilingual development. This is to say that children exposed to more than two languages from birth are, in principle, able to acquire multiple native competences. After all, their cognitive system can handle three and more languages, as I stated above. Multiple first language acquisition is thus indeed possible. This assumption is not only plausible; it is supported by empirical findings, even if the empirical basis is by far not as broad as in the research on various aspects of simultaneous bilingualism presented in the preceding chapters.

Importantly, however, if multilingual first language development is an attainable goal, this does not mean that it will be reached in all or even most cases. We must not forget that the Language Making Capacity has its limits, even if it is a very robust cognitive device. When certain minimum requirements are not met, it will be pushed to its limits, and one such condition is undoubtedly exposure to adequate amounts of the target languages. The question of what constitutes adequate input is a particularly difficult one that deserves careful attention. I will therefore deal with this topic in some detail in the next section of this chapter; see section 6.2. What should be obvious, independently of the details of this discussion, is that quantity of exposure is a more pressing problem, the more languages are acquired simultaneously. Yet even if the available input in each language of a multilingual individual reaches the required minimum for the development of a native competence – whatever that minimum may be – variable input quantities can affect acquisition rates and the nature of the acquired performance skills differently. In fact, the above-mentioned studies on cross-linguistic interaction, language dominance and preference, or on the development of weak languages in multilinguals suggest that quantity and possibly quality of exposure are particularly relevant factors in all these cases.

The following quote from an email by a mother of a trilingual daughter illustrates this point, especially with respect to how language preference, active use, and possibly rate of development of the three languages can depend on the amount of exposure to each of them.

Active Trilingualism?

Our daughter (age 27 months) is growing up trilingually. I talk to her in my native language, Armenian; her father speaks his native language Dutch with her. She is learning German in the nursery school. My husband and I speak German between ourselves.

Our daughter started talking early in all three languages, and she separates the languages very well. At home, she only speaks German when she plays 'kindergarten' or when she quotes what was said in the nursery school. Concerning her knowledge of German, I therefore have to rely on what the teachers tell me, and their feedback has always been positive. I noticed, however, that my daughter is more advanced in the family languages Armenian and Dutch. Moreover, she prefers to speak the family languages and has started to use Armenian outside the family. She now speaks Armenian when playing in the nursery school and answers her teachers in Armenian, although nobody understands her, of course. Two months ago, she entered a phase that I hope is a temporary one: she avoids speaking German. When the nursery teachers ask her something, she answers whispering in German. Yet she understands everything very well and can speak German, but does not do it. When I ask her at home how she is asking for water at the nursery school, for example, she reproduces the entire dialogue with the teacher in German.

(Translated from German, JMM)

The fact that this girl is reluctant to speak one of her languages is a by now familiar phenomenon, since we have seen in the preceding chapter (section 5.1) that some bilingual children try to avoid using one of their languages, except that this trilingual child speaks *two* of her languages actively. Note that the three languages apparently developed normally and that this girl separated the languages from early on. However, the active use of one language declined.

Interestingly, it is the community language that she seems to be avoiding. This is all the more remarkable because German is present in the family context, too, though not in the parents' child-directed speech. Importantly, the girl is able to quote entire dialogues in the language that she prefers not to use actively but that she can speak if adults insist. All of this demonstrates that she has acquired a trilingual competence and that her linguistic behaviour is indeed a case of avoidance rather than the result of insufficient knowledge of German. This is also indicated by the fact that she is whispering when she is obliged to speak the language that she would prefer not to use.

Based on the available information about the child, it is not possible to say why it is the community language that she does not want to use. Speaking more than one language is clearly not an issue; in fact, she expects other people to do so too, since she uses Armenian outside the family home. I can only speculate that she replicates in her linguistic behaviour the trilingual situation at home. There, she speaks Armenian and Dutch, but not German, although her receptive competence in that language is well developed. What matters ultimately is that her behaviour is not a reason for concern, as far as the development of her knowledge of the languages is concerned. It is in all likelihood a temporary phenomenon, as suspected by the mother.

The reports in the preceding chapter on bilingual children who do not speak one of their languages actively have shown that it is usually the minority language that is not used, once children interact more frequently with people other than their family members. The community language, on the other hand, typically ends up being the stronger one. This is likely to happen in the case of this trilingual girl as well. In other words, if a trilingual individual exhibits only receptive competence of one language, avoidance of the community language is the least worrisome case because it will receive increasingly more support as the child's social and communicative circles increase.

In sum, although there can be no doubt that children are able to acquire a native knowledge in more than two languages, they may exhibit marked preference or dominance patterns in their use of these languages. As we have seen in the preceding chapter, this is also the case in bilinguals, and these behavioural patterns change over the years, sometimes resulting in the preference of a language that had previously not been used actively. Receptive bilingualism is thus not in itself a reason for concern because it does not necessarily indicate acquisition failure. However, it may well be the result of reduced exposure to the target language, and insufficient exposure could also cause partial acquisition failure. This is why the next section of this chapter is dedicated entirely to this issue.

To Sum Up: Three Is Not Too Much

- The human Language Making Capacity is an endowment for multilingualism.
- It is possible to attain multiple native competences in trilingual or quadrilingual first language acquisition.
- There is no fixed upper limit on the number of languages the cognitive mechanisms can process. But the quantity of exposure in meaningful interactions that children must receive limits the number of languages an individual can acquire successfully.

The encouraging message throughout this book has been that children come equipped with a highly efficient Language Making Capacity that subserves multilingual as well as monolingual acquisition. The only requirement is early and adequate exposure to the target languages. However, precisely these two conditions may be more difficult to meet in multilingual settings. Not only are multilinguals likely to receive less input in each of their languages than monolinguals or bilinguals, they are frequently not exposed to all languages from birth. Age of onset of acquisition might thus represent another challenge that could push the LMC to its limits. A more in-depth discussion of this issue must wait until the next chapter, but in the present context, it is important to note that this could indeed be a problem concerning children growing up trilingually.

It will hardly come as a surprise if I say that the issue hinges on the distribution of the three languages in a child's communicative environment and, more generally, on the kind of trilingual settings in which the child is raised. In a particularly common one, the parents speak different native languages, both of which are minority languages. The community language is thus not present in the family. Consequently, adopting the one person, one language strategy does not create a situation of within-family trilingualism. Rather, parents frequently rely on the wider community to provide opportunities for the children to learn the majority language. Considering what we know about the role of the community language in multilingual acquisition, most importantly that it tends to become the dominant language, this does not seem to be an unreasonable strategy.

However, it implies that the societal language is not acquired from birth. Rather, first exposure and thus onset of acquisition of the third language happens at the time of entering daycare/kindergarten or even later, e.g. at school age, if children do not attend preschool. We are thus looking at cases of successive rather than of simultaneous acquisition of languages, and this delayed onset is likely to affect the outcome of acquisition; see the next chapter (section 7.3). If the goal is to enable children to acquire native competences in all three languages, first exposure to the third language should happen during the children's first three years. My advice is therefore to try to create opportunities for early exposure to the community language, either in the family or outside the family context. This may not always be possible, depending on whether or not parents can count on support from family members or from the wider community. But any attempt to avoid a delay of several years at the onset of acquisition is certainly worth the effort. How this can be achieved is discussed by this mother of a girl growing up trilingually.

Distribution of Languages in Trilingual Families

I am German, and I live with my family in Norway. My husband is Kurdish and speaks Sorani. Between us, we speak Norwegian, since he does not speak German, and I do not speak or understand Kurdish. I have a question about how to raise children multilingually. It concerns our one-year-old daughter. I read a book on multilingual education. As I understand it, parents of children growing up with three languages should speak their mother tongues. However, both should also use the third language once every day, at the same time and in the same situation. Is this correct? Since her birth, I have been speaking only German with our daughter, and my husband only Kurdish. So far, we have not spoken Norwegian with her, but she hears us speak it every day, and I take her to Norwegian playgroups. I find communication somewhat difficult when the three of us are together, not having a common language. I understand almost nothing when my husband speaks Kurdish with her, and he understands almost nothing when I speak German. What is your advice? Should we consistently stick to our native languages, anyway? For us, it is very important that our daughter speaks both German and Sorani very well. I believe that she will be able to speak Norwegian, anyhow, since this is the community language here.

(Translated from German, JMM)

As I have noted repeatedly, many parents who ask for advice have, in fact, a good idea of the approach that is likely to be the best one for their specific situation. Nevertheless, they need to know whether research on child bilingualism revealed facts that blatantly contradict the assumptions underlying their choice. Interestingly, this has rarely been the case in the many years of my parent counselling, and it is certainly not the case here.

These German-Kurdish parents follow the one person, one language strategy and use the majority language between themselves. In a trilingual setting, the OPOL principle creates situations similar to those where the mL@H strategy (minority language at home) is adopted. However, it does not result in a monolingual family situation, since two different minority languages are involved. In other words, one critical point that I raised against the mL@H strategy in Chapter 5 (section 5.3) does not apply in this case because it does not lead to a monolingual environment in the family. At the same time, it strengthens the minority language, a factor that crucially helps to enhance active bilingualism, according to the discussion in Chapter 5. Moreover, this Kurdish-German couple in Norway do not rely entirely on communicative opportunities outside the family home to ensure the child's exposure to the majority language, another critical point raised against the mL@H strategy. Rather, they speak Norwegian at home and make sure that their daughter meets and interacts with Norwegian-speaking children. She is thus exposed to the community language from early on, first exposure to the majority language is not delayed by several years, and onset of acquisition happens early, even if the amount of exposure to this language is limited.

However, although it is very likely that Norwegian will initially develop as the weaker language, this is not a problem: as the community language, it will soon become dominant in the child's social and communicative environment, certainly when she starts attending a nursery or school. It is therefore not necessary to further strengthen this language by introducing daily Norwegian sessions in the family, i.e. recurrent situations where the parents use Norwegian in addressing their daughter. Note that this is indeed a possible solution when the community language is not sufficiently present in a child's daily world. However, in the context under discussion, further support for the majority language is not required. It is already present in the family context and, importantly, in interactions with other children in the playgroup. Linguistic contact with peers is crucial and cannot be overrated as a decisive factor for language acquisition in general, and for the development of multilingualism in particular.

Let me add that the presence of the community language in the family can be reinforced if the OPOL principle is followed with some flexibility, as recommended repeatedly in the preceding chapters. This is to say that the parents can address the child in Norwegian when other speakers of this language are present and participate in the interaction, at home or outside the home. In sum, no special means in support of the third languages are required. Normal multilingual behaviour will do the trick: one person, one language – but switch languages out of courtesy for monolinguals.

6.2 Quantity and Quality of Input

Acquiring three languages simultaneously is not too much in early childhood. That much we can affirm with confidence. The human Language Making Capacity can subserve the simultaneous development of several linguistic systems and no principled reasons impose an upper limit on the number of languages that the LMC allows us to acquire. Native competences in three or four languages are attainable, if children are exposed to the target languages from early on. Yet this 'if' reveals that there are limits to what the LMC enables children to do, and it would be useful to know what these limits are and where multilingual acquisition is likely to fail. One necessary though not sufficient condition of successful acquisition is early exposure to the target languages. Properly speaking, these are two conditions, referring to the age of onset of acquisition (see Chapter 7) and to the input that a child receives. It is this latter issue that we need to address here because sufficient amounts of input from each language may be more difficult to attain when several languages are acquired.

Surprisingly, perhaps, the question of what constitutes an adequate amount of exposure is difficult to answer. In fact, I will only be able to offer an approximate answer. This is all the more regrettable since it is not only a question of utmost importance for parents raising multilingual children, it is also an issue that is crucially relevant for our understanding of the human language faculty. If, namely, the development of a native competence by mere exposure to the primary linguistic data during the optimal age period should indeed fail because the required minimal amount of exposure to the language is not attained, we must conclude that onset of acquisition during the critical phases for language development (see Chapter 7, section 7.2) is a necessary but not sufficient condition for native language acquisition. In other words, for practical as well as theoretical reasons, the task of determining the quantitative threshold for native language development is of high priority. However, quantifying the required minimal amount is extremely difficult, and this difficulty is due to a number of reasons.

First of all, it is impossible, for ethical reasons, to test this question empirically by reducing the quantity of input to some children gradually up to a point where they fail to develop native competences. Therefore, the only way to proceed is to examine language acquisition in settings where, for whatever reason, the amount of input is already reduced, as compared to what is normal in ordinary monolingual acquisition. Yet what, at first sight, may appear to be a straightforward solution, actually raises a number of new questions. Even if we ignore the problematic equation of monolingualism with the standard norm in acquisition (see Chapter 1), the more serious problem is that we do not actually know what is normal for monolinguals. In fact, studies measuring the amount of speech that monolingual children hear during one day have shown that it varies enormously, whether one looks at speech spoken in the presence of children or at child-directed speech. In some families, toddlers were exposed to eight or ten times the number of words that other children heard. These findings demonstrate that we cannot readily convert the number of hours that parents spend with their children into a reliable measure of quantity of child-directed speech. Moreover, the unexpectedly large variance in the quantity of adult speech production across families shows that it is extremely difficult to determine what is a 'normal' amount of exposure that a child must receive in order to be able to develop a native competence. We consequently lack an established benchmark when trying to assess the possible impact of reduced input quantities on language acquisition.

Thus, these studies do not reveal what the required minimum amount of exposure to a language is. Let me add that generalizations across individuals are not warranted, not even if it were possible to draw conclusions from findings about the threshold of native language development, e.g. by referring to the lowest recorded number of words or utterances directed at monolingual toddlers. In other words, if some children attained full competences in spite of being exposed merely to the minimally required amount of input, whatever it may be, it would not follow that all toddlers can succeed under similar circumstances. We are thus left without meaningful insights that might tell us how much exposure to each language multilingual children need in order to be able to develop native competences in all of them. Referring to what appears to be 'normal' in monolingual acquisition can at best give a very rough idea of what is necessary. Nevertheless, the studies measuring the amount of speech exposure do show very clearly that most monolingual children receive a much larger quantity of input than what is minimally necessary. It is therefore not necessarily a problem if the amount of speech directed to multilinguals in each of their languages is indeed smaller than that of the respective monolinguals.

This idea, that bi- or multilingualism necessarily implies that children receive reduced amounts of input in each of their languages, is rarely questioned, neither by parents nor by researchers. It is inferred from apparently solid facts, and the logic of the argument seems irrefutable: since bilinguals and monolinguals spend roughly the same number of waking hours with their parents and other family members, bilinguals' relative time of exposure to each of their languages amounts at best to 50 per cent of the total amount of child-directed speech. In fact, even this 50 per cent can only be attained if parents follow the one person, one language principle and adhere to it consistently. In most cases, input from one language will actually amount to less than 50 per cent, given that the two languages are rarely distributed equally in children's linguistic environments. Enticed by this logic, researchers jump to unwarranted conclusions, arguing that observed differences between monolinguals and bilinguals must be due to the reduced amount of input. The fallacy in this line of argument is that one cannot simply convert the number of hours parents spend with their children into a measure of quantity of child-directed speech, as we have seen above. It is correct that many bilinguals will indeed be exposed to a reduced amount of primary linguistic data in each of their languages, in comparison to monolinguals, but this is not always the case. It is therefore necessary to offer empirical evidence in every instance where one wants to explain observations on bilingual acquisition as a result of input deficits.

Matters are indeed more complicated than what is suggested by those who claim that children acquiring two or more languages simultaneously are likely not to receive an adequate amount of input. The assumption here is that bilinguals can at best get access to 50 per cent of the input quantity that monolinguals receive, trilinguals to 33 per cent, and so forth. However, as we have seen above, monolingual children are exposed to quite different amounts of adult speech, some of them to less than 10 per cent of that of others. It is therefore plausible to assume that the 33 per cent of trilinguals can easily amount to more than the required minimal quantity. Yet we do not know what the facts really are. Since we cannot refer to a benchmark defining the necessary minimum, all attempts to determine the minimally required input quantity in terms of *relative frequency* of exposure cannot offer more than an approximative idea of what the quantitative condition for native language acquisition may be.

On the other hand, attempts at defining a quantitative threshold in *absolute numbers* of child-directed words or utterances have also failed, mainly due to the fact, mentioned above, that parents vary considerably in the quantity of their language use. This means that 33 per cent of one family's child-directed speech can amount to more utterances than 66 per cent of another family's. It is therefore possible that the quantity of input that bilingual children receive in each of their languages is equal to or larger than that of monolinguals in these languages, provided the parents raising the bilinguals speak to them more frequently.

For a long time, this possibility had not been considered seriously. However, more recently, De Houwer (2014) investigated it in an empirical study of Dutch-French Belgian children. Importantly, in order to determine input quantity, this study collected data on the absolute amount of input children actually received, rather than relying on information on the relative amount of exposure to languages. It compared the use of Dutch by mothers of monolingual and bilingual children at ages 1;1 and 1;8, applying different measures of maternal input frequency, including frequency of utterances, words, morphemes and syllables per utterance. The analysis revealed no group differences across these measures. This is to say that the quantity of Dutch input that the group of bilingual Dutch-French children received was not lower than that offered to the monolingual Dutch group, although mothers *within* both groups differed considerably in how much they spoke to their children.

In other words, this result does not support the assumption that bilinguals' amount of input is necessarily reduced in comparison to that of monolinguals. However, it does confirm the observation that extensive variation exists between mothers with respect to speech rate per hour, and this applies to both groups. This means that several bilingual children heard more Dutch than some monolingual children, and also that some bilinguals had a lower number of utterances addressed to them in the dominant language than in the one in which they receive proportionally less input.

In sum, there is at least one important lesson to be learned from studies on the effects of input quantity on linguistic development: children acquiring languages profit enormously from verbally rich environments. This is true for all children, but it is particularly pertinent to those acquiring two or more languages simultaneously. Although relative frequency of exposure to each language is necessarily lower for the latter than for monolinguals, their absolute quantity of input need not be reduced, in comparison to monolinguals; it can even be richer.

Recall that I am looking for acquisition settings in which exposure to the target languages is limited to such an extent that it may not be sufficient for the development of native competences. The preceding summary of research findings has shown that neither bilingual nor trilingual acquisition is likely to create situations that qualify as such contexts. In fact, the discussion in Chapter 5 (section 5.2) led to the conclusion that the acquired knowledge is ordinarily not deficient, not even in settings where one language is weaker than the other one, although it typically develops at a slower rate. Yet there cannot be any doubt that a minimum threshold does exist and that it is not possible to develop a full competence if the amount of exposure to the target language does not reach that minimum. Trivially speaking, zero input results in acquisition failure.

The challenge is to determine the point at which decreasing amounts of input affect the quality of language acquisition and to quantify the threshold for successful acquisition of grammars, although it may vary across individuals. Interestingly, this is one point on which expectations of parents diverge considerably. Whereas some express concerns because the children are not exposed to their languages to exactly the same degree, others believe that even limited amounts of input suffice for toddlers to acquire languages.

Amount of Exposure to the Third Language

The following is an excerpt from a request for counselling by the father of a Finnish-German boy. The mother speaks Finnish with the child, the father German, but he is of Hungarian extraction. German is also the language used between the parents. They would like to introduce Hungarian as a third language:

We would like to know whether the father's grandparents should speak Hungarian with the child in order to transmit this language too. They are both fully competent in Hungarian and speak German very well. Once or twice a week, they spend approximately two hours with the child. However, we want to emphasize that we are primarily interested in the transmission of Finnish and German. It is also very important for us not to ask too much of the child by adding a third language. We would therefore only ask the grandparents to speak only Hungarian with the child if you can recommend this without any reservations.

(Translated from German, JMM)

This is an example of the more optimistic kind. These parents wonder whether they might be asking too much of their son if they introduce a third language, but these reservations concern the number of languages, not the quantity of input. For a counsellor, it is frustrating not to be able to give straightforward and clear advice. Parents ask for information about the required minimum of exposure in terms of daily or weekly hours of contact. Yet I have to remain vague on the quantity of necessary input, and I even have to mention that it will vacillate across individuals, some requiring more exposure than others.

Nevertheless, two to four hours per week, as suggested in this email, is definitely not enough. On the positive side, I know of no reason why the grandparents should not speak Hungarian with their grandson. It will not have negative effects on the development of the two other languages, and he will undoubtedly learn Hungarian words and perhaps develop a receptive grammatical competence. Thus, if the boy enjoys being immersed in another language when spending time with his grandparents, adding a third language is certainly an option. However, if the child participates only reluctantly or rejects this situation, my advice is not to persist in it. It is more likely that he will develop negative attitudes towards multilingualism rather than a trilingual competence.

As I said before, the challenge is to determine the point at which decreasing amounts of input affect the quality of language acquisition and to quantify the threshold for successful acquisition. As we have seen, quantifying the required amount of input in relation to what might be considered as normal in monolingual acquisition is not a viable solution. Defining the threshold in absolute numbers of words or utterances is not possible either, since we lack the necessary information. This is why I had to confess that I can only offer an approximate indication of the necessary quantity of input from the target language. It means that I have to rely on findings from studies relating success of acquisition to the relative amount of exposure to each of the languages of multilingual individuals. Thus, calculated percentages refer to the frequency of contact with one language in relation to the total amount of exposure to speech per day/week/month, across all languages present in the child's environment. This can only provide an approximate idea of the developmental threshold because the absolute amount of input depends crucially on the speech rate of the children's interlocutors, as is always the case when input quantity is assessed in terms of time of exposure.

Not surprisingly, the results of the studies reviewed resemble those summarized in the preceding chapter (section 5.2) because we are looking again at the weaker languages of multilinguals, this time focusing on the question of whether they can inform us about the required minimum of input. The best-documented effect of limited exposure to the target language concerns *lexical* development. Although bilinguals' total vocabulary in both languages combined is virtually the same as that of monolinguals, their vocabulary in each language is normally smaller than that of the respective monolinguals at the same age, and it frequently develops more slowly. However, these findings are not really revealing with respect to our quest for the acquisition threshold. After all, we know that bi- and multilinguals do not normally use all languages in all sociolinguistic domains. Lexical gaps are therefore to be expected and are due to this functional distribution of languages. Whether amount of exposure also plays a role here is an open question. As for the reported delay of lexical development, this is a relevant finding, even if it does not tell us what the necessary input minimum is. It shows that varying frequencies of exposure to the input data have effects on acquisition. Delays in lexical learning have been reported to occur when relative frequency of exposure to a language amounts to no more than approximately one-third (30–40 per cent) of the total exposure to the target languages. Thus, as far as lexical development is concerned, the likely input quantity for each language in trilingual settings is sufficient. Note, however, that effects of reduced amounts of exposure are quantitative in nature. Slower learning rates do not result in lasting negative effects because new words can be acquired throughout the lifespan, although some aspects of lexical learning may deteriorate due to age-dependent changes of the acquisition mechanisms, as we will see in the next chapter (section 7.2).

The more pertinent question with respect to the issue of whether reduced input can cause qualitative deficiencies in the acquired linguistic knowledge is how limited exposure to a language affects *grammatical* development. Let us first look at the 30 per cent range again. It is of particular interest for those who raise trilingual children, and it has been investigated in longitudinal as well as cross-sectional studies dealing with different grammatical phenomena in various languages. The overall result is that grammatical development, too, is dependent on the amount of exposure to the languages. However, the observed effects are more subtle than in the lexical domain, and, most importantly, they too merely concern developmental rates. In other words, grammatical development may be slower when children are dealing with reduced amounts of input. However, this delay, if it happens, falls within the normal range of variation for monolingual children. Crucially, these bilinguals proceed through the same sequences of developmental milestones as monolinguals. In sum, we can retain that studies examining language acquisition in settings where children have only limited access to the primary linguistic data of one of their languages confirm the expected relation between the available amount of input and grammatical development with respect to the rate of development. However, none of the cases studied, with relative frequency of exposure to a language of approximately 30 per cent, provided evidence for qualitative deficits in the ultimately attained grammatical knowledge.

These findings necessarily lead to the conclusion that the acquisition threshold, defining the minimum amount of input quantity for the successful acquisition of native grammars, must be lower than 30 per cent. In order to determine the minimum more precisely, it is necessary to examine cases where access to the target language is radically limited, i.e. where children are exposed to an even smaller amount of primary linguistic data.

As mentioned above, it is, of course, not admissible to test children's language acquisition capacity in a minimal input

context, designed to offer a decreasing amount of speech directed
to them or uttered in their presence. The goal would be to reduce
it to a point where acquisition fails, at least partially, in that the
attained grammatical knowledge differs in some respects from
that of monolingual or bilingual first language learners. However,
acquisition settings where input quantities are extremely limited
do exist naturally. In multilingual contexts, for example, they exist
where more than three languages are acquired simultaneously
and where interaction in one non-dominant language accounts
for considerably less than 30 per cent of daily or weekly verbal
communication. Or in situations such as the one mentioned in
the email above where grandparents, who spend a few hours
every week with their grandchildren, are the only interlocutors in
a language. A similar situation can also arise in the acquisition
of oral languages by hearing children of deaf parents. Acquisition
under such difficult conditions of drastically reduced exposure
to the target language is thus not as rare a phenomenon as one
might suspect. It typically happens in multilingual contexts where
access to *one* of the languages is severely limited. However, studies
investigating how children cope with these unfavourable learning
conditions are scarce, and the few that exist do not always specify the amount of the available input, or they do not analyse the
attained linguistic knowledge in much detail.

Consequently, the emerging picture is still blurred. Nevertheless,
some case studies show that it is possible to acquire a competence
that is not qualitatively different from that of a monolingual or a
balanced bilingual learner, if exposure to a non-dominant language
comprises 20–30 per cent of weekly interactions. Development
under these conditions typically happens at a slower rate, but it
proceeds through the same developmental phases and in the same
order as in monolinguals. This is the most precise estimate of the
acquisition threshold that is currently possible. In fact, it may not
be possible, for principled reasons, to be more specific. Even if we
could draw on more research, the fact remains that relative frequency of exposure does not capture the actual amount of input
in absolute terms. Moreover, not all children behave identically;

some are more successful than others, and we do not know what the causes are for these individual differences. Nevertheless, in the final analysis the estimated threshold is good news for parents raising children with more than two languages. It implies that trilingualism should not be a problem for the children's acquisition mechanisms, confirming other findings presented in this chapter. Moreover, it suggests that the simultaneous acquisition of four languages is also possible, assuming that the amount of exposure to each of them is more or less the same, i.e. approximately 25 per cent of verbal interactions with the child.

But what if the relative amount of exposure to a language drops below 20 per cent? In trying to answer this question, I must venture an educated guess, based on the very small body of empirical research on this issue. On the positive side, one finds that language acquisition does happen, even if weekly exposure is limited to 8–10 hours. However, linguistic development not only proceeds at a markedly slower rate, the attainable grammatical knowledge will most likely consist of an incomplete system or subsystem of the target language. Moreover and not surprisingly, the lexical repertoire that can be learned under these circumstances will be rather limited compared to that of the stronger language of simultaneous bilinguals. In fact, the children studied mostly developed a receptive multilingualism, some with good comprehension skills, but rarely able or willing to use the language actively.

To Sum Up: Defining the Necessary Input Minimum

- We do not know what the 'normal' amount of exposure to a language is. The number of child-directed utterances or, more specifically, of verbal interactions varies enormously across families, monolinguals as well as bilinguals.
- Consequently, we have an only approximate idea of what the minimum amount of input is for a child to be able to develop a native competence. It should definitely not

drop below 20 per cent of the total amount of verbal interactions a child receives.

- More reduced amounts of exposure to a language may suffice to trigger linguistic development, but this will happen at a significantly slower rate and it is unlikely to result in a native competence.

I hasten to add that this summary sounds perhaps more pessimistic than it is intended to be. Let me emphasize some positive aspects, most importantly the fact that even such dramatically reduced amounts of input suffice to kick off a developmental process. This means that the foundations of a linguistic knowledge system have been laid and can be developed into a more complete system later on. Not to forget that it is no mean achievement to be able to understand at least substantial parts of a language and to interact with family members or friends. If, for example, it allows children to communicate with grandparents who speak only that language, this alone is reason enough to encourage children to acquire a basic knowledge of the family language. After all, no harm is done if they succeed only partially because their other languages will not be affected negatively. Also, the amount of input that can be offered in eight or ten weekly hours can be quite considerable. Remember the recommendation in Chapter 3: talk, talk, talk!

So far, this discussion of the role of input has been restricted to the question of what constitutes an adequate amount of input. However, the success of acquisition also depends on the kind of input a multilingual child receives. The point I want to make here is that it is not only the quantity of input that counts, but also the *quality*. It can differ in various ways from that of monolinguals, and the question is what the consequences are of such differences for the acquired linguistic knowledge and skills. In the present context, I will focus on issues related to family bilingualism.

However, I should at least mention one aspect of societal bi- or multilingualism that can affect the quality of the input. In settings where the target is the societal minority language and it has been in contact with the majority language for a long time, it may have undergone contact-induced changes. Moreover, if its speakers immigrated from various countries where different varieties of this language are spoken, these have probably also contributed to the emergence of a new variety. Children growing up in this environment will obviously acquire the newly emerged variety, the one to which they are exposed, rather than some traditional standard variety. Their input is thus of a different quality. Importantly, 'quality' does not imply that one variety is better or worse than the other – they are different. Although all this should be fairly obvious, problems arise if the differences between the input variety and the respective standard are not taken into account. In this case, multilingual acquisition may be held responsible for the emergence of certain non-standard forms that are really properties of the speech to which the children were exposed. As trivial as this may appear, the point I am trying to make is that assessments of the success of multilingual acquisition must refer to the actual input rather than to some assumed standard.

A conspicuous property of multilingual settings is that the number of speakers interacting with the language-learning child in a non-dominant language tends to be considerably smaller than in monolingual contexts. In fact, in many cases of family bilingualism, children have only one interlocutor and thus only one role model in the minority language. Now, if you recall from Chapter 1 (section 1.2) the discussion of the notion of multilectal speakers of a language, it should be obvious that in order to become multilectal, one needs to be exposed to various situational, social and perhaps also regional varieties of the target languages. Yet with only a small number of interlocutors, such opportunities are rare. Consequently, the variation space of learners is likely to be more reduced, i.e. they are likely to exhibit less flexibility in adapting to changing communicative contexts in their non-dominant as compared to their dominant languages. However, a more limited range of lects is a small price to pay for the opportunity to acquire another language. Moreover, such limitations can be avoided or overcome if the children are offered opportunities to interact in socially more complex environments in the non-dominant languages. Crucially, these should allow them to interact with a larger variety of interlocutors, including other children.

A potentially more serious issue relating to input quality arises when parents or other caregivers are themselves not native speakers of the language that they speak with the children. This is an increasingly frequently chosen option, especially by parents with a secondary education. The reasons why they find it attractive vary considerably from case to case, but most of the time they hope for better educational and job opportunities for their children. The following short excerpts from three emails by parents illustrate different motivations as well as some shared concerns about ensuing educational opportunities.

Non-Native Input – Intentional Bilingualism

The first email is from a German couple living with their 13-month-old twins in Brussels. They speak German between themselves but are fluent in French. Their nanny is a native speaker of Spanish.

Up to now, we asked the nanny to speak French with the children, so that a third language would not confuse them. However, her knowledge of French is limited, and she speaks it with a heavy Spanish accent. It is very important for us that the children end up speaking perfect German and French. So far, we have only spoken German to them. However, since they will not start kindergarten until 18 months from now, they will only then have intensive contact with French native speakers. Would it thus not make more sense to allow the nanny to speak Spanish with the children? She spends about five hours every day with them.

(Translated from German, JMM)

A university professor from the Spanish-Basque Country with two daughters, one recently born, the other one two-and-a-half years old, wonders whether he should not speak English with them, so that they will learn the language early and easily. He does not trust foreign language instruction in schools because he finds most of his students' English poor.

The idea that I could speak English with my daughters occurred to me some time ago when I realized that a colleague did just that. Recently, I met a mother (an English teacher) who also does this. Nevertheless, I have many doubts. Firstly, concerning our limited knowledge. My wife and I both have the Cambridge Advanced English Certificate. Secondly, about how to proceed. Thirdly, whether it will be good for the girls or whether it might harm them. My niece, who studied English, does not recommend it, whereas the above-mentioned mother does. My wife and I speak Basque between us, our mother tongue. Our older daughter attends a Basque-speaking daycare. I am not worried about her Spanish because I am convinced she will learn it in the streets. What do you recommend?

(Translated from Spanish, JMM)

The third email is from a Turkish-Iranian father.

I am writing this to get an idea about how to help our three-month-old daughter to learn English in addition to our native language. My wife and I are from Iran, and our native language is Turkish. Our second and official language of the country is Farsi. Since we live in a Turkish region of Iran, the spoken language is Turkish whereas educational courses and all media are in Farsi. We speak both languages interchangeably. Both my wife and I studied ELT. We are not native English speakers, but we can manage our daily conversations in English. In the region where we live, people never communicate in English, but this is gradually changing among young people. So, we do not have a very rich source of daily interactions in English, except for the language use between ourselves and the media via satellite (English cartoons, sitcoms, talk shows…).

It is a big question whether we should try to speak English most of the time at home, to each other and to our daughter. Will she be able to learn English in addition to one of our native languages even if English is not our native language? Or can it cause mental or cognitive problems for our daughter? Which language should we emphasize more at home?

Two concerns are mentioned by most parents. The first is that family, friends, educators, paediatricians and others reject this kind of multilingual education as artificial and not in the best interest of the children. The second worry is that parents who address children in a non-native language might not speak this language perfectly well, that their vocabulary is limited and that they might make errors when speaking to the children. Let me say right away that neither of these arguments is a reason to abandon the idea of a multilingual education, provided the non-native speakers are fluent in this language and can commit themselves to this kind of language choice for an extended period of time. Although I find it understandable that parents and family members might regard it as a potential problem, I must admit that I have no understanding for paediatricians, educators and even linguists who advise against this option. They reject it without giving good reasons – because empirical studies do not provide good reasons against this kind of acquisition setting.

As for the first of the two objections, treating this kind of multilingual environment as 'artificial' is not justified, given that no plausible counterarguments have been offered against this solution. Certainly not from the perspective of children who have been shown to experience it as normal if they are raised in this context from birth. Nor from an adult perspective because it is not unusual to speak a second language in the presence of interlocutors who share one's first language. It is, indeed, common practice, in family as well as business contexts, to switch to a second language when at least one person does not understand the speaker's first language. In fact, several of the bilingual strategies discussed in Chapter 5 (section 5.3) require that one parent uses a language other than his or her native tongue when addressing the child. Moreover, all these strategies imply that parents can and should use a non-native language in the presence of bilingual children when this is the only common language in a given situation. What harm this perfectly normal multilingual behaviour could possibly cause for children is entirely mysterious. My suspicion is that the aversion to the use of a non-native language when addressing children is a relic from the well-known negative attitudes against child bilingualism in the past. Only monolingualism used to be considered as appropriate and normal for young children. In its contemporary version, this prejudice is expressed by the claim that it would be inadequate or artificial for a parent to use a non-native language in child-directed speech.

What some believe to be an artificial situation is really a viable option for parents who want to raise their children in more than one language. It is indeed an instance of *intentional bilingualism*, as it has been referred to quite adequately, I believe, because it is the result of a legitimate choice by parents. However, one point that parents considering this option should take to heart is that they will have to interact with their children for many years in the second language. They must remember that a language is not merely a means of communication but also the expression of the speaker's personality. It is probably for this reason that many children react strongly when parents switch languages and start addressing them in a different one. In fact, a change of language can also have negative consequences for the children's linguistic development. After all, an acquisition process comes to an abrupt end before it is complete, and a different one is not initiated at birth, but with some delay. These potentially detrimental effects are, of course, not specific to situations in which parents change back from a non-native to their native language. They exist in all cases where parents switch to a different language in their child-directed speech. The reason why I insist on this issue at this specific point is that some parents find it difficult to communicate mostly or exclusively in a second language with their children. It is undoubtedly a demanding task, especially when it comes to expressing strong feelings like love or anger. However, for those parents who feel that they are up to this challenge, raising their children in a non-native language is definitely an option.

The first author to show that children can be raised successfully as bilinguals when a parent talks to them in a language that is not his/her native tongue was the Australian linguist and language teacher George Saunders (1982, 1988). Both he and his wife are native speakers of English, but he decided to speak German with his three children. His insightful reports on their bilingual acquisition demonstrated that it is possible for children to acquire a parent's second language as their first language.

As for the second objection against this acquisition setting – insisting on the fact that the non-native model is probably not perfect – it is indeed an issue that must be addressed, although Saunders and others after him have shown that it need not be an obstacle to successful language development. Quite obviously, children acquire the language variety to which they are exposed. If it contains systematic grammatical errors, these are likely to appear in the children's speech as well. However, the parent who is a second language learner need not be the only one to provide input in this language. Rather, various media (internet, Skype, TV, audio recordings, videos, etc.) can complement and enrich the input with speech samples by native speakers. If at all possible, the children should also meet native speakers in the neighbourhood and spend time in countries where the parent's second language is the societal language. What is particularly important is that they meet other children who are native speakers of the target language, monolinguals or bilinguals. It is well known that peers tend to be more influential as role models than parents. This is why children easily pick up dialects or non-standard varieties that they do not hear at home. At any rate, if the potential bilinguals are exposed to the speech of native speakers, in addition to their parent's non-native speech, they are very likely to succeed in acquiring a native variety of the target language.

Does this mean that children exposed to a non-native variety in the family will acquire a 'perfect' knowledge of that language, as many parents hope, not only the father of the twins growing up in Brussels? Perhaps! It depends on the quantity and quality of input outside the family and on the children themselves. However, considering this kind of acquisition context, the question of whether it is possible to develop a native competence may not be the most urgent one. After all, even if the attained knowledge or the acquired skills should not be perfect, the result of this acquisition process will almost certainly be vastly superior to what is normally achieved in foreign language classrooms. Let me add that in a context like the one in Brussels, it might actually be preferable if the nanny spoke Spanish with the children. Not because of her less than perfect French – since it is the dominant language outside the family, the twins will certainly acquire a native French competence – but why not allow them to learn a third language?

6.3   How Many Is Too Many?

The first question raised at the beginning of this chapter was whether three languages were too many to be acquired simultaneously from birth. This is clearly not the case. Reports by parents of multilingual children as well as results obtained by acquisition research leave no doubt that trilingual acquisition is not too much for young children. In fact, they are even able to acquire native competences in three languages. What makes this possible is that they come to this task equipped with a highly efficient Language Making Capacity that subserves multilingual, not only monolingual, acquisition. No principled reasons impose an upper limit on the number of languages that the LMC enables children to acquire. It operates whenever and as often as children are exposed to language in meaningful social interaction.

However, as we have seen in this chapter, one necessary requirement for acquisition to be successful is adequate exposure to primary linguistic data. Unfortunately, we only have a vague idea of what 'adequate' means in this context. Yet although we are not able to determine the minimally required amount of exposure with the desirable precision, the discussion of qualitative and quantitative properties of the necessary input leaves little doubt that quantity of exposure is a decisive issue when we try to assess the chances of children becoming multilinguals. Trivially, the more languages are acquired simultaneously, the more difficult it is to provide the child with a sufficient number of opportunities to meet and interact with interlocutors in each language. Does this mean that trilingualism represents the upper limit? Not necessarily. As we have seen in the preceding section, some children, whose exposure to one language amounted to 20–30 per cent of weekly interactions across all languages, succeeded in acquiring a full competence, although at a slower rate compared to the development of this knowledge in dominant languages.

In other words, it is possible to acquire four first languages simultaneously. Even more than four languages can be acquired simultaneously, although I doubt whether native competences will be attained in all of them. What, then, is the limit? To be honest, I cannot answer the question in the title of this section: How many is too many? The few existing reports on early multilinguals simply remain too vague in their assessment of the acquired lexical and grammatical knowledge. Moreover, as I have emphasized repeatedly, we find considerable variation across children in this respect. Finally, language acquisition is not an Olympic discipline where the one who speaks most languages at preschool age wins. I do not believe that more is better, unless speaking and understanding several languages serves communicative and social purposes, as is the case in the situation on which the following email reports.

More Than Three Languages

I am from Poland, and I live in Luxemburg. Multilingualism is an interesting but also a challenging topic for my family, because we raise our children here, and this country is a real tower of Babel. There are no bilingual children here – they are all multilingual. 50 per cent of the population are immigrants from all over the world. When I am at the playground with my three-and-a-half-year-old daughter, I have a hard time recognizing all the languages spoken there.

I follow my daughter's linguistic development carefully, and I am wondering whether this multilingualism is not too much for her. She speaks Polish at home and refuses to speak another language with us, answering in Polish when I address her in French. The nursery-school teachers speak French and German. Yet with some children she speaks English, and at the preschool (mandatory in Luxemburg as of the fourth year of life), she will have to learn a fifth language, Luxemburgish! In primary school, the three official languages are used, French, German and Luxemburgish. English is taught as a foreign language, and, not to forget, our child speaks Polish at home. I find all this a bit crazy, but I try not to panic and to trust the Ministry of Education. It seems that our daughter, who was born here, finds this linguistic diversity totally normal and unproblematic.

(Translated from German, JMM)

This girl seems to cope very well with the multilingual situation in which she is growing up, probably because each language serves a specific purpose in her life. Children who have opportunities to interact regularly with different interlocutors speaking their languages are most likely to acquire a native or native-like knowledge and adequate performance skills in each of them. I do not know how proficient the girl in Luxemburg is in her languages but the family language, Polish, is clearly developing as the strongest one, and she communicates successfully in her other languages as well.

However, in settings where children acquire several languages simultaneously, we should be prepared to find that they do not attain the same level of knowledge and proficiency in all of them. This is what we find in the following example.

Variable Degrees of Proficiency in Multilingual Individuals

Husband and wife grew up in Germany. He is a native speaker of German with a good knowledge of English; she is trilingual, having acquired Croatian from her mother, English from her father, and German in kindergarten and in school. She now speaks English with her three-and-a-half-year-old daughter, her husband German, and they use German between themselves. One grandmother speaks Farsi with the child (at least twice per week for several hours), the other one Croatian (once per week for a few hours).

Our daughter seems to understand all four languages well or very well. As for her active use, she speaks German like monolinguals of her age, English rarely on her own initiative and only in simple sentences, Croatian and Farsi only with single words inserted into German sentences. *She consistently replies in German* (all interlocutors understand and speak German very well). Measures to support English: Once per week two hours in a playgroup with English native speakers; occasional visits with other German-English families with children. 70% of the children's books that we own are in English, and 90% of the songs and rhymes for children are in English. So far, all videos for children have been in English, and we only listen to English radio stations. What else can we do to enhance the active use of the other languages, especially English? My wife is planning to go for a two-week trip to England with our daughter. Would it be useful to introduce an English day, e.g. Mommy and Daddy speak only English on Saturdays?

(Translated from German, JMM)

German is quite obviously this girl's dominant and strongest language and English the weak one. In Farsi and Croatian, she seems to have acquired some basic knowledge that allows her to act as a receptive bilingual in these languages.

The picture that emerges here is not uncommon in multilingual settings, i.e. children develop a native competence and active performance in one of their languages, a possibly full competence but receptive bilingualism in another, and basic knowledge without active usage in a further one. Although it is not impossible to achieve an active quadrilingualism, this goal will frequently be difficult to attain, depending on constraints imposed by specific situations and, importantly, on individual attitudes of children (see section 5.3).

A secret formula performing linguistic miracles does not exist. Rather, parents may have to make choices and establish a linguistic hierarchy, reflecting the needs of the child and the family. In the present example, a receptive competence seems to be the optimal solution for both Croatian and Farsi, and this is indeed what the parents are aiming for. Yet although it is not surprising that German, the family as well as the community language, is the girl's strong language, the current status of English is not what the parents were hoping for, and it should indeed possible to strengthen this language. The measures introduced by the parents are all appropriate and correspond to what I recommended in Chapter 5 (section 5.3) as strategies that can strengthen weak languages, i.e. trips to England, encounters with other bilingual children, reading books to the child, English-language media, etc. In fact, research studies suggest that reading books aloud is particularly useful, whereas two-year-old bilingual children apparently do not learn languages from sources like video or audio or from watching TV. Nevertheless, such media offerings are likely to make the minority language more attractive and can thus be helpful. What still can and should be done is to enhance the presence of the minority language in the family, as recommended in section 5.3. English should be the family language that is used between the parents, and they should indeed introduce an English day or two, as proposed by the father in his email – provided the child accepts this change of language, as emphasized in section 5.3. Multilingualism is a goal well worth all these efforts by parents, other family members and the children themselves, but not at the price of a linguistic war within the family. Children have their own opinions on the matter – opinions that adults do not always understand and that can change over time in a lifespan.

6.4   Reading Suggestions

I must confess that I do not have reading suggestions that might be of interest for non-specialists and that are easily available, concerning the three main issues dealt with in this chapter: the simultaneous acquisition of three or more languages, the minimally required input, and the role of non-native input in bilingual first language acquisition. However, readers who would like to get more information about the effects of contextual factors in early trilingual acquisition may want to read Chapter 6 of the following sociolinguistic case study of two trilingual children during their third year of life:

Chevalier, S. (2015). *Trilingual language acquisition*. Amsterdam: John Benjamins.

I think that readers of this book would be interested in learning more about the efforts by George Saunders and his wife to raise their three children bilingually, English-German, although neither of them speaks German as a first language. Unfortunately, both books by George Saunders are out of print and are difficult to obtain. Nevertheless, I want to mention the following title, hoping that you might get hold of it.

Saunders, G. (1988). *Bilingual children: From birth to teens*. Clevedon: Multilingual Matters.

7 The Age Question

7.1 Multiple First Languages or Second Language Acquisition in Childhood?

Bilinguals come in all shapes and sizes. They are individuals who use more than one language in daily life. This definition, quoted in Chapter 1 (section 1.1), covers a wide range of possibilities concerning their linguistic competences, performance skills, attitudes towards bilingualism, frequency of use of the languages, and so forth. Some of these differences are due to the social and linguistic contexts that characterize their daily lives, others are consequences of particularities of the acquisition process. In other words, bilinguals do not necessarily have an equally good command of their two languages. In many cases, the individuals themselves – or their parents, for that matter – do not have control over the factors that determine the nature of their bilingualism. Rather, it is a reflection of the social and communicative settings in which they acquire and use the ambient languages.

In those cases, however, where it is possible to control at least the major influencing factors, it is important to know how these determine the attainable linguistic competence, the attitudes towards bilingualism, etc. Only then is it possible to decide on one's goals, weighing up needs and possibilities against required actions. In settings of family bilingualism, this is a task that parents face. It can be a formidable one, especially if the goal is to enable the children to become native speakers of two or more languages. Yet even if the goal is more modest, aiming, for example, at basic abilities to communicate with speakers of other languages, the task can still be huge. Just recall the expectations and concerns listed in the boxes in Chapter 1 (section 1.1) that parents may have to consider when making their decisions. Most of the alleged disadvantages do not actually represent serious obstacles, as should be apparent by now. We have seen that bilinguals differentiate their languages from early on and are able to keep them apart, that one of their languages may be stronger and/or develop faster, but that they can nevertheless acquire a full competence in the weaker one. In sum, the task of acquiring two or more languages does not exceed very young children's mental capacities. Rather, adequate input and early exposure suffice to enable them to acquire multiple native competences.

Some readers may have been wondering why I insisted so much on these two requirements, adequate input and early exposure. The reason is that they are necessary – though not sufficient – conditions for an L1-like linguistic development. As I have tried to show in the preceding chapter, successful acquisition indeed requires a minimum amount of exposure to the target language, even if it is difficult to quantify the threshold with the desirable precision. What we still need to examine in more detail is the age question. What does 'early' mean in terms of age? And what are the possible consequences if onset of acquisition does not happen early? These are the two main issues that I propose to address in this chapter in order to enable parents and educators to make an informed decision on the age at which they expose children to another language.

The age question arises as soon as we look at bilinguals who acquired their languages not simultaneously, as was the case with almost all those whose linguistic development has been discussed so far, but *successively*. If we find that successive bilinguals differ systematically from simultaneous bilinguals in their linguistic knowledge or in the way this knowledge is put to use, we may plausibly assume that this is due to the fact that onset of acquisition of the target languages necessarily happens at different ages in successive acquisition. This is, of course, not the only possible explanation because age of onset of acquisition (AOA) is not the only point at which simultaneous and successive acquisition differ. To mention just one other potentially decisive difference between these two types of bilingualism, we must take into account the fact that, in successive acquisition, a linguistic knowledge system is already in place at the time of first exposure to another language. It is therefore possible that the previously acquired knowledge interferes with the developing one in subsequent acquisition processes. Still, age is undoubtedly the most significant factor making an impact on the course of development and on the knowledge that can ultimately be attained in successive language acquisition, as will become evident in what follows.

Trivially, AOA is a relevant issue only if it is the cause of *substantial* differences between acquisition types. That this is indeed the case becomes most obvious when we compare monolingual (L1) or bilingual first language (2L1) development with adult second language (L2) acquisition. No matter whether the L2 is acquired as a foreign language in classroom settings or in interactions with native speakers in so-called natural or naturalistic L2 acquisition, it is evident that such differences do exist. The certainly most important one is that all (2)L1 children develop full competences in their languages, whereas very few, if any, L2 learners are able to achieve this. In fact, research suggests that less than 5 per cent of learners attain near-native competences in an L2 and even fewer or none at all – this is a controversial issue – develop native competences. Moreover, most of those who are credited with a gift for language learning behave like native speakers in only some linguistic domains, e.g. either the use of syntax is native-like or the pronunciation is. Neonates and toddlers, on the other hand, are all equally 'gifted' for language; they can even develop two or more native competences simultaneously, as we have seen throughout the preceding chapters of this book.

In L2 research, the nature of (2)L1-L2 differences and their implications have been the subject of a controversial debate for many years. It is not possible to summarize this ongoing debate in a few words, and for our current purposes it would not be of much interest anyway. What matters in the context of this chapter is that such differences exist, and this is not a matter of controversy. That the overwhelming majority of adult L2 learners does not attain native-like competences is the most crucial point but not the only one. The two learner types already differ at the starting point because L2 learners can rely on previously acquired linguistic knowledge and skills as well as on more mature and further developed cognitive capacities. This is why L2 acquisition is not characterized by an early one-word stage, as we know it from L1 development, cf. Chapter 2 (section 2.2). In fact, although invariant developmental sequences exist in L2, too, they are not the same as the ones through which the respective L1 children proceed. A further particularity of L2 acquisition is that L2 learners exhibit a much larger range of variation, across individuals and within learners over time, than L1 children. This concerns the rate of acquisition as well as the use of target-deviant constructions and also the level of grammatical competence that they attain.

Researchers mostly agree that such differences exist, but they disagree on whether they are of a fundamental nature, reflecting differences in the acquired linguistic knowledge. Ultimately, the issue is whether the observed differences indicate that age-related changes affect the availability of some components of the Language Making Capacity (LMC) or more specifically of the Language Acquisition Device (LAD); see Chapter 2 (section 2.1). This can mean that the LAD itself has changed over time or that access to the LAD is partially inhibited. Alternatively, the causes of observable L1-L2 differences might be of a more superficial nature, consisting, for example, of interferences either from previously acquired linguistic knowledge or from other cognitive systems that are not involved in L1 acquisition. The latter can be due to the fact that older learners possess more mature and high-performing cognitive capacities and that these are activated where it would be preferable to let the specialized LAD do its job.

I must refrain from a more in-depth summary of this issue. Let me merely say that there exist good reasons to believe that (2)L1 and aL2 differ in fundamental ways. Recall that L2 learners do not proceed through the same developmental sequences as L1 children and that they exhibit much more variation in their language use as well as in the knowledge that they ultimately attain. These observations strongly suggest that the cognitive capacity responsible for uniformity and success in L1 development (see Chapter 2, section 2.1) does not operate in entirely the same fashion any more in L2 acquisition. My conclusion therefore is that the LAD becomes partially inaccessible over time, although this is admittedly a controversial issue in acquisition research. This kind of age-dependent change in the capacity to acquire and use languages seems to be primarily the result of neurological maturation, as I will explain in the next section (section 7.2) of this chapter.

In order to avoid misunderstandings, let me add that partial inaccessibility of the LAD does not exclude the possibility for L2 learners to acquire a near-native proficiency of the target language. Rather, it accounts for the fact that L2 learners differ strongly in how successful they are in achieving this goal. Moreover, in those cases where they cannot rely on guidance by the LAD, they need to resort to inductive learning. As a result, L2 acquisition processes are more protracted and less uniform than L1 development, because inductive learning includes hypothesis-testing by trial and error over several months in grammatical domains where the LAD enables L1 children to succeed within a short period of time, sometimes within a couple of weeks.

In sum, the major differences between first and second language acquisition correspond to just the kind of effects one expects to find if acquisition is not guided by the LAD. This observation thus lends support to the claim that the acquisition device becomes partially inaccessible over the course of the first years of life. Still, irrespective of whether this explanation of the facts will prove to be correct, what matters for our discussion of successive acquisition are the empirical facts themselves, leaving no doubt that the observed differences between (2)L1 and adult L2 acquisition are substantial ones. The inevitable conclusion is that the capacity to acquire language is undergoing changes during childhood years, no matter whether we consider them as more or less fundamental or superficial in nature.

What transpires from these considerations is that sometime between early childhood and adulthood something must be happening that affects the Language Making Capacity. It is thus plausible to assume that age of onset of acquisition plays an important role as a cause of the observed changes. The question that arises immediately concerns the age period during which these changes occur: at the end of childhood or already during the first years of life? We want to know whether successive bilinguals who are first exposed to another language during childhood resemble simultaneous bilinguals who acquire two languages from birth or whether they are more like adult L2 learners and should therefore be regarded as child *L2 learners*. In order to answer this question without engaging in the controversial debate about what causes these changes, we need to look for constructions shared by acquisition types. For example, if successive bilinguals first exposed to another language in childhood use target-deviant constructions that are also attested in the speech of adult L2 learners but never in that of monolingual or bilingual L1 children, we may conclude that they resemble L2 learners in the acquisition of this particular phenomenon. The logic underlying this argument is that shared construction types reveal shared acquisition mechanisms.

Such commonalities between early successive and adult L2 learners in areas where both differ from L1 children do indeed exist, and they occur frequently enough to justify the classification of successive acquisition in childhood as an instance of child second language acquisition. The grammatical domain in which L2 properties have been detected most frequently in the speech of child successive bilinguals is inflectional morphology. For example, in languages where the finite verb carries tense and aspect markers and agrees in person and number with the subject, as in Spanish *yo hablé, tu hablas, ellos hablan* 'I spoke, you speak +2nd $_{sg}$, they speak+3rd $_{pl}$', these markings represent learning problems. Target-deviant uses – errors, if you prefer to call it that – also occur in first language development, and they are also attested in these domains of inflectional morphology. However, the error rate is much lower in L1 than in L2 acquisition, errors disappear after a short time, and some error types are not attested in L1 speech at all. For example, one finds virtually no errors in person agreement markings in L1 acquisition, and errors in number agreement markings are infrequent. In L2 acquisition, on the other hand, errors in person as well as in number marking occur frequently and during extended periods. Successive bilinguals who acquired both languages in childhood are therefore regarded as L2 learners if they exhibit characteristics of adult L2 acquisition, most importantly 1) high error rates or error rates oscillating between high and low values over time; 2) protracted acquisition processes; 3) L2-type errors not attested in L1.

Importantly, such L2-like phenomena also appear in the speech of successive bilinguals who started learning the second language at an early age. An example is grammatical gender marking, a notoriously difficult task for L2 learners. This is perhaps not surprising if their L1 lacks grammatical gender, like English does. However, a study of German children acquiring French (Meisel, 2018) revealed that they encountered the same kinds of problems with the two French genders, masculine and feminine, although German has three gender classes: neuter, feminine and masculine. What is really surprising is that the children were between three and four years old when they were first exposed to French.

Although these L1 German children started acquiring French at such an early age in an immersion context in a French-language preschool, their error rates in marking gender were high and persistent. After two or three years, they still oscillated in their use of articles encoding feminine and masculine gender, apparently not following specific rules or a particular system. This becomes apparent in that they combine both articles with one and the same noun, as in *le/la souris* 'the+masc/the+fem mouse' or *un/la maison* 'a+masc/the+fem house'. Moreover, when a noun is resumed by a pronoun, conflicting gender choices emerge, e.g. *la souris il fait* ... the+fem mouse, he makes...'. In fact, some children simply use the same article all the time, e.g. *le* or *une*, thus avoiding the choice between gender forms. Interestingly, these early learners do not rely on the meanings of nouns in their choice of gender, as the following examples show: *mon Schwester* 'my+masc sister', *le madame* 'the+masc lady', *une frère* 'a+fem brother',

le maman 'the+masc mom'. Nor can transfer explain their use
of gender markings, since less than one-quarter of the incorrect
French markings corresponded to the ones required in German. It
thus seems that these early successive bilinguals acquired gender
marking by lexical learning, in a word-by-word fashion, rather
than as a grammatical phenomenon that applies to all nouns.
Quite obviously, grammatical gender is a real challenge, even
when onset of acquisition happens as early as at age three or four.

But gender is not the only challenge for children acquiring
languages successively. The German-French successive bilinguals
who acquired French as of age three to four also behaved
like adult L2 learners in their use of French clitic subjects. As
mentioned in Chapter 4 (section 4.1), *clitics* are elements that
must be attached to others and cannot stand alone. French subject and object pronouns like *je* 'I' or *le* 'him, it', for example, must
be attached to the finite verb. In fact, they can *only* be combined
with *finite* verb forms, as in *je joue* 'I play'. Interestingly, this
constraint is never violated in L1 acquisition. Errors committed
during early L1 phases consist in the omission of the pronoun
(*joue* '(I) play'), or they are replaced by a 'strong' pronoun that
normally serves to express emphasis (*moi joue*). In the speech
of children, these strong pronouns are occasionally combined
with non-finite verbs (*moi jouer* 'me to play'), but clitic subjects
never appear in this context. In other words, constructions like
*je jouer 'I to play' are not attested in L1 child language. Early
successive bilinguals, on the other hand, do combine clitics with
a non-finite verb. In the following examples, verb endings are
rendered phonetically as [e] to avoid a commitment on whether
the child is using an infinitive *–er* or a past participle *–é*, homo-
phone non-finite verb form.

> Et là c'est un jeu il cass[e]   Paul
> 'And there that's a game he to break/broken'

> Ils jou[e] dehors   Erich
> 'They to play/played outside'

> Et le canard là, elle dessin[e]   Nadja
> 'And the duck there, she to draw/drawn'

Errors like these suggest that these children, who all started acquiring French before the age of four, do not make a distinction between finite and non-finite verbs. This conclusion is confirmed by the fact that they occasionally combine two finite verbs, a construction that is illicit in French as well as in German.

> Mon papa fait joue au football   Ludwig
> 'My dad makes plays soccer'

In fact, non-finite verbs are not only combined with clitic subjects, they appear in other finite contexts as well:

> Un petit [n]enfant qui mang[e] une pomme   Nadja
> 'A small child that to eat an apple'
>
> Et là jou[e] dehors   Paul
> 'And there to play outside'
>
> Et après il(s) devenir cop-, deux
> copains   Veronika
> 'And later they to become friends'

Constructions like these, in which non-finite verbs occur in positions that require finite forms, indicate that the children's grammars differ from native grammars not only in morphology but also in morphosyntax, because finiteness and verb placement verbs are tightly connected, as explained in Chapter 2 (section 2.2). In adult L2 acquisition, this connection can be interrupted, and this dissociation of morphology and syntax is a defining property of L2 acquisition. Consequently, non-finite verb forms are placed in finite positions, a phenomenon never attested in L1 speech. In SVO languages lacking the verb-second (V2) effect, like English, French and other Romance languages, placement errors are not easily detectable because finite and non-finite verbs appear in superficially identical positions. Erroneous inflectional markings, on the other hand, are readily identified. This is why some acquisition researchers concluded that, at this early age, syntactic knowledge is not affected by age-dependent changes of the LAD, only inflectional morphology.

However, if one examines contexts where finite and non-finite verbs may not appear in superficially identical positions, a different picture emerges. French negative constructions are contexts of this type; see Chapter 2 (section 2.2). In French negated clauses, finite verbs must precede the negative element *pas*, whereas non-finite verbs must follow it. Yet in the recordings with the German-French children, one finds a fair number of utterances where this is not the case. Rather, some of these successive bilinguals behave like adult L2 learners, placing finite verbs after *pas*.

*moi pas connais ça	'me not know (finite) that'
*moi aussi pas connais ça	'me too not know (finite) that'
*je crois mais pas je sais	'I believe but not I know (finite)'

Other studies have confirmed the claim that early successive language learners use L2-like syntactic constructions. Sopata (2011), for example, has shown that Polish children, who acquired German after their families moved to Germany (AOA 3;8–4;7), use word order patterns in German where verbs do not appear in the required OV order, possibly transferring VO order from Polish. Moreover they initially place finite verbs frequently in a target-deviant *V3 position, while at the same time moving non-finite verbs to the V2 position, an unambiguous feature of L2 acquisition. These and similar findings leave no doubt that successive language acquisition is affected by changes in the LMC and that these occur earlier than expected, already between age 3 and 4 (AOA).

To Sum Up: Age-Related Changes of Acquisition Capacities

- First and second language acquisition differ substantially, probably due to age-related changes of acquisition

> capacities, particularly of the Language Acquisition Device.
>
> - Although acquisition remains possible at all ages, some acquisition mechanisms become inaccessible in successive acquisition. Learners intuitively resort to others to replace them. However, this does not necessarily enable them to develop native competences.
> - Child and adult second language learners therefore use some constructions that neither monolingual nor bilingual first language learners use. These are therefore defining properties of L2 acquisition, distinguishing it from (2)L1.

It has been known for a long time that age-dependent changes of the capacity to acquire languages do occur. It is also widely agreed that brain maturation is a major cause, if not *the* most important one for these developments. The latter view reflects the *Critical Period Hypothesis* (CPH), as originally suggested by Lenneberg (1967). I will discuss this hypothesis and related topics in the following section (section 7.2). This discussion will show that the original CPH had to be revised and that one of the points that needed to be changed was the claim that critical period effects emerge at around age 11. In fact, Long (1990) already argued that major changes happen at around age 6–7, and Johnson and Newport (1989) were the first to point out that critical age limits may lie before age 7, possibly between ages 4–6. This comes close to the more recent findings by neurological research and by the above-mentioned studies of child second language acquisition according to which morphosyntactic knowledge is affected even before age 4.

Before ending this section, I want to add one further remark, concerning the emergence of unusual, non-native constructions in the speech of language-learning children. Some such usages, identical or similar to those by L2 learners, have also been detected in the speech of children with developmental language disorders, bilinguals as well as monolinguals. This has sometimes led to quite some confusion among acquisition researchers and speech therapists. Rather serious cases are the ones where bilingual children were misdiagnosed as being language impaired when they were not, or, conversely, impairment was not detected and, as a result, children did not receive the necessary clinical care. Fortunately, due to recent research, we have reached a better understanding of these phenomena, enabling us to disentangle quite reliably bilingualism from language impairment; see, for example, Armon-Lotem, de Jong and Meir (2015). Most importantly, bilingualism is definitely *not* the cause of developmental disorders. The unusual constructions are attested in the speech of monolinguals, too, and can therefore not be attributed to bilingualism. Moreover, if bilinguals show signs of language impairment, these appear in both languages and language disorders are not worsened by the fact that a child acquires two languages. There is thus no reason not to raise children with developmental language disorders bilingually.

To finally conclude this section, I want to answer the questions raised at the beginning, namely what it means that 'early' exposure is a necessary condition for the development of two (or more) first languages and what the possible consequences are if first exposure does *not* happen early.

As the preceding discussion has shown, 'early' indeed means much earlier than at age 11, as is still assumed by many. So far, the earliest effects of age-dependent changes in the morphosyntactic domain have been observed at around age 3;6 (AOA). However, phonological knowledge and the skills implied in perceiving and pronouncing sounds of a language are affected even earlier, and it would not be surprising if further research discovered that certain aspects of morphosyntax can also be subject to changes at earlier ages. These are, of course, only approximate age ranges because children are not all affected at exactly the same age. Just as the rate of acquisition varies across individuals, the effect of maturational changes varies. In the study with German-French children, for example, AOA ranged from 2;8 to 4;0, and some learners of the AOA 3;3–3;7 group behaved like L1 children, others like L2 learners. However, those exposed to French at age 3;2 or earlier were all indistinguishable from L1 children, and those first exposed to French after age 3;7 all exhibited L2 properties. Findings like these strongly suggest that the ability to develop native morphosyntactic competences begins to change during the period between 3 and 4 years of age – and 'change' unfortunately means that it deteriorates.

As for the question asking about the consequences of later onset of acquisition in successive bilinguals, we have seen that these learners resemble adult L2 learners in a number of ways and that they differ from monolingual and bilingual L1 children in just these respects. They are thus *child second language* learners. Importantly, only some parts of grammatical knowledge are subject to age-dependent changes of the sort discussed here, and those that *are* affected do not all change simultaneously. Incremental deterioration of the language acquisition capacity also means that early effects are rather subtle and not necessarily detectable by interlocutors in daily interactions. It is certainly not a reason not to offer children the opportunity to acquire another language. Successive bilinguals, at least those first exposed to the L2 between ages 3 and 6, are mostly very successful language learners who achieve more than what instruction in foreign language classes can hope for.

In sum, successive language acquisition at preschool age can result either in another native language competence or in child second language acquisition, depending on the age of first exposure to the other language. Child L2 acquisition is, in fact, an acquisition type in its own right. Child L2 learners resemble in some respects children acquiring first languages but they share characteristics with adult L2 learners in other domains of linguistic competence. Their acquisition rate tends to be faster than that of adult L2 learners, and they mostly outperform adults in the ultimately attained linguistic competence.

7.2   Critical Periods for Language Development

Biological or neurological explanations of human behaviour inevitably lead to controversial discussions. But if it is indeed the case that the human Language Making Capacity changes over time and that substantial aspects of the alterations that happen during a child's first years are due to maturational changes in the brain, some further comments explaining these claims are in order. This may not be of crucial interest to all readers, but I believe that for others it would be an inexcusable omission if this topic was not addressed here.

Let me start by emphasizing that 'age' is obviously not exclusively a biological issue. From the day of our birth, body and mind change, and a number of these changes affect our capacity to acquire language as do the previously acquired linguistic knowledge and skills. Simultaneously, our roles as members of social groups change, and in the course of socialization social-psychological conditions evolve, as do attitudes and motivations; all this exerts influence on our behaviour, including our linguistic behaviour.

Thus, age-dependent changes concerning the acquisition and use of language are by no means limited to the ones that affect the structure and the functioning of the brain. In fact, a wealth of research indicates that the development of linguistic knowledge and skills is influenced by age-related factors from birth up to approximately age 15, when the maturational period ends. And yet, neural maturation plays a special role in language acquisition, especially during early years, i.e. roughly during the first half of this period. It is of particular importance not only because all children are subject to very much the same changes, proceeding through identical phases of development; it is also special because the Language Making Capacity, as a subsystem within the overall cognitive system, enjoys a certain degree of autonomy. Although it interacts with other subsystems, its development does not have to be in pace with them, nor does it depend on them. This becomes obvious when one considers the fact that adults can rely on more mature cognitive capacities than toddlers, yet in spite of their high-performing processing and rich memory capacities, they do not fare better in acquiring language – just the opposite. This developmental autonomy is the main reason why I suggest taking a look at how maturational changes affect children's capacity to acquire language.

The LMC common to all children can account for the success, uniformity and rate of first language development, as I explained in Chapter 2. Crucially, however, acquisition does not develop at a steady pace. Rather, it proceeds through periods of heightened activity, alternating with others during which not much change is attested. Since this is the case for all children, it is plausible to assume that it is not due to particular learning conditions of individuals but to age-dependent changes to which the LMC is subject. The developmental commonalities across individuals, most importantly the invariant acquisition sequences introduced in Chapter 2 (section 2.2), lend strong support to this assumption. Although the precise age at which children attain a given phase varies considerably across individuals, the order of phases within sequences is invariable and, importantly, there exist age limits for the onset of specific developments. In other words, even for precocious children it is more than unlikely that they will produce multi-word utterances at age 12 months, i.e. constructions typically emerging at around 18 months of age.

What this means is that changes in the LMC open windows of opportunities. This is to say that at specific points of development, the acquisition device is ready to process information encoded in properties of the input data that it could not deal with previously. The new information is then integrated into the currently available knowledge system – it has now been learned. Successful learning is thus an indication that the acquisition device was ready at this point for the new task. The question is whether it remains permanently in this state of readiness, once this has been attained. Findings from research on successive language acquisition, some of which I mentioned in the preceding section, suggest that this is not always the case. Faced with morphosyntactic acquisition tasks, successive learners do not consistently attain the same results as L1 learners. In some instances, they come up with L2 solutions instead. Note that acquisition has not become impossible; rather, it must rely on some means of expression not used in L1 development. These differences indicate that, in successive language acquisition, learners resort to distinct learning mechanisms. This, in turn, leads to the conclusion that age-related changes of the LMC do not only open but also close windows of opportunities. The developmental phases during which the learning device is optimally prepared for particular learning tasks have been referred to as *critical periods*.

Critical periods have been studied extensively in developmental biology. Some songbirds, for example, will only learn their species-specific song if they have the opportunity to listen to a song tutor, usually the father, during a specific age period. Further critical periods have been identified in a number of species, including humans, for the development of vision and of hearing, for example. What the various cases across species have in common is that they concern developments where internal and external factors interact. Organisms come equipped with preprogrammed capacities or knowledge systems that will only develop, however, if they are triggered by external stimulation. This situation contrasts with others where developments are either fully preprogrammed and happen even without interaction with the outside world, or they are fully learned by experience, without guidance by innate capacities. The situations that are of interest here are those where internal and external factors interact, e.g. guidance by the innate LMC and exposure to the input data. In some of these cases, optimal results can only be attained when this interaction happens during a well-defined developmental period.

The hypothesis that such a critical period (CP) also exists in language acquisition was first proposed by neurologists Penfield and Roberts (1959) and subsequently elaborated by linguist and neurologist Eric H. Lenneberg (1967). This *Critical Period Hypothesis* (CPH) establishes a causal relationship between neural maturation and changes in the capacity to acquire language. Initially, it only referred to first language acquisition, claiming that it was not possible to develop a native competence in a first language if age of onset of acquisition was seriously delayed. Confirmation came from studies of children who were not sufficiently or not at all exposed to language during their early years. Profoundly deaf children, for example, who up to age 5 or later were not exposed to sign language, never acquired a full competence in this language, not even after many years of exposure. Furthermore, there are a number of studies of so-called feral children. However, due to the dramatic circumstances under which these children lived and were studied, most of this research does not provide the kind of information needed to either corroborate or refute the CPH. Nevertheless, the one on *Genie*, on which Curtiss (1977) reports, does give strong support to this hypothesis.

This does not necessarily mean that critical periods still play a role in developmental processes that happen later on, in successive language learning. In principle, it is imaginable that acquisition mechanisms, once activated in L1 development, remain permanently accessible and can be reactivated during later age periods, in successive acquisition. The question of whether critical period effects exist in L2 is indeed a controversial issue. As in the discussion summarized in the preceding section, it is widely acknowledged that non-L1-like constructions do appear in the speech of successive bilinguals. The controversy concerns, once again, the explanation of this fact, i.e. whether qualitative differences between simultaneous and successive bilingualism can be caused by maturational changes in the brain, effectively closing windows of acquisition opportunities. As I pointed out at the beginning of this section, other factors undoubtedly come into play when such differences emerge. However, given that they appear uniformly across learners and that very few of these attain near-native competences and probably none a native competence, the most plausible conclusion seems to be that neural maturation does play a role here and that successive acquisition is subject to critical period effects. This is why I want to spell out some implications of the CPH, primarily with respect to the age of onset in successive acquisition, even if there remain doubts as to whether the observed effects are indeed caused by neural maturation.

It was Lenneberg (1967) himself who first extended the CPH to L2 acquisition, pointing out that the capacity to acquire a language by mere exposure to input data disappears at a certain age, although a person can still learn to communicate in that language at a later age. His basic insight, that it becomes impossible to develop a native competence but that language acquisition continues to be possible, was confirmed by subsequent research. However, new research methods that became available during the five decades since the publication of this seminal book have led to revisions of the initial version of the CPH. Most importantly, perhaps, brain imaging studies and psycholinguistic research have demonstrated that crucial changes happen much earlier than during the age period at around puberty (age 10–12) that Lenneberg identified as the critical one.

Let us thus have a brief look at this revised version of the CPH in order to better understand the relevance of critical periods for successive language acquisition and to get a realistic idea of the age question. The first point that needs clarification is that the notion of critical period does not imply abrupt changes, overnight, so to say. Rather, the *optimal period*, during which acquisition happens easily, triggered by exposure to the primary linguistic data, is preceded by a fairly short *onset* period and followed by a period of gradual *offset* during which the optimal period fades out. We can think of these developments as like a slowly closing door (or window of opportunities). For some time, it may still be possible to squeeze through, yet it becomes increasingly more difficult. Note that this implies gradual changes. It is therefore only possible to identify approximate age ranges, not precise ages at which the changes happen. In what follows, I am referring to the beginning of the transition period, i.e. the time when the optimal period starts to fade out, when I mention critical ages.

The first major insight leading to revisions of the original CPH concerns the fact that there exist several age periods during which the Language Acquisition Device is affected by age-dependent changes. Consequently, postulating the existence of one critical period cannot be an adequate solution. Rather, there clearly are several sensitive periods affecting language development. Moreover, we know that the various components of grammar – phonology, morphology and syntax – do not follow the same developmental agenda. In fact, even within these domains, one finds asynchronous developments, related to specific grammatical phenomena. This amounts to saying that for every property of grammar that is subject to age-related changes, one can identify an optimal period during which it is easily acquired by exposure to the input data. In principle, we should therefore expect to find a multitude of critical periods. In reality, we observe that a number of optimal phases begin to fade out during more or less the same age span, and we can refer to such phases as critical periods. Consequently, critical periods are best understood as clusters of *sensitive phases* during which the LAD is optimally prepared to integrate new information into developing grammars.

In sum, we are not talking about one big critical period after which the learnability of all phenomena that are subject to maturational changes deteriorates. Rather, we are looking at various critical periods, each representing an age span during which a number of linguistic phenomena are acquired easily and successfully if the child is exposed to the relevant input data. In other words, although maturational changes affecting language acquisition happen at virtually every point of development, children proceed through certain periods during which sensitive phases for different grammatical phenomena cluster, thus constituting particularly crucial periods. I should emphasize again that this reinterpretation of the CPH predicts that critical period effects do not all happen simultaneously and that it is not language as a whole that is affected by maturational changes, but some domains of grammar. Lexical learning, on the other hand, is not subject to age-dependent changes of the acquisition mechanisms in quite the same way as grammar, although the ability to learn new words may also deteriorate.

Since we are now dealing with several critical periods, each a cluster of a number of sensitive periods, the challenge is to identify the respective age ranges. As we have already seen in the preceding section, important changes happen long before the frequently quoted age of approximately 10–12 years. Linguistic evidence from studies of successive language acquisition revealed that there indeed exist several critical age periods. In the morphosyntactic domain, crucial changes have been observed at around ages 3;6–4 and between 6 and 7. In fact, some studies reported on subtle effects as early as of age of onset of acquisition 3;6, and massive effects after AOA 6. Not to forget, language acquisition is influenced by age-related changes from birth up to approximately age 15. However, after age 6–7, social-psychological factors like attitudes and motivation play an increasingly more important role, whereas their influence is negligible during early childhood.

To Sum Up: Sensitive Phases in Language Development

- Maturational changes open and close windows of opportunities for language acquisition. During these *sensitive phases*, children's cognitive systems are optimally prepared for the acquisition of specific grammatical phenomena.
- It is not 'language' as a whole that is affected by age-related changes of the acquisition mechanisms, and there is not just one critical period. Rather, certain parts of grammar are best acquired during specific sensitive phases that happen at different age periods.
- Certain age periods are of particular importance for language development. These are critical periods during which various sensitive phases cluster. The age spans at around 3;6–4 and 6–7 years have been found to be crucial for the acquisition of morphosyntax.

There is one more point that I would like to add to this summary of research findings on critical ages. As mentioned repeatedly, the Critical Period Hypothesis maintains that maturation of the brain is the most important cause of these developments. If this is correct, it should be possible to detect changes happening at approximately the same ages in the brain and in the speech of successive language learners. Insights into these kinds of issues can be attained by neuroimaging techniques. They are based on the assumption that changes in the functional organization of the brain result in different *activation patterns* as well as in a different *spatial organization* of the brain in language processing. This is expected to happen if first exposure to a language does not fall within the optimal period. Supporting evidence for this assumption comes from studies using electrophysiological (electroencephalography, EEG) or haemodynamic methods (e.g. functional magnetic resonance imaging, fMRI). Modified activation patterns are primarily expected to be found in areas of the brain that are typically involved in language processing, most importantly Broca's area and Wernicke's area.

EEG research has demonstrated that the spatial distribution of activation patterns in the left hemisphere does indeed change at later ages of onset of acquisition, i.e. the specialization in the left hemisphere is reduced and the right hemisphere is increasingly activated. Electroencephalography is a non-invasive method by which electrical variations induced by neural activity are recorded at the surface of the scalp. From these recorded variations, event-related brain potentials (ERPs) are derived. The critical age ranges lie around 4 and 7 years, i.e. if AOA happens at age 4 or later, this effect of more diffuse spatial distribution and more right hemispheric processing becomes increasingly stronger. Importantly, differences between L1 and L2 learners are only detectable when subjects are exposed to syntactically deviant sentences, whereas exposure to semantically ill-formed ones does not produce this type of effect. Similar results have been obtained by studies using haemodynamic methods. They find differences with respect to spatial differentiation as well as intensity of brain activation between native speakers and L2 learners, and this refers again to morphosyntactic, not to semantic or pragmatic, processing.

In sum, neuroimaging studies speak in favour of the claim of functional differentiation, syntax being dissociated from semantics and pragmatics. They furthermore support the hypothesis that AOA is a major cause of the observed differences between L1 and L2 learners. They also confirm the claim according to which important changes happen around age 6–7, and some ERP results further show that crucial changes occur at age 4 or shortly before. These findings corroborate the hypothesis that postulates multiple sensitive periods, some of which cluster at around age 4 and at around age 6–7. Importantly, the fact that the age ranges identified as critical periods (3;6–4, 6–7) by neuroimaging studies coincide with the ones that emerged from linguistic analyses of the speech of successive bilinguals lends further strong support to the hypothesis according to which maturational changes in the brain cause alterations of the language acquisition mechanisms.

One last point concerning maturational changes of the LMC must be mentioned here. Although the period from approximately 3–4 to 6–7 years of age is the crucial one for the acquisition of native grammatical competence, age effects are not limited to these phases. Rather, once acquired, grammatical knowledge needs to be consolidated. Studies of language attrition in individuals have shown that grammatical knowledge is most likely to suffer from attrition if speakers lose contact with a language before age 11. Thus, there exists a period of stabilization up to age 11–12 that ensures that the acquired knowledge remains permanently accessible. Without sufficient exposure to the language during this age range, an individual's ability to control the acquired knowledge is likely to dwindle. In sum, early exposure, preferably before age 4 but certainly not later than age 7, is a necessary condition for the acquisition of a native competence, but this knowledge is vulnerable for some time and needs to be stabilized during a period when adequate exposure to the language continues to be possible.

7.3   Successive Bilingualism

Throughout this book, I have insisted that early onset of acquisition and adequate exposure to the target languages is basically all it takes for children to become bilinguals. They come equipped with a Language Making Capacity that enables them to develop the necessary linguistic knowledge and the skills required to put it to use. In the preceding sections of this chapter, I could finally present some more detailed information on what *early* exposure means in terms of age at the time of first exposure to a language. The importance of AOA follows from the fact that the LMC changes in the course of the first years of life of an individual. It optimally prepares the acquisition device for various upcoming learning tasks, successively opening various windows of opportunities. However, some optimal periods for the acquisition of grammatical knowledge eventually fade out in the course of further developments. Consequently, successive bilinguals cannot fully rely on the guidance by the LMC, any more. Rather, when facing certain acquisition tasks, they must resort to different learning mechanisms, as compared to simultaneous bilinguals or monolinguals. Unfortunately, 'different' means 'less successful' in most or all of these cases.

Yet what are the implications and consequences of these and related facts for parents raising bilingual children who are not exposed to another language from birth? Recall that the earliest signs in the morphosyntactic domain indicating that successive bilingualism resembles in some respects non-native acquisition appear between ages (onset of acquisition) 3 and 4. It thus seems that successive acquisition starting later than age 1;0 but earlier than age 3;0 enables children to develop native morphosyntactic knowledge. However, studies of successive acquisition during the first three years are sparse, and it is imaginable that L2 characteristics in very early successive bilinguals will be detected by future research. In fact, some of the currently available evidence does point in this direction. It seems, for example, that insufficient exposure to the target language during the second half of the first year, e.g. in cases of severe *otitis media*, can result in long-lasting linguistic deficiencies. Moreover, non-native features can emerge in phonology even if onset of acquisition happens as early as during the second year of age.

Further evidence comes from a particular case of successive language acquisition, namely *internationally adopted children*. They are not bilinguals in the usual sense because the development of their first language ends abruptly at the time of adoption, and the adoption language is the only one acquired from then on. This is why they have been referred to as monolinguals in an L2. There can be no doubt that AOA is not the only factor responsible for the fact that the acquisition of the adoption language deviates in some respects from the acquisition of the same language by non-adopted children. Preadoptive environments, for example, may not have been optimal, and the abrupt termination of L1 development may well have a negative effect on subsequent acquisition processes. Nevertheless, most of the children adopted at age 24 months or younger attain native-like proficiency and perform within normal range. However, when tested and compared to children exposed to the same language from birth, almost all of them turned out not to be entirely native-like. They attained lower scores on several measures, e.g. receptive grammar or sentence recall. In fact, one finds considerable variation across individuals, some performing at the same level as non-adopted children, others significantly worse. In other words, most of them are near-natives, although they were perceived as native-like in everyday conversation, and this so-called non-perceivable non-nativeness has been argued to be primarily due to the delayed onset of exposure to the adoption language. It remains to be seen whether the non-nativeness of internationally adopted children actually reflects knowledge deficits or whether it is merely due to performance limitations.

What matters for the present purpose is that the non-L1 properties are of a rather subtle kind and difficult to detect in spontaneous speech. In fact, the majority of successive bilinguals who started acquiring another language by age 6 seem to be able to behave in their language use like monolinguals and are thus largely indistinguishable from L1 speakers. Moreover, some of the early L2-L1 differences can be levelled out during later phases of acquisition. Still, the grammatical competence of successive bilinguals is very likely to exhibit qualitative differences if onset of acquisition happens after age 4, even if these are not always noticeable in spontaneous speech. And as of AOA 6 or later, non-native properties are definitely more noticeable. These (approximate!)

age ranges should be taken into account when deciding on the possibility of a successively bilingual education. Early exposure to the other language is crucial in situations where the goal is to attain a native or native-like competence, e.g. when this is the societal language and the language of the educational system in the years to come. On the other hand, near-native competence, too, is a goal worth pursuing. Not to forget that it is, of course, still possible to learn languages later on, at age 40, as Lenneberg wrote, or even later.

Nevertheless, child L2 acquisition is almost always more successful than adult L2 acquisition, and I think this is a good reason to decide in favour of a bilingual education, even after some early monolingual years. If such an opportunity presents itself, parents should seize it. Everything we know about child bilingualism speaks in favour of this option. However, it is not always obvious how to proceed if one opts for successive bilingualism, as the following email from the mother of two monolingual daughters shows.

Successive Bilingualism?

I have two daughters, aged 17 months and 3 years. Until now, my husband and I have only spoken German to them. As of January, I will be teaching English in the kindergarten of my three-year-old daughter, and already now she enjoys very much practising English words. This is what made us wonder whether I should from now on only speak English to our children and my husband German. My English is far from being grammatically perfect, but due to a year that I spent in Ireland, my pronunciation is very good.

Is speaking only English with my daughters a possibility? Does it make sense to switch from a monolingual to a bilingual education? Should there be a transition period?

(Translated from German, JMM)

She actually raises three different issues. First of all, she asks whether successive bilingualism is a viable option. The preceding sections of this chapter already contain the answer to this question, namely that first exposure to English at ages 1;5 and 3:0 is definitely a possibility. The second issue, too, has already been answered, i.e. whether non-native input might be problematic; see Chapter 6 (section 6.2). Intentional bilingualism is certainly feasible and not at all problematic if certain requirements are met.

The third issue, however, concerning possible transition periods, raises a question that has not yet been addressed explicitly and to which I cannot offer a plain answer. The potential problem follows from the fact that the additional language is not introduced by additional interlocutors but by the mother who intends to change the language she speaks to the children. One must, of course, make sure that this does not result in an interruption of the development of the children's first language. But this is not really the issue here because the goal is to create a bilingual situation where the father continues to speak German, the societal language.

However, a potentially serious concern is that the children might react negatively to an abrupt language change by their mother. As mentioned before, language is perceived as an expression of the personality of the speaker, and some children react negatively when a parent changes as a result of her or his use of a different language. Even if a child likes to play language games, e.g. using foreign language words, switching to another language altogether is an entirely different matter. It therefore depends largely on the reaction of the children whether a change of language by a parent is an option. Only if they accept this change without being pressured should parents consider switching from a monolingual to a bilingual education. If they do, a gradual transition is in my opinion the best way to proceed. One could start with an English day or by using English in certain situations of everyday life, carefully monitoring how the children react to a parent's language switching.

Similar issues arise when a family moves temporarily to another country or to a region where a different language is spoken – or a third language, in the case of bilingual families. In a globalized world where employees are expected to be mobile, this is not an uncommon situation. In at least one respect, it is a less challenging setting than the previous one because it does not require that parents switch languages in child-directed speech. In fact, it is up to them to decide whether they really want to raise their children bilingually, and if yes, whether this will be a temporary or a permanent change. After all, successive bilingualism is not inevitable in this context. Rather, parents can continue to speak their first language at home and have the children attend daycare centres or schools where this language is the medium of instruction. This obviously means that they deny their children the opportunity to become bilinguals in a situation where this could easily be achieved. A rather unfortunate decision, in my view, and I suppose that most readers of a guide for parents of bilingual children will share this opinion. The crucial question to be addressed here is therefore how monolingual families can become bilingual, and how bilingualism can be maintained, once back in the home country. These are, in fact, the issues frequently addressed in requests for counselling, as in the following one by the mother of a three-year-old girl.

Temporary Multilingualism?

We are about to go from Berlin to Canada for probably two years, to the Ottawa/Gatineau/Hull region at the Ontario/ Québec border. We are wondering what kind of childcare (English, French, German) will be best for our daughter. Many daycares in that region – especially the Francophone ones – follow the immersion principle. We are not sure whether this would not be too much for our daughter, if she was to be exposed to two new languages simultaneously. There is a German-speaking daycare in Ottawa that we also consider as a possible choice, since our daughter will probably attend a German school on our return. Could you help me find answers to the following questions?

1) Will it be sufficient for the development of her German that we continue to speak German in the family?
2) Will it be too much for her if she is exposed to two new languages? Or is this perhaps less problematic for a young child than what we imagine from our adult perspective?
3) How can we prepare our daughter? Currently, we sometimes read English or French books together, and we occasionally use English words when meeting with our Canadian colleagues.

(Translated from German, JMM)

These parents have decided to take advantage of their stay in Canada to raise their daughter bilingually. It will hardly come as a surprise that the author of this book strongly supports this decision. From all we have seen in the current chapter and in the preceding ones, we can predict with much confidence that this girl will become bilingual. Moreover, what we know about the role of parents' language choice suggests strongly that continuing to use German as the family language will enable the child to further develop her native competence in much the same way as monolingual children of her age. I therefore recommended that she should attend a French or English-language rather than a German daycare.

As for the question of whether a bilingual French-English daycare is also a possibility, this is again difficult to answer in a straightforward fashion. As we have seen in Chapter 6, trilingualism is certainly a possibility. Furthermore, the Language Making Capacity undoubtedly enables children to acquire two languages simultaneously, even if first exposure occurs only at age 3. I nevertheless recommended a monolingual French or English daycare for this girl. Adapting to a new environment, meeting new friends, etc. is quite a challenge, not only for a three-year-old. Some children cope easily with this situation; others encounter serious difficulties. It is difficult to predict how this child will react, but exposing her to two new languages may just be too much. One could, of course, have her attend a bilingual daycare to find out how she copes with this situation. But it would be unfortunate if she had to change her social environment, newly found friends, etc., once again, after a few weeks. At any rate, a multilingual education for *two years* does not make much sense. The competences acquired at an early age need to be developed further and stabilized, as we have seen in the preceding section. Otherwise, they will be lost over the following years. In other words, a trilingual education for this girl only makes sense if the three languages are maintained upon return to Germany.

Concerning the third question, it is certainly possible to prepare children for what they will experience after a move to a foreign-language region or country. Occasional exposure to the new language via media (children's books, videos, etc.) or by introducing a day per week or daily situations when parents or other caregivers interact with the children in this language; all this is possible and may be helpful. However, it is not really necessary. At this early age, if onset of acquisition happens before age 6, the most important requirement that must be met for successive bilingual development to be successful is sufficient exposure to the language in meaningful interactions. A daycare where children meet other children of approximately their age is very likely to offer what is needed.

7.4 Reading Suggestions

To my knowledge, the topics of this chapter, especially the role of age of onset of acquisition, are not treated in easily available non-technical publications. However, readers who wish to know more about the importance of critical periods in first language acquisition will find Curtiss (1977) interesting.

Curtiss, S. (1977). *Genie: A psycholinguistic study of a modern-day 'wild child'*. New York: Academic Press.

Similarities and differences between first and child second language acquisition are explored in Chapter 6 of Meisel (2011). Note, however, that this is a university textbook that presupposes some familiarity with linguistics.

Meisel, J. M. (2011). *First and second language acquisition: Parallels and differences.* Cambridge: Cambridge University Press.

Readers interested in issues related to developmental language disorders and child bilingualism will find the following book particularly useful:

Genesee, F., Paradis, J., & Crago, M. (2010). *Dual language development & disorders: A handbook on bilingualism & second language acquisition.* Second edition. Baltimore: Paul H. Brookes Publishing.

8 Benefits and Advantages of Child Bilingualism

8.1 Making the Most of One's Endowment

L'homme qui parle deux langues vaut deux hommes. The person who speaks two languages is worth two people. This is what the *Conseil pour le développement du français en Louisiane* (Council for the Development of French in Louisiana) claims on a poster that is meant to encourage the use of French in Louisiana. Admittedly, this may be slightly exaggerated, but it conveys an idea that asserts, correctly, I believe, that speaking another language enables you to become part of another social world. As a bilingual, you are not merely able to express the same ideas in two languages, you have the opportunity to be immersed in cultures in which these ideas may have slightly or even fundamentally different meanings or express distinct value systems. In this context, 'culture' does not necessarily refer to Culture with a capital C. That too: it implies being able to read the works of great authors in the languages in which they were written, to be exposed to art and music you might not have encountered in the other cultural space.

Primarily, however, I am referring here to culture as it is expressed by social practices in everyday life: lullabies or nursery rhymes you hear in early childhood, what is served for breakfast (porridge, cappuccino and biscotti, pancakes and bacon, miso soup, shakshuka or sirniki, etc.), going for a paseo before dinner, having dinner at 6 pm or at 10 pm, and so forth. Importantly, different cultures imply differences in value systems defining socially acceptable behaviour as opposed to behaviour that is frowned upon or might result in the exclusion from a social group. An example of the not so serious sort is turn-taking in informal conversations: should one wait until the person speaking pauses, or may one interrupt, and if yes, how does one do this? In some

Benefits of bilingualism

cultures, it is totally acceptable for the speaker to carry on, two or more people speaking simultaneously, competing in trying to catch the attention of other participants in the conversation. In other cultures, this kind of behaviour is regarded as rude and socially unacceptable.

A rather special case is linguistic exogamy. It is practised, for example, in Tucano (or Tukano) communities in the Colombian-Brazilian border area where Eastern Tucanoan languages are spoken. Family membership is defined by the language an individual speaks, more precisely by one's father's language. People speaking the same language are therefore considered to be brothers and sisters. Since marriages between brothers and sisters are not tolerated, one can only marry someone who speaks a different language. Consequently, married couples are all bilingual, and since adult sons typically live in their father's house, this is normally a multilingual environment because their wives speak different languages, too, but not necessarily all the same one. The patrilineal tradition implies that children are expected to exclusively use their father's language. This is remarkable from an acquisition perspective because babies and toddlers spend more time with their mothers and other women in the house or the village. They are thus expected to act as active bilinguals in the non-dominant language and as receptive bilinguals in the dominant language. I am not aware of any studies on the acquisition of Tucano, but this situation does not seem to represent a problem for the members of these communities who are mostly multilingual or at least bilingual. Lexical and grammatical differences between their languages resemble in some cases dialectal variation. In other cases, however, they differ to the same degree as Romance languages, e.g. Portuguese, Spanish or Italian, differ from each other, and they are not all mutually comprehensible. If interlocutors do not understand each other's paternal languages, they resort to one of their other languages. Interestingly, though, in the Tucano languages one uses the verb *speak* only for the paternal language, whereas one is said to 'imitate' the other ones, like a parrot 'imitates' human languages. I should add that the Tucanos consider societies that do not practise linguistic exogamy, such as the Colombian majority society, as incestuous because their members marry their 'sisters'.

Different cultures can thus represent distinct value systems, and although differences are frequently not of such a fundamental nature as in this example, gaining an understanding of another culture can be extremely difficult. In fact, subtle differences are particularly difficult to perceive, and their significance will easily go unnoticed by those who are not members of the social group. Paradoxically, violations of social norms are more likely to be tolerated if committed by someone who does not speak the language well – precisely because linguistic and social skills both reveal that this person is an outsider. Native or native-like bilinguals, on the other hand, do not necessarily benefit from the same degree of tolerance because their linguistic and their social behaviour are in conflict, the former suggesting group membership, the latter ignorance or deliberate violation of social norms. This is one of many reasons why bilinguals should seize the opportunity to be immersed in two cultures and become bicultural. In section 8.3, I will have more to say about this, and I will try to explain why I think it is preferable for bilinguals not to remain monocultural.

Bilingualism is undoubtedly a key to biculturalism, not the only one, but probably the most efficient one, and acquiring two or more languages simultaneously in early childhood is not only possible; it is the easiest and the most successful path towards bilingualism. This is the message I have tried to convey in this book. I have presented a wealth of arguments, based on findings from research investigating child bilingualism, all leading to the conclusion that it is possible and indeed recommendable to learn more than one language from early on. The slogan stating that monolingualism is curable is thus not much of an exaggeration. Although for someone to be considered bilingual does not necessarily require that this person have an equally good command of the two languages, exposure to two or more languages from birth does enable children to develop native competences in these languages. Their Language Making Capacity is an endowment for multilingualism. This, in turn, means that children exposed to only one language are deprived of the opportunity to make the most of this endowment.

Most of these insights into bilingual acquisition have been known for many years by now, yet the rumour still runs that acquiring more than one language during early childhood might contain risks for the children's linguistic or cognitive development. Understandably, parents who have a choice between raising their children bi- or monolingually are likely to decide against a bilingual education if there remain doubts as to whether it is possible to develop a competence in each language equivalent to that of the corresponding monolinguals. This is why I addressed in Chapters 3 to 7 the most pressing concerns expressed by parents. As it turns out, none of them actually represents a serious obstacle to the development of two or more first languages. Returning briefly to the concerns listed in Chapter 1 (section 1.1), let me remind you of some of the findings that confirm that possible doubts are indeed unwarranted.

The most alleged problem of early child bilingualism frequently mentioned concerns language differentiation. Fortunately, it is also the most extensively studied issue and the one where all relevant studies agree that it is really not a problem at all. The findings summarized in Chapter 3 leave absolutely no doubt that children exposed to more than one language at an early age are well able to keep them apart. None of the available pieces of evidence oblige us to believe that they fuse two linguistic systems into a single one, neither temporarily nor permanently. Moreover, once separated, the linguistic systems of the bilinguals' languages are not fused during later developmental phases, either; see Chapter 4. Importantly, even young bilinguals do not speak a macaronic language mix. They sometimes switch languages between or within utterances, but this does not mean that they confound their languages in the use they make of them in everyday communication. Rather, switching typically serves specific communicative purposes in bilingual interactions. It is not chaotic but systematic, in its sociolinguistic functions as well as in its structural properties, because possible switch points within a sentence are constrained by grammatical principles.

Switching and similar kinds of bilingual language use are clear indications that there is constant interaction between the linguistic systems in the minds of bilinguals. The effects of interaction on the outcome of acquisition processes have been the object of controversial debates among bilingualism researchers; see section 4.2. Importantly, however, grammatical interaction has been demonstrated to be a temporary phenomenon, if it happens at all. It does not entail that the acquired grammatical knowledge is qualitatively distinct from that of monolinguals. In other words, the ultimately attained grammatical competence is not affected by possible cross-linguistic interaction during early years of linguistic development.

This does not necessarily mean, however, that bilinguals will always be ready to use both languages in all possible contexts or at least in those situations where they are expected to use them. We must keep in mind that they constantly have to choose which of their languages to use, at least in all potentially bilingual settings. As we have seen in Chapter 5 (section 5.1), this mostly implicit choice is determined by a network of external factors. In cases of family bilingualism, parental language use is probably the most important one. But children's bilingual behaviour also follows personal preferences that cannot always be influenced by family members or other caregivers, and it may not be in accordance with contextual factors. Rather, they may be more at ease in one language, or they feel that they are more proficient in one of them. In fact, one language may indeed be weaker and thus less advanced in its development. Developmental delay or a lower proficiency in a language, real or imagined, can result in its avoidance and in the preference of the other one. Importantly, however, this does not mean that it is impossible to acquire a native competence in the weaker language. On the contrary, it can become the stronger or the preferred language, later in childhood, and this kind of change can happen repeatedly over the lifespan.

This also means that the claim that balanced bilingualism is not possible and that one language will always be stronger than the other one is not correct. It is definitely wrong if it is meant to imply that early bilinguals cannot acquire full competences in both languages and that the attainable knowledge of one language will necessarily be incomplete. If, however, it is merely supposed to mean that one language is normally the preferred or the stronger one, it is at least misleading. Balanced bilingualism may well be the exception in that individuals tend to prefer one of their languages, because dominance and balance are reflections of a person's social interactions, and these are rarely perfectly balanced with respect to occasions to use one or the other language. Yet this does not imply that one language must be weaker than the other one – and if it is, this is frequently a temporary phenomenon. Most importantly, in the present context, it is certainly not the case that the attainable competence in the weaker or disfavoured language is deficient in comparison to that of monolingual native speakers and that it resembles the linguistic knowledge of foreign language learners.

From all this, it follows that bilingual children who do not actively speak one of their languages, or are reluctant to use it, are nevertheless bilinguals, provided they understand that language. In virtually all cases that I encountered over the years, this was indeed what I could observe, i.e. children who did not speak actively one of their ambient languages turned out to be receptive bilinguals who understood this language reasonably well. They had not failed to acquire a competence in the language that they chose not to use actively. This is demonstrated unmistakably by their ability to comprehend the disfavoured language. Quite obviously, it is not possible to understand a language that one has not acquired. Language comprehension requires the same kind of grammatical and lexical knowledge as production.

Another objection frequently raised against a certain type of family bilingualism that has proven to be unwarranted concerns parents' interaction with their children in a language that is not their native language. There simply does not exist any empirical support for the claim that children must fail to acquire a native competence if parents or caregivers are themselves second language learners of the language in which they address the children. Intentional bilingualism is a perfectly viable option. It is therefore rather irritating that some researchers and educators warn against using non-native languages in child-directed speech, arguing that it constitutes an unnatural setting for the children or that the acquisition process is likely to be hampered if children are exposed to errors. Some counsellors even go as far as to contend that bilingual children should only be exposed to 'high-quality, first-class input'! Be assured that these recommendations are not based on facts; they belong to the realm of fiction. Moreover, arguments cited in their support are not valid. In reality, no child encounters only error-free, 'first-class' input. Empirical studies reveal that a considerable percentage of (monolingual!) children's input consists of ungrammatical utterances: people do not finish a sentence, drop obligatory elements, commit speech errors, and so forth. Fortunately, children's acquisition mechanisms enable them to filter out a certain amount of 'noise', and this is obviously also the case with bilinguals. However, if specific errors occur systematically in the speech to which they are exposed, they will, of course, incorporate them into their linguistic systems. These may thus differ in some points from those of the respective monolinguals, but they are not 'incomplete', and if the children are also exposed to the speech of native speakers, they are very likely to acquire a native competence in the target language.

The summaries and discussions of research findings presented in the preceding chapters have shown, I think, that a number of concerns about early child bilingualism needed to be considered seriously and had to be scrutinized for evidence possibly confirming them. In other cases, like the one just mentioned, their sources and motivations remain mysterious because they are not based on any kind of empirically testable observations. There exist others of the same nature, and I am perplexed by the fact that they are occasionally still brought up, given that so many multilingual children attest to the contrary. Further examples of this kind of prejudice-based objection are the claim that children exposed to more than one language from birth end up as semilinguals in two languages, with incomplete competences in each of them, or the contention that the task of acquiring two languages simultaneously puts excessive strain on the mental capacities of young children, or that it negatively affects children's cognitive development because they are torn between languages and cultures. Not only does one not find empirical support for these alleged dangers, but recent research suggests that, if anything, early bilingualism might actually be advantageous in just these domains. I will return to this issue below (section 8.2).

As irritating as such warnings against presumed risks of child bilingualism are, it is not difficult to deal with them. In most cases, one merely needs to ask for empirical evidence, and this is the end of the debate, since the required evidence simply does not exist. In some cases, however, one needs to have a closer look because they are apparently supported by empirical facts. Only careful scrutiny reveals that the observed effects are not actually caused by the factors mentioned or at least not in the alleged fashion. The latter comment applies, for example, to developmental delays. The claim is that the rate of linguistic development in bilinguals is slower than in monolinguals and that this delay can have negative effects on the children's success in preschool or in school. Whether bilingual development indeed proceeds at a slower rate is a controversial issue, primarily because of the considerable variance in developmental rates across monolinguals as well as bilinguals.

Yet even granting that this assumption is correct, the worry that this will result in problems when the children enter institutions of formal education is unwarranted, because possible delays among bilinguals fall within the range of what is also attested among monolinguals. Moreover, slower learners typically catch up with the faster ones by the time they enter school.

An even more irritating and serious case of false alarm refers to bilingualism as an alleged cause of language impairments. It is not uncommon that parents report that paediatricians recommend abandoning the bilingual education when children begin to stammer or when they are diagnosed with Specific Language Impairment (SLI), claiming that both occur significantly more frequently among bilinguals. This is blatantly false; neither stammering nor SLI or other language (development) disorders are caused by bilingualism. As for SLI, for example, most researchers agree that it is caused by genetic mutations. It is diagnosed when otherwise normally developing children show signs of severely delayed or disordered language development. Crucially, SLI does not occur more frequently among bilinguals, nor is it aggravated by bilingualism.

Let me finally comment briefly on one more point, namely that the psychological development of bilingual children might be affected negatively, because they are torn between languages and cultures. I am not aware of systematic studies investigating these issues. However, based on my experience with bilingual families, I do not find it implausible to expect that conflicts triggered by disagreement about educational or more generally social values are more likely to happen in multilingual than in monolingual families, precisely because they represent multicultural settings. Such conflicts can undoubtedly be detrimental to children, but raising them monolingually would not make them vanish because they are rarely caused by the presence of two or more languages. Rather, disagreement about social values or conflicting educational styles are more likely causes. Not that these could not arise in monocultural and monolingual settings – here too parents differ, for example, in being more or less strict or in adopting *laissez-faire* attitudes. But differences of this kind may very well emerge more frequently in multicultural settings. It is therefore in the best interest of the children and probably of the entire family if multilingual families are multicultural environments where all members are willing to respect common as well as conflicting values. Giving up one language will certainly not make cultural differences disappear. In fact, this can be the cause of further conflicts.

In sum, none of the concerns listed in Chapter 1 represents a potential disadvantage for children acquiring two or more languages simultaneously and could thus be a reason to decide against a bilingual education. Rather, it is possible to develop a competence in each language equivalent to that of the corresponding monolinguals. This is not to say that it will always be easy; in fact, it may sometimes be difficult. But parents, other family members and caregivers can influence the acquisition process and should not give up too early when problems arise. Children's Language Making Capacity is an endowment for multilingualism, and the best way to support them in the process of becoming competent speakers of two or more languages is to offer as many opportunities as possible to hear and speak their languages, preferably with different interlocutors. As mentioned in Chapter 6 (section 6.2), children who have only a single interlocutor and thus only one role model in the minority language are likely to exhibit less flexibility in adapting to changing communicative contexts in their non-dominant as compared to their dominant language. Remember that the quantity of child-directed speech matters. So, let me repeat the simple advice: talk, talk, talk! This will enable language learners to make the most of their endowment for multilingualism.

In this first section of this last chapter, I briefly recapitulated some of the reasons that demonstrate that there exist no real disadvantages for bilinguals as compared to monolinguals. I think it is important to emphasize this fact once again. However, there is really no need to constantly compare your children or yourself, if you are bilingual, to monolinguals, neither for the better nor for the worse. The defensive attitude, arguing that bilingualism does not entail disadvantages, is increasingly often replaced by an offensive one that emphasizes possible advantages of bilinguals over monolinguals. This is why I will briefly review some of these alleged advantages in the following section, although I do not think that any of them is a decisive reason to raise children bilingually. In my opinion, the most important advantage of being bilingual is the fact that one can speak another language and understand another culture.

8.2 Benefits Beyond Linguistic Skills

In Chapter 1 (section 1.1), I listed some of the supposed benefits of bilingualism that parents mentioned when they explained why they are raising their children bilingually. As we have seen in the subsequent chapters, the most crucial and most frequently mentioned one of those referring to linguistic knowledge and skills is indeed well founded: children exposed to more than one language from birth can become native speakers of these languages.

At least one expectation, however, could not be confirmed: If onset of acquisition happens later in childhood, children will at best attain a near-native competence in that language, but they will not become native speakers if they are first exposed to a language later than at the age of approximately six years. However, early bilinguals seem to have advantages over monolinguals in learning additional languages at a later age. Although this is one of the questions that still need to be researched more extensively, there exists sufficient evidence from psycholinguistic and neurolinguistic research confirming this assumption, and it is also supported by a number of informal observations and self-reports. Another language-related advantage concerns reading and writing skills. Bilinguals have indeed been shown to outperform monolinguals in their reading and writing abilities, possibly because they develop metalinguistic awareness earlier than monolinguals, i.e. knowledge about language. It helps them to understand that words are arbitrary labels for the objects or ideas they refer to. More generally, they become more easily aware of formal properties of languages, as they experience that their languages differ in these properties, and this can give them an advantage over monolinguals when it comes to learning to read and write.

Turning to possible benefits beyond linguistic competences and skills, the picture is somewhat blurred, as far as I can see. As you may recall from Chapter 1, bilinguals are said to outperform monolinguals in their mathematical abilities, achieve higher scores in intelligence tests and even make better financial decisions than monolinguals. Moreover, bilingualism has been claimed to entail cognitive benefits and to delay neurological disorders. I must admit that I am not really in a position to assess competently the validity of all these claims. This is not to deny that they are all based on serious research, but it is not easy to decide to what degree the conclusions drawn from these findings are well-motivated.

The reasoning that has led to these and a few other claims postulating benefits of bilingualism is that bilinguals are credited with an enhanced mental flexibility, resulting from the fact that speaking two or more languages forces them to recognize distinct linguistic systems, to actively choose one of them, to inhibit the other one, and to switch between languages when their communicative intentions or the setting requires it. The crucial argument is that the thus acquired and practised capacities and skills are carried over from the purely linguistic to other cognitive domains where cognitive flexibility matters, where it is necessary to switch between tasks, or where one must focus on one task and ignore others, because they are irrelevant at this moment.

This can explain, so the argument goes, why bilinguals have sometimes been found to achieve higher scores in intelligence tests for tasks that require meta-knowledge or selective attention. It would also account for the finding that bilinguals obtained significantly better results than monolinguals on tests of verbal and, importantly, non-verbal, working memory. Furthermore, bilinguals' capacity for divergent thinking has been argued to be the reason why, in some studies, they outperformed monolinguals in verbal creativity. Moreover, the fact that children being raised bilingually have to follow social cues to figure out which language to use with which person and in what setting may be the reason why bilinguals as young as 3 years have demonstrated a head start on tests of fundamental social and emotional skills like perspective-taking and theory of mind. *Theory of mind* refers to the ability to attribute emotions, intents, beliefs and other mental states to oneself and to others.

The reason why I see a blurred picture of the cognitive benefits of bilingualism is that not all of the many recent studies investigating these issues actually show that significant bilingual advantages exist. Whereas some failed to find any evidence for this hypothesis, others detected only minimal effects in its support. Nevertheless, the good news is that virtually all studies agree that bilinguals do not do worse than monolinguals. In fact, there can be no doubt that at least some of the beneficial effects attributed to bilingualism are real. What is less certain, however, is the nature of the cause–effect relationship. Bilingualism may not be the only cause of some of the observed benefits, and some of them may not be related to bilingualism at all. Yet if they are, we need to know what kind of cognitive operations lead to these results. Only then can we draw conclusions that might enable us to alter the education of children being raised bilingually in a way that could allow them to benefit from possible advantages.

Psychologists suggest that *executive function* plays the crucial role here, because it subserves the mental activities involved in the kinds of language use that have been found to result in cognitive advantages of bilinguals. In order to stay within one language or to switch between languages, individuals rely on executive function controlling language use, and this is hypothesized to have an impact on non-linguistic executive control processes, in switching between tasks, filtering out superfluous information, and so forth. To avoid misunderstandings, I should hasten to add that speech production and perception by monolinguals also demand the activation of executive processes, in selecting the right lexical item, the appropriate morpho-syntactic properties of a word, etc. Nevertheless, bilingual speech production and perception require further control processes and perhaps also a more frequent activation of these cognitive mechanisms. The cognitive benefits hypothesized to result from these mental activities consist in superior executive function and, perhaps surprisingly, delayed onset of dementia.

These claims have led to a wealth of research activities, and they have also attracted much attention beyond academia. Unfortunately, the alleged benefits, to the extent that they do exist, are much less impressive than what is reported in the media and in recent textbooks. In reality, the findings concerning allegedly enhanced performance of executive function and less demented ageing are actually contradictory in a number of aspects. This is partly due to the fact that the research methods by which they were obtained vary in such a way that it is not always possible to compare the results – a problem that I will ignore here.

More importantly for the present discussion, there is no single executive mechanism, but a number of different ones, and not all studies actually investigated the same ones. In fact, they do not even agree on which cognitive activities should be subsumed under the term 'executive function'. However, there seems to be consensus that executive functions manage, integrate, coordinate or supervise other cognitive processes. Early studies, investigating the hypothesis according to which bilingual language use results in enhanced performance of executive function in domains not directly related to language comprehension or production, focused mainly on inhibitory control. However, more recent work on this topic has focused increasingly on different components of executive function: switching between tasks, working memory, attentional control, cognitive flexibility, etc.

The reasons why it is difficult to arrive at unambiguous conclusions on the bilingual benefit hypothesis are manifold. If, for example, studies that investigate different components of executive function disagree on whether bilingual advantages do exist, it may well be that the various components do not play an equally important role. Yet the inconsistencies in the results can also be due to other variables, e.g. age, intelligence or socioeconomic status of the subjects, length of exposure to their languages, and so forth. In fact, most tasks that subjects had to carry out in tests typically involve not only several executive functions but also other cognitive processes. It can therefore be difficult, if not impossible, to decide which one is the primary cause of an observed effect. In addition, some studies found that the expected benefits of bilingualism did not emerge in the results of all the tasks that were predicted to activate identical components of executive function. Perhaps even more seriously, tasks did not always trigger converging results across different studies. In sum, these and a few more problematic aspects of the research studying the bilingual benefit hypothesis make it extremely difficult to take a firm position on this issue.

Nevertheless, I believe that there exist good reasons to adopt a moderately optimistic view, although some studies found no effects or no significant ones that would support the idea of bilingual advantages in executive function. After all, null effects do not constitute counterevidence to the hypothesis under investigation, although, admittedly, one hopes for statistically significant effects supporting it. Still, as mentioned above, some inconsistencies in the research results may be due to the interaction of other cognitive processes with those of executive function. This, in turn, is likely to vary across types of bilinguals, who are obviously not all subject to the same preconditions and intervening factors. Thus, if we concede that not all bilinguals should be expected to exhibit equally positive effects, the moderately optimistic conclusion that I am propagating may be plausible, after all.

I largely follow here the well-balanced and fairly comprehensive research review by Valian (2015). She concludes that the most convincing results were obtained with older adults whereas studies of bilingual children showed weak or no effects and those with young adults are inconsistent. Her explanation of these findings is that monolinguals, children and young adults, who perform as well as bilinguals, succeed because they have other experiences that are equally suitable as bilingualism to enrich cognitive mechanisms and processes. Old adults, on the other hand, benefit more from bilingualism because they tend to spend less time on challenging cognitive activities. In other words, other cognitively enriching and challenging activities, too, contribute to superior performance of executive function. In the absence of other stimulation, the benefits of bilingualism are stronger and can be detected more easily. Consequently, elderly bilinguals tend to perform better than monolinguals with respect to executive function.

Unfortunately, however, I have to add a note of caution to this already not overwhelmingly positive summary of the state-of-the-art. Critical reviews of the research on alleged bilingual cognitive advantages suggest a possible distortion of the overall research results by biases influencing scientific publishing. It appears that null and negative findings were underreported, at least in publications that appeared up to the year 2014. Not to be misunderstood: we are not dealing here with fraudulent scientific activities. Rather, we are looking at a situation that reflects biases of which the people involved are normally not aware.

At a time when the idea that bilinguals might have cognitive advantages was new and surprising, researchers were eager to publish their results if they could corroborate this idea – and scientific journals were particularly interested in publishing them. If, however, a study arrived at a result that did not support this hypothesis, either because it could not detect any difference between bilinguals and monolinguals, or if the bilingual advantage was not statistically significant, it was less likely to be published. Authors, referees reviewing the article and editors of scientific journals, all seemed less convinced that these results deserved to be published. This interpretation of the facts is supported by comparisons of studies presented at conferences with those that were eventually published. They revealed that positive results were more likely to be submitted and also more likely to be accepted for publication. In other words, a publication bias in favour of positive results seems to have skewed the overall literature on bilingualism and cognitive function. The broadly accepted view that bilingualism confers a cognitive advantage may thus not accurately reflect the full body of existing scientific evidence. Let me add that now that the alleged bilingual advantage is considered to be common wisdom by many, there is evidence for a publication bias favouring negative results. But why should we be surprised to discover that scientific publications reflect trends, preferences and fashions, much like most domains of public life?

This consideration also applies to the discussion of the claim that bilingual benefits include the possibility of less demented ageing. The idea underlying this hypothesis is that using two or more languages can increase what psychologists refer to as *cognitive reserve*, enabling individuals to maintain cognitive function despite brain pathology. As for the connection between bilingualism and dementia in older age, the assumption is that 'whatever contributes to better executive function will also protect against cognitive decline, and vice versa' (Valian, 2015: 8). Not surprisingly, in view of the dramatically increasing social significance of issues relating to ageing populations, the reverberation of the claim that bilingualism might lead to a delay of onset of cognitive decline and dementia, including Alzheimer's disease, has been enormous. The hypothesis triggered a number of further studies, and the popular media reported on the most spectacular findings. For many, a protective effect of bilingualism against dementia seems to be a fact, and it is even presented as such in some psycholinguistic textbooks.

In reality, the state-of-the-art is, once again, more intricate than the widespread narrative suggests because the results obtained by studies investigating this issue are not consistent. Importantly, almost no prospective study, following older individuals over a number of years, found any evidence of advantages of bilingualism. Only retrospective studies, which record the age at which patients were first diagnosed with cognitive impairment, tend to find protective effects of bilingualism. Whatever the explanation for this disagreement may be, it suggests that findings supporting the idea of bilingual advantages in this domain need to be interpreted cautiously. According to these positive results, onset of dementia is delayed by four to seven years; but once it happens, the decline is more rapid and people die sooner. Interestingly, in some studies strong positive effects emerged only with multilinguals speaking four languages or more.

If I were to come up with a concise summary of the state-of-the-art on this issue, I would say that it is quite likely that bilingualism can contribute to better ageing, but that bilingualism alone does not guarantee that this will actually be the case. Not only can other enriching cognitive experiences help to achieve this goal, they can have the same or similar effects on monolinguals. Higher educational levels, for example, better levels of occupation, or music training also correlate with a delayed onset of cognitive decline. Even physical exercise is beneficial, in this respect. Although for each of these factors the supporting evidence is inconsistent, it is safe to conclude that they can all contribute to a cognitively better ageing.

In fact, consistent cognitive challenges not only protect against premature cognitive decline, they also improve executive function. One such challenge is the acquisition (and use) of two or more languages. In spite of mixed results within and across studies, there exists sufficient evidence to conclude that bilingualism can affect individuals' cognitive development and that the effects are generally positive when they do occur. However, bilingual acquisition is not unique in this sense – other enriching experiences can lead to similar results.

To Sum Up: Does Bilingualism Make You Smarter and Less Prone to Demented Ageing?

- Bilinguals do seem to have advantages over monolinguals, e.g. in learning additional languages at a later age or in their reading and writing skills.
- As for benefits beyond language-related domains, these do exist, yet they are less impressive than what is expected

by many. Enhanced mental flexibility, for example, is well documented, but it is not entirely clear whether it is indeed due to bilingualism. The same comment applies to allegedly enhanced performance of executive function and less demented ageing.
- In sum, bilingualism can contribute to better executive function and consequently also to better ageing, but other cognitive activities can have similar effects.

Before concluding this section, I would like to add a personal comment. I wonder to what extent these findings will be useful for parents who have to decide whether to raise their children bilingually. In my opinion, a possible bilingual advantage in cognitive development should at best play a marginal role in this decision-making process. Not to be misunderstood: these are fascinating insights into the working of our mind and our brain. And there is at least one lesson to be learned that is definitely important for parents of bilingual children, namely that a bilingual upbringing does not put children's cognitive development at risk. This is why I felt I could not simply ignore this discussion and skip the topic in this book. Yet this does not mean that I want to propagate bilingualism as a means of making children smarter or cognitively better performing. At any rate, as the summary of this research has shown, there is as yet no evidence for a clear bilingual advantage in childhood, although it has been shown to be more marked in simultaneous than in successive bilinguals.

In my view, an important goal of bilingual education should be a harmonious development, as explained by Annick De Houwer (2009). If this entails cognitive advantages in comparison to monolingual children – all the better. From this perspective, it is obvious that some particularly important benefits of bilingualism are lacking in the list of potential benefits, e.g. to be able to communicate with grandparents who do not speak the community language.

8.3   Living Multicultural Lives

At the beginning of this chapter, I alluded to the possibility of becoming part of other social worlds by speaking other languages. At this point, before concluding this book about child bilingualism, allow me to repeat and emphasize that bilinguals are not only able to express ideas in two languages, they also have the opportunity to be immersed in two cultures. I want to encourage parents, family members and other caregivers to seize this truly life-changing opportunity. As announced at the beginning of this book, it has been primarily about the *acquisition* of two or more languages, on what is possible and what the limits are. But in order to achieve what is possible in principle, one must consider other aspects than the psycholinguistic ones. My claim is that individuals are only making the most of their endowment for multilingualism if they become bicultural. I therefore think that bilinguals should not remain monocultural if the social contexts in which they live offer opportunities for multicultural lives.

Those who are willing to consider this option, for themselves or for their children, are likely to face similar questions to the ones they had to address when deciding in favour or against children's bilingual upbringing: Why should a person want to be bi- or multicultural? Is it really possible to live multicultural lives? The risks versus advantages and benefits issue all over again! And assuming it is indeed desirable and feasible, how does one go about it?

There is, of course, no single valid answer to the 'why' question. But one important reason to become bicultural has already been mentioned: a person who speaks two languages is worth two people. I interpret this as meaning that bicultural individuals are at home in two communities. This allows them to build bridges and act as go-betweens among members of different cultures. In my mind, this role as mediators is the essential and outstanding property distinguishing bicultural from monocultural individuals. It can materialize in a virtually infinite number of different ways, ranging from a child's ability to bring together family members adhering to different and perhaps conflicting social values, to the adult who excels in personal and professional networking. In other words, there are as many good reasons to strive for a bicultural identity as there are opportunities to act as intermediary or to simply enjoy living in two distinct social worlds.

Admittedly, this is not always an enriching experience. If two social worlds represent conflicting and perhaps incompatible value systems, living in both or rather alternating between them may be more than what a person can reasonably be expected to accomplish or endure. These very difficult situations are precisely the reason for doubts over whether it is really possible to live a multicultural life without being torn between incompatible worlds. This is indeed a problem and a possible reason for concern. However, it would not disappear if bilingual individuals decided to identify with the culture of only one of their languages because they would still find themselves in a situation of conflicting loyalties. In other words, monoculturalism is not the solution to the problem, and biculturalism is not the cause. Rather, if there is a way out of conflicting situations, familiarity with both value systems is perhaps the only key that can open locked doors.

There are, in fact, reasons for optimism concerning these issues. Social scientists have demonstrated that learning other languages and having close interactions with people of other cultures result in openness towards and respect for others. Moreover, bicultural bilinguals seem to have social and emotional benefits; they have been shown to internalize negative states like anxiety, aggression, anger, loneliness or low self-esteem less frequently. They have also been found to possess greater tolerance towards other cultures and to be less prone to racist attitudes. It thus seems that they are more tolerant of value differences and more open to diversity.

Let me add a remark of clarification. Being bicultural does not necessarily mean that individuals must harbour two separate identities in their inner self. They do not have to develop split personalities. Rather, it is not only possible but indeed desirable that one personality embraces two cultural identities. Most bilinguals, monoculturals and biculturals alike, are probably familiar with the frequently asked questions that urge them to choose between loyalties: Are you really more X or Y? If, for example, in sports, an X-team faces a Y-team, which one do you support? Questions like these offer false alternatives. Monolingual monoculturals must learn to accept that a person can be X as well as Y. To be more precise, the true identity of a person may be just that, a unification of two or more cultural components. This does not exclude the possibility of preferring certain options in some situations and different ones in other contexts. Why should a Canadian-German not support Team Canada in hockey and die Mannschaft in football (or soccer, for those who do not play football with their feet)?

In this context, it may be useful to remember that bilinguals are not two monolinguals in one person, even if they attain the same competences in their languages as monolinguals. Note that this observation applies not only to their linguistic but also to their cultural knowledge. As correctly pointed out by Grosjean (2008), being bicultural implies a cultural competence consisting of two interacting cultures, to be able to take part in the life of two or more cultures and to adapt, at least in part, attitudes, behaviours and values, to these cultures. Importantly, this view of biculturalism includes the possibility of blending aspects of the cultures involved, rather than keeping them separated at all times.

Returning, finally, to early child bilingualism, my advice is to aim for a multicultural rather than a language-only monocultural bilingual education. All it takes is to offer children a multicultural environment from very early on. This may sound more ambitious and demanding than it actually is. It really only requires the presence of both cultures in a child's everyday life, in nursery rhymes, fairy tales, picture books, videos, and so forth. Quite obviously, time spent in countries where the other language is the community language is particularly helpful in this respect, as are visits by friends and family members from these countries. I am, of course, aware that this is not always easy to arrange, but it should be possible to apply at least some of these measures. They will definitely prove useful not only for the bicultural but also for the bilingual development of the child, especially if a parent is the only interlocutor in one language, particularly in settings where a parent addresses the child in a second language.

Let me take this opportunity to add a remark that is not based on scientific research but on my experience of many years studying and, more importantly, participating in the everyday life of bilingual families. It concerns the attitudes of adults interacting with children being raised bilingually – attitudes towards bilingualism as well as towards cultures or, more specifically, countries. I have come to the conclusion that young children can already perform what social psychologists call evaluative assertion analyses. What I mean by this is that value judgements on apparently trivial phenomena are transferred to the culture that they represent. For example, if a parent frequently makes derogatory comments on the food typically served in a country or on its habitually bad weather, children might interpret this as a rejection of the country, its culture, and perhaps also its language. Parents and other adults interacting with bilingual children should be aware of the possibility that covert negative value judgements on the culture associated with one of the family languages can result in its rejection by the child. Let me also remind you of a point made before, namely that parents' attitudes towards bilingualism are conveyed by their linguistic behaviour. I therefore want to encourage them to make an effort to learn the other family language and to become at least receptive bilinguals. It not only makes communication and probably even life in the family easier, since no one will feel excluded, it also conveys to children that bilingualism is something positive and valuable.

My last recommendation is perhaps an obvious one. Make sure that the bilingual education continues beyond early childhood! As explained in Chapter 7 (section 7.2), language development proceeds through a period of stabilization that ranges at least up to age 11–12. It ensures that the acquired knowledge remains permanently accessible, later in life. Without sufficient exposure to the language during this age range, the ability to control the acquired knowledge is likely to dwindle and can eventually become inaccessible. Moreover, in order to become a balanced bilingual and a bicultural individual, literacy in the two or more languages is crucial. It is therefore particularly important that bilingual children learn to read and write in both their languages. Multilingual schools are of course an obvious solution. But if this is not a possibility or not the parent's first choice, I strongly recommend making sure that children become literate in both languages. They should acquire and develop cultural knowledge and skills in both languages. It will enable and encourage them to live bilingual and bicultural lives beyond childhood.

8.4   Reading Suggestions

It is perhaps not necessary to suggest further articles or books to read, now that we have reached the end of the *child bilingualism tour* for which I offered my services as a guide. Nevertheless, let me mention an article by an eminent linguist from Brazil, who reports on her own experience as a child growing up with two, and later three, languages: first Japanese, then Brazilian Portuguese at the age of 6, and English at age 12. What is of particular interest is that Portuguese, arguably a second language, became her strongly dominant language, and her proficiency in her first language is much less developed.

Kato, M. A. (2003). Child L2 acquisition: An insider account. In N. Müller (Ed.), *(In)vulnerable domains in multilingualism*, pp. 271–93. Amsterdam: John Benjamins.

Bibliography

Primary Sources

Armon-Lotem, S., de Jong, J., & Meir, N. (Eds.) (2015). *Assessing multilingual children: Disentangling bilingualism from language impairment*. Bristol: Multilingual Matters.

Baars, C. (2002). *Sprachdifferenzierung in früher Kindheit bei gemischtsprachlichem Input: Eine Untersuchung von bilingual Wolof-Französisch sprechenden Kindern im Senegal*. Hamburg: Unpublished MA Thesis.

Barron-Hauwaert, S. (2004). *Language strategies for bilingual families: The one-parent-one-language approach*. Clevedon: Multilingual Matters.

Bialystok, E. (2016). Bilingual education for young children: Review of the effects and consequences. *International Journal of Bilingual Education and Bilingualism*, 21(6), 666–79. doi:10.1080/13670050.2016.1203859.

Bonnesen, M. (2009). The status of the 'weaker' language in unbalanced French/German bilingual language acquisition. *Bilingualism: Language and Cognition*, 12, 177–92.

Caldas, S. J. (2006). *Raising bilingual-biliterate children in monolingual cultures*. Clevedon: Multilingual Matters.

Chevalier, S. (2015). *Trilingual language acquisition*. Amsterdam: John Benjamins.

Choi, J., Cutler, A., & Broersma, M. (2017). Early development of abstract language knowledge: Evidence from perception-production transfer of birth-language memory, 4. *Royal Society Open Science*. doi:10.1098/rsos.160660

Clark, E. V. (2017). *Language in children*. London: Routledge.

Curtiss, S. (1977). *Genie: A psycholinguistic study of a modern-day 'wild child'*. New York: Academic Press.

De Houwer, A. (2005). Early bilingual acquisition. In J. F. Kroll & A. M. B. de Groot (Eds.), *Handbook of bilingualism*, pp. 30–48. Oxford: Oxford University Press.

De Houwer, A. (2007). Parental language input patterns and children's bilingual use. *Applied Psycholinguistics*, 28, 411–24.

De Houwer, A. (2009). *Bilingual first language acquisition.* Bristol: Multilingual Matters.

De Houwer, A. (2014). The absolute frequency of maternal input to bilingual and monolingual children: A first comparison. In T. Grüter & J. Paradis (Eds.), *Input and experience in bilingual development*, pp. 37–58. Amsterdam: John Benjamins.

Ethnologue: Languages of the World. (2017). 20th edition, 21 February 2017. www.ethnologue.com/

Genesee, F., Paradis, J., & Crago, M. (2010). *Dual language development & disorders: A handbook on bilingualism & second language acquisition.* Second edition. Baltimore: Paul H. Brookes Publishing.

Grammont, M. (1902). Observations sur le langage des enfants. *Mélanges linguistiques offerts à M. Antoine Meillet par ses élèves*, pp. 61–82. Paris: Klincksieck. www.worldcat.org/title/melanges-linguistiques-offerts-a-m-antoine-meillet/oclc/9952299

Grosjean, F. (2008). *Studying bilinguals.* Oxford: Oxford University Press.

Johnson, J. S., & Newport, E. (1989). Critical period effects in second language learning: The influence of maturational state on the acquisition of English as a second language. *Cognitive Psychology*, 21, 60–99.

Kato, M. A. (2003). Child L2 acquisition: An insider account. In N. Müller (Ed.), *(In)vulnerable domains in multilingualism*, pp. 271–93. Amsterdam: John Benjamins.

Lanza, E. (1997). *Language mixing in infant bilingualism: A sociolinguistic perspective.* Oxford: Clarendon Press.

Lenneberg, E. H. (1967). *Biological foundations of language.* New York: Wiley and Sons.

Leopold, W. F. (1939–1949). *Speech development of a bilingual child: A linguist's record.* Evanston, Illinois: Northwestern University Press, vols. 1–4; New York: AMS Press, 1970.

Long, M. H. (1990). Maturational constraints on language development. *Studies in Second Language Acquisition*, 12, 251–85.

Meisel, J. M. (1989). Early differentiation of languages in bilingual children. In K. Hyltenstam & L. Obler (Eds.), *Bilingualism across the lifespan: Aspects of acquisition, maturity, and loss*, pp. 13–40. Cambridge: Cambridge University Press.

Meisel, J. M. (2011). *First and second language acquisition: Parallels and differences*. Cambridge: Cambridge University Press.

Meisel, J. M. (2017). Bilingual acquisition: A morphosyntactic perspective on simultaneous and early successive language development. In H. Cairns & E. M. Fernández (Eds.), *Handbook of psycholinguistics*, pp. 635–52. New York: Wiley Blackwell.

Meisel, J. M. (2018). Early child second language acquisition: French gender in German children. *Bilingualism: Language and Cognition*, 21(4), 656–673.

Pavlovitch, M. (1920). *Le langage enfantin. Acquisition du serbe et du français par un enfant serbe*. Paris: Champion.

Penfield, W., & Roberts, L. (1959). *Speech and brain mechanisms*. New York: Athenaeum.

Pinker, S. (1994). *The language instinct*. New York: William Morrow and Company.

Poplack, S. (1980). Sometimes I'll start a sentence in Spanish Y TERMINO EN ESPAÑOL: Toward a typology of code-switching. *Linguistics*, 18, 581–618.

Ronjat, J. (1913). *Le développement du langage observé chez un enfant bilingue*. Paris: Librairie Ancienne H. Champion.

Saunders, G. (1982). *Bilingual children: Guidance for the family*. Clevedon: Multilingual Matters.

Saunders, G. (1988). *Bilingual children: From birth to teens*. Clevedon: Multilingual Matters.

Schlyter, S., & Håkansson, G. (1994). Word order in Swedish as the first language, second language and weaker language in bilinguals. *Scandinavian Working Papers on Bilingualism*, 9, 49–66.

Sopata, A. (2011). Placement of infinitives in successive child language acquisition. In E. Rinke & T. Kupisch (Eds.), *The development of grammar: Language acquisition and diachronic change*, pp. 105–21. Amsterdam: John Benjamins.

Valian, V. (2015). Bilingualism and cognition. *Bilingualism: Language and Cognition*, 18, 3–24.

Volterra, V., & Taeschner, T. (1978). The acquisition and development of language by bilingual children. *Journal of Child Language*, 5, 311–26.

Yip, V., & Matthews, S. (2000). Syntactic transfer in a Cantonese-English bilingual child. *Bilingualism: Language and Cognition*, 3, 193–208.

Other Sources

Abrahamsson, N., & Hyltenstam, K. (2009). Age of onset and nativelikeness in a second language: Listener perception versus linguistic scrutiny. *Language Learning*, 59, 249–306.

Allen, S. (2007). The future of Inuktitut in the face of majority languages: Bilingualism or language shift? *Applied Psycholinguistics*, 28, 515–36.

Antonova-Ünlü, E., & Wei, L. (2016). Aspect acquisition in Russian as the weaker language. *International Journal of Bilingualism*, 20, 210–28.

Argyri, E., & Sorace, A. (2007). Crosslinguistic influence and language dominance in older bilingual children. *Bilingualism: Language and Cognition*, 10, 79–99.

Au, T. K. F., Knightly, L. M., Jun, S. A., & Oh, J. S. (2002). Overhearing a language during childhood. *Psychological Science*, 13, 238–43.

Barnes, J. D. (2006). *Early trilingualism: A focus on questions.* Clevedon: Multilingualism Matters.

Barreña, A., Ezeizabarrena, M.-J., & García, I. (2008). Influence of the linguistic environment on the development of the lexicon and grammar of Basque bilingual children. In C. Pérez-Vidal, M. Juan-Garau, & A. Bel (Eds.), *A portrait of the young in the new multilingual Spain: Issues in the acquisition of two or more languages in multilingual environments*, pp. 86–110. Clevedon: Multilingual Matters.

Bergman, C. R. (1976). Interference versus independent development in infant bilingualism. In G. D. Keller, R. V. Teschner, & S. Viera (Eds.), *Bilingualism in the bicentennial and beyond*, pp. 86–96. New York: Bilingual Press/Editorial Bilingüe.

Bialystok, E. (2009). Bilingualism: The good, the bad, and the indifferent. *Bilingualism: Language and Cognition*, 12, 3–11.

Blom, E. (2010). Effects of input on the early grammatical development of bilingual children. *International Journal of Bilingualism*, 14, 422–46.

Carroll, S. E. (2017). Exposure and input in bilingual development. *Bilingualism: Language and Cognition*, 20, 3–16.

Costa, A., & Caramazza, A. (1999). Is lexical selection in bilingual speech production language specific? *Bilingualism: Language and Cognition*, 2, 231–44.

Costa, A., Colomé, A., Gómez, O., & Sebastián-Gallés, N. (2003). Another look at cross-language competition in bilingual speech production: Lexical and phonological factors. *Bilingualism: Language and Cognition*, 3, 167–79.

de Bruin, A., Treccani, B., & Della Sala, S. (2015). Cognitive advantage in bilingualism: An advantage of publication bias? *Psychological Science*, 26, 99–107.

De Houwer, A. (1990). *The acquisition of two languages from birth: A case study*. Cambridge: Cambridge University Press.

De Houwer, A. (2011). Language input environments and language development in bilingual acquisition. *Applied Linguistics Review*, 2, 221–39.

Delcenserie, A., Genesee, F., & Gauthier, K. (2013). Language abilities of internationally adopted children from China during the early school years: Evidence for early age effects? *Applied Psycholinguistics*, 34, 541–68.

Döpke, S. (1992). *One parent – one language: An interactional approach*. Amsterdam: John Benjamins.

Döpke, S. (2000). Generation of and retraction from cross-linguistically motivated structures in bilingual first language acquisition. *Bilingualism: Language and Cognition*, 3, 209–26.

Fantini, A. E. (1985). *Language acquisition of a bilingual child: A sociolinguistic perspective*. Clevedon: Multilingual Matters.

Flores, C., & Barbosa, P. (2014). When reduced input leads to delayed acquisition: A study on the acquisition of clitic placement by Portuguese heritage speakers. *International Journal of Bilingualism*, 18, 304–25.

Fuentes, C. (1998). Los Estados Unidos por dos lenguas. *El País Digital*, 18 June 1998.

Gawlitzek-Maiwald, I., & Tracy, R. (1996). Bilingual bootstrapping. *Linguistics*, 34, 901–26.

Genesee, F. (1989). Early bilingual development, one language or two? *Journal of Child Language*, 16, 161–79.

Genesee, F., Nicoladis, E., & Paradis, J. (1995). Language differentiation in early bilingual development. *Journal of Child Language*, 22, 611–31.

Gleitman, L., & Newport, E. (1995). The invention of language by children: Environmental and biological influences on the acquisition of language. In L. Gleitman & M. Liberman (Eds.), *Language: An invitation to cognitive science* (Second edition), pp. 1–24. Cambridge, MA: MIT Press.

Gómez Imbert, E. (1995). Puesto que hablamos distinto, quiere ud. casarse conmigo? *Glotta*, 18–22.

Granena, G., & Long, M. H. (2013). Age of onset, length of residence, language aptitude, and ultimate L2 attainment in three linguistic domains. *Second Language Research*, 29, 311–43.

Granfeldt, J., Schlyter, S., & Kihlstedt, M. (2007). French as cL2, 2L1 and L1 in pre-school children. *Petites Études Romanes de Lund*, 24, 5–42.

Green, D. W. (1998). Mental control of the bilingual lexico-semantic system. *Bilingualism: Language and Cognition*, 1, 67–81.

Grosjean, F. (1989). Neurolinguists, beware! The bilingual is not two monolinguals in one person. *Brain and Language*, 36, 3–15.

Grosjean, F. (1998). Studying bilinguals: Methodological and conceptual issues. *Bilingualism: Language and Cognition*, 1, 131–49.

Guasti, M. T. (2002). *Language acquisition: The growth of grammar.* Cambridge, MA: The MIT Press.

Hoff, E., Core, C., Place, S., Rumiche, R., Señor, M., & Parra, M. (2012). Dual language exposure and early bilingual development. *Journal of Child Language*, 39, 1–27.

Hoffmann, C. (1985). Language acquisition in two trilingual children. *Journal of Multilingual and Multicultural Development*, 6, 479–95.

Hulk, A., & Müller, N. (2000). Bilingual first language acquisition at the interface between syntax and pragmatics. *Bilingualism: Language and Cognition*, 3, 227–44.

Hyltenstam, K., & Abrahamsson, N. (2003). Maturational constraints in second language acquisition. In C. Doughty & M. H. Long (Eds.), *Handbook of second language acquisition*, pp. 539–88. Oxford: Blackwell.

Hyltenstam, K., Bylund, E., Abrahamsson, N., & Park, H.-S. (2003). Dominant-language replacement: The case of international adoptees. *Bilingualism: Language and Cognition*, 12, 121–40.

Jekat, S. (1985). *Die Entwicklung des Wortschatzes bei bilingualen Kindern (Französisch/ Deutsch) in den ersten vier Lebensjahren.* University of Hamburg: M.A. Thesis.

Kielhöfer, B., & Jonekeit, S. (1983). *Zweisprachige Kindererziehung.* Tübingen: Stauffenburg Verlag.

Köppe, R. (1996). Language differentiation in bilingual children: The development of grammatical and pragmatic competence. *Linguistics*, 34, 927–54.

Köppe, R. (1997). *Sprachentrennung im frühen bilingualen Erstspracherwerb: Französisch/Deutsch.* Tübingen: Narr.

Köppe, R., & Meisel, J. M. (1995). Code-switching in bilingual first language acquisition. In L. Milroy & P. Muysken (Eds.), *One speaker, two languages: Cross-disciplinary perspectives on code-switching,* pp. 276–301. Cambridge: Cambridge University Press.

Kuhl, P. K. (2007). Is speech learning 'gated' by the social brain? *Developmental Science,* 10, 110–20.

Kupisch, T. (2007). Determiners in bilingual German-Italian children: What they tell us about the relation between language influence and language dominance. *Bilingualism: Language and Cognition,* 10, 57–78.

Lakshmanan, U. (1994). *Universal Grammar in child second language acquisition.* Amsterdam: John Benjamins.

Lehtonen, M., Soveri, A., Laine, A., Järvenpää, J., de Bruin, A., & Antfolk, J. (2018). Is bilingualism associated with enhanced executive functioning in adults? A meta-analytic review. *Psychological Bulletin,* 144, 394–425.

Lindholm, K., & A. M. Padilla (1978). Language mixing in bilingual children. *Journal of Child Language,* 5, 327–35.

Liu, L., & Krager, R. (2016). Perception of a native vowel contrast by Dutch monolingual and bilingual infants: A bilingual perceptual lead. *International Journal of Bilingualism,* 20, 335–45.

Locke, J. L. (1997). A theory of neurolinguistic development. *Brain and Language,* 58, 265–326.

Lust, B., Flynn, S., Blume, M., Park, S. W., Kang, C., Yang, S., & Kim, A.-Y. (2016). Assessing child bilingualism: Direct assessment of bilingual syntax amends caretaker report. *International Journal of Bilingualism,* 20, 153–72.

Meisel, J. M. (1994a). Code-switching in young bilingual children: The acquisition of grammatical constraints. *Studies in Second Language Acquisition,* 16, 413–39.

Meisel, J. M. (1994b). Getting FAT: Finiteness, Agreement and Tense in early grammars. In J. M. Meisel (Ed.), *Bilingual first language acquisition: French and German grammatical development,* pp. 89–129. Amsterdam: John Benjamins.

Meisel, J. M. (2001). The simultaneous acquisition of two first languages: Early differentiation and subsequent development of grammars. In J. Cenoz & F. Genesee (Eds.), *Trends in bilingual acquisition,* pp. 11–41. Amsterdam: John Benjamins.

Meisel, J. M. (2004). The bilingual child. In T. K. Bhatia & W. C. Ritchie (Eds.), *The handbook of bilingualism*, pp. 91–113. Oxford: Blackwell.

Meisel, J. M. (2007a). On autonomous syntactic development in multiple first language acquisition. In H. Caunt-Nulton, S. Kulatilake, & I.-H. Woo (Eds.), *Proceedings of the 31st Boston University conference on language development*, pp. 26–45. Somerville, MA: Cascadilla Press.

Meisel, J. M. (2007b). The weaker language in early child bilingualism: Acquiring a first language as a second language? *Applied Psycholinguistics*, 28, 495–514.

Meisel, J. M. (2009). Second language acquisition in early childhood. *Zeitschrift für Sprachwissenschaft*, 28, 5–34.

Mishina-Mori, S. (2005). Autonomous and interdependent development of two language systems in Japanese/English simultaneous bilinguals: Evidence from question formation. *First Language*, 25, 291–315.

Montanari, E. (2002). *Mit zwei Sprachen groß werden*. Munich: Kösel.

Montrul, S., Davidson, J., de la Fuente, I., & Foote, R. (2014). Early language experience facilitates the processing of gender agreement in Spanish heritage speakers. *Bilingualism: Language and Cognition*, 17, 118–38.

Nicholas, H. (1987). *A comparative study of the acquisition of German as a first and as a second language*. Melbourne, Monash University: Unpublished Ph.D. Thesis.

Onysko, A. (2016). Enhanced creativity in bilinguals? Evidence from meaning interpretations of novel compounds. *International Journal of Bilingualism*, 20, 315–34.

Paradis, J., & Genesee, F. (1996). Syntactic acquisition in bilingual children: Autonomous or independent? *Studies in Second Language Acquisition*, 18, 1–15.

Park-Johnson, S. K. (2017). Crosslinguistic influence of wh-in-situ questions by Korean-English bilingual children. *International Journal of Bilingualism*, 21, 419–32.

Patterson, J. L. (2002). Relationships of expressive vocabulary to frequency of reading and television experience among bilingual toddlers. *Applied Psycholinguistics*, 23, 493–508.

Pearson, B. Z. (2008). *Raising a bilingual child*. New York: Living Language.

Pienemann, M. (1981). *Der Zweitspracherwerb ausländischer Arbeiterkinder*. Bonn: Bouvier.

Pirvulescu, M., Pérez-Leroux, A.-T., Roberge, Y., Strik, N., & Thomas, D. (2014). Bilingual effects: Exploring object omission in pronominal languages. *Bilingualism: Language and Cognition*, 17, 495–510.

Quay, S. (1995). The bilingual lexicon: Implications for studies of language choice. *Journal of Child Language*, 22, 369–87.

Quay, S. (2001). Managing linguistic boundaries in early trilingual development. In J. Cenoz & F. Genesee (Eds.), *Trends in bilingual acquisition*, pp. 149–99. Amsterdam: John Benjamins.

Qi, R. (2011). *The bilingual acquisition of English and Mandarin: Chinese children in Australia*. Amherst, NY: Cambria Press.

Redlinger, W., & Park, T. (1980). Language mixing in young bilinguals. *Journal of Child Language*, 7, 337–52.

Rodina, Y., & Westergaard, M. (2017). Grammatical gender in bilingual Norwegian-Russian acquisition: The role of input and transparency. *Bilingualism: Language and Cognition*, 20, 197–214.

Schlyter, S. (1993). The weaker language in bilingual Swedish-French children. In K. Hyltenstam & A. Viberg (Eds.), *Progression and regression in language: Sociocultural, neuropsychological and linguistic perspectives*, pp. 289–308. Cambridge: Cambridge University Press.

Sebastián-Gallés, N., & Bosch, L. (2005). Phonology and bilingualism. In J. F. Kroll & A. M. B. de Groot (Eds.), *Handbook of bilingualism*, pp. 68–87. Oxford: Oxford University Press.

Serratrice, L., Sorace, A., & Paoli, S. (2004). Crosslinguistic influence at the syntax-pragmatic interface: Subjects and objects in English-Italian bilingual and monolingual acquisition. *Bilingualism: Language and Cognition*, 7, 183–205.

Silva-Corvalán, C. (2014). *Bilingual language acquisition: Spanish and English in the first six years*. Cambridge: Cambridge University Press.

Štefánik, J. (1996). Intentional bilingualism in children. *Human Affairs*, 6, 135–141.

Strik, N., & Pérez-Leroux, A.-T. (2011). Jij doe wat girafe? Wh-movement and inversion in Dutch-French bilingual children. *Linguistic Approaches to Bilingualism*, 1, 175–205.

Taeschner, T. (1983). *The sun is feminine. A study of language acquisition in bilingual children*. Berlin: Springer.

Takeuchi, M. (2006). *Raising children bilingually through the 'one parent-one language' approach: A case study of Japanese mothers in the Australian context*. Bern: Peter Lang.

Thordardottir, E. (2011). The relationship between bilingual exposure and vocabulary development. *International Journal of Bilingualism*, 15, 426–45.

Thordardottir, E. (2015). The relationship between bilingual exposure and morphosyntactic development. *International Journal of Speech-Language Pathology*, 17, 97–114.

Ünlü, E. A., & Li, W. (2018). Examining the effect of reduced input on language development: The case of gender acquisition in Russian as a non-dominant and dispreferred language by a bilingual Turkish-Russian child. *International Journal of Bilingualism*, 22, 215–33.

Unsworth, S. (2016). Quantity and quality of language input in bilingual language development. In E. Nicoladis & S. Montanari (Eds.), *Lifespan perspectives on bilingualism*, pp. 136–96. Berlin: De Gruyter.

Vihman, M. (1985). Language differentiation by the bilingual infant. *Journal of Child Language*, 12, 297–324.

Weisleder, A., & Fernald, A. (2013). Talking to children matters: Early language experience strengthens processing and build vocabulary. *Psychological Science*, 24, 2143–52.

Yip, V., & Matthews, S. (2007). *The bilingual child: Early development and language contact*. Cambridge: Cambridge University Press.

Index